Projected Fears

Projected Fears

HORROR FILMS AND AMERICAN CULTURE

Kendall R. Phillips

Westport, Connecticut
London

Library of Congress Cataloging-in-Publication Data

Phillips, Kendall R.
    Projected fears : horror films and American culture / Kendall R. Phillips.
        p. cm.
    Includes bibliographical references and index.
    ISBN 0–275–98353–6 (alk. paper)
1. Horror films—United States—History and criticism.   I.   Title.
PN1995.9.H6P44   2005
791.43'6164—dc22   2004028376

British Library Cataloguing in Publication Data is available.

Library of Congress Catalog Card Number: 2004028376
ISBN: 0–275–98353–6

First published in 2005

Praeger Publishers, 88 Post Road West, Westport, CT 06881
An imprint of Greenwood Publishing Group, Inc.
www.praeger.com

Printed in the United States of America

The paper used in this book complies with the
Permanent Paper Standard issued by the National
Information Standards Organization (Z39.48–1984).

10 9 8 7 6 5 4 3 2 1

I dedicate this book to my family: to my father for jumping with me at Jason's appearance in the final moments of *Friday the Thirteenth*, to my brother for taunting me into seeing *Halloween*, and to my mother, who never wanted me to watch these "ugly films" in the first place.

Contents

Acknowledgments

The work in this book could not have been accomplished without the amazing love, support, and counsel of my wife, Catherine Thomas. The work has also benefited from innumerable conversations with the many groups of students who have taken my film courses, and in particular, Alyssa Vleck, for help on *The Silence of the Lambs*, and Ani Mandera, for help on *Dracula*. I would also like to acknowledge the outstanding support from the folks at Praeger, especially Eric Levy, without whom this book would truly not exist.

Portions of the argument in Chapter 7 appeared previously in my "Consuming Community in Jonathan Demme's *The Silence of the Lambs*" in *Qualitative Research Reports in Communication* in 1999 (volume 1, pages 26–32).

Introduction

When I tell people that I'm working on a book about horror films there are two typical reactions. The first is a mildly incredulous, "Oh." For some, including many within academic circles, horror films hardly constitute worthy cultural texts for analysis. This reaction is compounded as I explain that, rather than pursuing arcane film history or neglected cult classics, I'm focusing on those films that gained a wide mainstream audience. While it is certainly true that the study of popular culture has gained great ground in academic circles over the last few decades, there is still a strong strain of contempt for those cultural artifacts and icons that attain wide levels of popularity. So, due to this first reaction, I've found myself being strategically vague about my current work when in certain company.

The vast majority of the people in my life, fortunately, have a different and much more positive reaction, which focuses on what I call the "top-ten list." This reaction sometimes comes as a question—"So, what is the best horror film of all time?"—and is usually followed by a story—"I remember when I first saw film *X*. I was fourteen and I ..." Over the past few years of these conversations, I've been struck by the variety of narratives people spin about their memorable encounters with scary films. These stories certainly vary in the kinds of films people recall as frightening. While many are traditional horror films, it's surprising how often films from other genres appear, including the remarkably pervasive fear evoked by *The Wizard of Oz*. I'm also surprised by the variety of reactions reported. My father recalls riding along dusty gravel roads in the back of a pickup truck after seeing *Dracula* in the early 1930s and starting at every shadow and overhanging limb. A friend tells the story of being terrified by an afternoon showing of *Nightmare on Elm Street* as a child but sneaking back into the theater to watch it again. Over the years, people have described to me their sleepless nights and locked doors and romantic interludes.

After listening to literally hundreds of these stories, I'm particularly impressed by the impact these films have had on individuals. People carry these stories with them, recount the most disturbing moments, and recall their peculiar reactions. Horror films, perhaps more than any other type of film, seem to impact people's lives. In fairness, the biggest impression is often when we are children or adolescents and are beginning to struggle with societal boundaries and forbidden knowledge. The film that I recall scaring me the most—and it's a question I often get asked—was *Halloween*. I was far too young to see *Halloween* in its first run. However, my brother, who is several years my elder, had seen the film and crept into my bedroom late one evening to recount the tale of Michael Myers coming home. So, with remarkable ease, the next night my older brother helped me sneak into a crowded theater, where we illicitly watched John Carpenter's classic.

When I watch the film now I'm always struck by how different it seems from my recollection of it. In particular, I recall being most horrified by the sequence in which Laurie (Jamie Lee Curtis) is running down the block, desperately banging on the doors of her neighbors. Her cries are ignored, and she eventually must face the killer Michael Myers on her own. Of course, the sequence lasts only a few seconds, but in my memory, the memory of a nine-year-old boy sitting in a crowded north Texas theater, the sequence of suburban pursuit lasted forever.

When I think about this memory now, it makes a great deal of sense. I was a young boy living in a neighborhood not entirely unlike the one depicted in the film—indeed, the filmmakers intended the neighborhoods of Haddonfield to have this generic quality—and like most young people, I was dependent on the adults in my life (family, neighbors, teachers, etc.) for safety. Laurie's terrified flight through a neighborhood of closed doors, while utterly fantastic, was not entirely alien to me, or in all likelihood, to the millions of other adolescents who flocked to the film in the late 1970s.

While my anecdote, and those of others, depicts the impact that frightening films have on us as individuals, I think it also opens up a broader question about culture—a question that sits at the heart of this book. Each of us experiences a film individually, and our different tastes in films demonstrate how unique our individual reactions are. Yet, what are we to make of those films that seem to have tapped into the collective fears of an entire generation? Can we have what film theorist Robin Wood calls "collective nightmares"?[1] If so, how should we seek to understand those "projected nightmares" that seem to affect our broader culture? In other words, while any given film can be frightening to any given individual, certain films become the touchstone of fear for an entire generation. It is as if, at certain points, a particular film so captures our cultural anxieties and concerns that our collective fears seem projected onto the screen before us. Not every horror film achieves this effect, indeed, very few do, but when a film does so touch our collective nerve, our reactions to it are unmistakable. We talk about these films, debate their meaning, praise and condemn them. These films that touch upon our collective fears become part of our culture.

This is a book about horror films. More specifically, it's a book about those horror films that made such an impression on American culture that they became instantly recognizable and, indeed, redefined the notion of what a horror film is. In my estimation—an estimation I'll try to justify in the course of these pages—there are ten films that can be thought of as having this kind of connection to American culture: *Dracula* (1931), *The Thing from Another World* (1951), *Psycho* (1960), *Night of the Living Dead* (1968), *The Exorcist* (1973), *The Texas Chainsaw Massacre* (1974), *Halloween* (1978), *The Silence of the Lambs* (1991), *Scream* (1996), and *The Sixth Sense* (1999). It is not my contention that these are, necessarily, the most frightening films ever made—a line of argument far too subjective to make seriously—or that they are necessarily the most original—a line of argument more of interest to the film historian. Rather, my argument in this book is that these are the most "successful" and "influential" horror films in American history and that their level of success and influence can be correlated to broader cultural anxieties into which they somehow tapped.

When I say these films were successful, I mean not only that they achieved financial success but also that each of these films became "cultural moments." Of course, all ten of these films achieved huge box-office success, and several did so with very little production value, promotion, or even major studio backing. Financial success, however, is not enough to argue that these films are important. The history of film is replete with financially successful but instantly forgettable films. Still, these ten horror films have achieved a level of cultural immortality far beyond their monetary profit. They have become part of our culture. What is particularly interesting about these films is that they became part of our culture almost instantly. To attain this kind of broad success, these films had to reach out to more than just the hardcore horror fans. As Elizabeth Cowie notes, "Successful horror films succeed in horrifying both those who love the horror of horror films and those who loathe the horror of horror films."[2] These were films that people talked about, not that this talk was always positive. Some of these films were widely embraced and praised; others were roundly condemned, even censored. Even the vehemence of this condemnation, however, is evidence of their cultural impact.

Additionally, these films have remained instantly recognizable, even among people who have never seen them. When I talk about the films I'm studying, I'm struck by how almost everyone knows them all and how most can recount the general plot and feel of each film, even those they have never watched in their entirety. *Psycho* always gets this reaction. Everyone can imitate the striking string musical theme, and most can even describe the shower scene in vivid detail. However, surprisingly few people have actually sat down and watched the entire film, and when they do, they often report to me how surprised they are at its depth, subtlety, and humor. Everyone "knows" *Psycho*—even if few of us really *know Psycho*.

In part, the cultural immortality of these films stems from their influence on other films. The success of each of these films spawned—at least in part—a whole new trend in the development of the horror genre: The success of *Dracula* gave rise to the era of the Universal Monsters; *The Thing* spawned the creature features of the 1950s; *Night of the Living Dead* brought the grotesqueries of splatter to American cinema; and even the most recent film in this study, *The Sixth Sense*, can be said to have heralded a return of Gothic art to American horror films, such as *The Blair Witch Project* and *The Others*. To put it simply—and perhaps too boldly—the impact of each of these films was such that, after each one was released, it became very difficult to think of horror films in the same ways. While the Universal Monsters (Dracula, Frankenstein, the Wolfman, etc.) have remained a vital part of our collective imaginary, their capacity to evoke fright, already waning by 1951, became almost impossible after the emergence of *The Thing* from its icy saucer.

The dynamic, sometimes dramatic, evolution of the horror films makes it difficult to talk about the genre as a whole. How, for instance, can one seek to put the haunting elegance of, say, *Picnic at Hanging Rock* in the same genre as the assaulting gore of *House of 1,000 Corpses*? The answer to this problem is suggested by James Naremore, who contends that genres are not constituted so much by essential similarities between the films as they are constituted by the ways we talk about these films. Genres are, as he puts it, "a loose evolving system of arguments and readings, helping to shape commercial strategies and aesthetic ideologies."[3] In other words, if we talk about a film as if it is a horror film—market it that way, respond to it that way, interpret it as one—then it is, effectively, part of the horror genre. Andrew Tudor summarizes the point, "Genre is what we collectively believe it to be."[4]

If genre is essentially our collective understanding and expectation, then the evolution of genres involves the skillful violation of those expectations. S. S. Prawer observes that the speed with which conventions become established and expectations set allows the talented filmmaker to "use the conventions as a kind of grid against which to draw their own rather different picture."[5] The violation of an audience's expectations contributes to their experience of terror and, in so doing, redraws the contours of the horror genre. Upon their release, each of the ten films examined here redefined fear for a generation and revealed something about the contours of our culture at those moments.

At this point, I want to make my overarching argument a bit clearer. While it might be tempting to claim that these particular films influenced our culture in specific, causal ways, this is not my argument. The logic of causality is appealing but far too simplistic for discussions about film and culture. The films I examine in this book did not *cause* American culture to go in one particular direction or another. Rather, these films connected to existing cultural drifts and directions in such peculiarly poignant ways as to be recognized as somehow "true." This is not, of course, to suggest that audiences emerged from these films fearing the undead or ghosts or aliens but that they emerged knowing that somehow what they saw upon the screen was an accurate, if allegorical, depiction of their own collective fears and concerns.

Allegory, however, is not an entirely accurate way of thinking about the connection between certain horror films and the broader culture that embraces them. Allegory, while a useful way of thinking about representation, suggests, on the one hand, too much intention upon the part of the producers of a text and, on the other hand, too much awareness upon the part of the audience. While allegories are powerful fictional tools, they are generally unsuccessful in creating horror. *1984*, for example, contains within it numerous horrific images and is a largely disturbing tale. However, as a reader or viewer we can never fully escape the overt allegorical relationship between Orwell's fictive kingdom and his very real concerns about his contemporary global political situation. Horror fiction may contain elements that upon later inspection contain an allegorical relation to external objects, but if horror bares its allegory too overtly, it fails to produce its primary product—fear. Edward Ingebretsen notes that every monster is, essentially, a political entity and that our production of monsters is always part of our broader political understanding of the world and of notions of good and evil.[6] However, if those politics are too overt, then we read the monster as a symbol and not as a threatening entity. Allegory, as Tzvetan Todorov points out, removes the literal reading of a monster or fantastic event and, thus, removes the space for fear and suspense.[7] It is, in other words, difficult to be frightened by a political symbol.

A more productive way of thinking about the subtle relationship between film and culture is suggested by Stephen Greenblatt's discussion of literature's relationship to culture.[8] Greenblatt contends that works of fiction "resonate" with elements in a particular culture, and I think this is a potentially powerful metaphor for thinking about films and the broader culture within which they become meaningful. Consider the more literal, physical sense of resonance. If we were to sound a tuning fork of the right frequency in a room full of crystal wineglasses, we would find a sympathetic hum emerging from the glasses. This physical act of re-sounding—or vibrating in sympathy with a similar frequency—gives a sense of the way that certain literary or filmic texts impact with the broader culture. An influential horror film does not necessarily create a certain pattern of anxiety or fear within a culture; instead, elements within the film resonate—connect in some sympathetic manner—to trends within the broader culture. Rather than creating cultural fears or reflecting them (as in allegory), the kinds of films with which we are here concerned can be said to attain influence by resonating with the broader culture.

Resonance, while vitally important to a film's reception, cannot be sufficient. Was resonance enough, then we would watch the same films over and over again. Film, like literature, cannot continue to offer us only the familiar but must, if it is to appeal to the wider collective imagination, offer something new. Greenblatt calls this the "wonder" provoked by a novel text. The broad cultural success of a given work of fiction, then, can be said to rest, in part, upon the balance the work maintains between its resonance with familiar cultural elements and the unfamiliar elements that create in its audience a sense of wonder.

In my analysis of popular horror films, I have found this balance to be vital. In my reading of these films, I find a strong resonance between the elements within the film and various anxieties existing in the broader culture. However, of equal importance, the groundbreaking films—those films that became real cultural events—shock their audiences. In this way, Greenblatt's notion of wonder seems even more important for horror films. If in love familiarity breeds contempt, in horror it can be said that familiarity breeds boredom and derision. The history of horror figures gives easy evidence of this claim. While Gothic ghouls such as Dracula and Dr. Jekyll provoked fright in their early audiences, after a few years they lost their fearsome potential and ended up costarring with Abbott and Costello. This can be seen in any number of genres from the laughable Styrofoam creatures of the B-movies to the recent success of the *Scary Movie* trilogy. As a general rule of thumb, monsters that are too familiar become the objects of ridicule.

To be horrific, to fulfill their primary narrative function, horror films must not simply offer us something novel, they must shock us. In the truly groundbreaking horror films of American history this level of shock is caused not merely by the introduction of some new monster but through an almost systematic violation of the rules of the game. The truly shocking—and, thus, successful—horror films are those that make us start in our seats and want to cry out, "Hey, you can't do that!" In a way, we come to a horror film with some general sense of what a horror film looks like, what its topics are, and what kinds of moves we expect the film to take. However, the groundbreaking films use our expectations to set us up for something new and unexpected. Just as we've become comfortable with the way that horror films in general operate, along comes a film that so violates our expectations that it becomes the start of a whole new form of horror—thus the cycle begins again.

Of course, just as resonance alone would breed too much familiarity, so too, violation alone would produce exasperation. While there are any number of "art house" films that strive for a level of incomprehensibility, for a horror film to achieve an impact on the broader cultural landscape, it must balance resonance and violation. Thus, in my reading of the history of influential American horror films, I find the central, crucial element to be that combination of familiarity and shock—a combination I refer to as resonant violation.

Each of the ten films I examine in this book attained this resonant violation at the moment of their release. It is not just that they each contain elements that can be seen as resonating with broader cultural elements—most films achieve this to some extent. Nor is it just that they violate audience expectations in shocking ways. Indeed, each of these films had precursors. What these ten films did, and did with considerable elegance, was to combine familiarity and shock—resonance and violation—in such a way that audiences left the theater feeling that each film was both vitally important and disturbingly new. This strange relationship between the recognizable and the shocking is suggested by James Ursini who contends, "Horror is based on recognizing in the unfamiliar something familiar."[9]

The concept of resonant violation does more than simply explain the success of certain horror films. It is my contention that this combination of the familiar and the unexpected suggests the broader cultural importance of horror films. By drawing upon our collective anxieties—projecting them, even if indirectly, upon the screen before us—horror films can be said to be vitally interested in the broader cultural politics of their day. If resonance connects the horror film to the broader politics of its day, what does the violation of expectations accomplish? It seems to me, that the systematic violation of our narrative expectations almost forces us to think differently about those anxieties, or at the very least, to think about our normal patterns of dealing with those anxieties. Prawer suggests this relationship when observing, "If the terror film is thus connected to our social concerns, it also, paradoxically, helps us to cope with our ordinary life by jolting us out of it."[10]

I believe this "jolting" is most evident and most effective in the kind of violation of expectations achieved by groundbreaking horror films. These moments of resonant violation demonstrate to audiences, at the very least, that our habitual ways of thinking about the world can get us into trouble and that we'll have to find new ways of coping. Some initial evidence for this claim can be offered in the often-made observation that horror films tend to become more popular during times of social upheaval.[11] Paul Wells, for instance, asserts that "the history of the horror film is essentially a history of anxiety in the twentieth century."[12] When the culture is in turmoil, for some reason audiences flock to the horror film. Perhaps, during these times of great, generalized social anxiety, the horror film functions to shock its audience out of their anxiety. Anxiety tends to promote a sense of helplessness; fear, on the other hand, provides an impetus for change.[13] Of course, anxieties and tensions exist at all times, not just those of upheaval. By resonating with these anxieties, whether explicit or implicit, horror films provide a space for reflecting on them.[14]

Following this line of argument, we should be able to gain a great deal of insight into American culture at particular moments in time by focusing on those films that attained the kind of widespread success and influence I've suggested above. Indeed, this is the ultimate aim of the present book: to examine the potential points of resonant violation between influential horror films and the particular cultural moments in which they emerged. I pursue this purpose by examining each of these films with a particular eye towards the broad cultural issues and anxieties surrounding its release.[15]

The critic's job, in essence, is to slow the film down—pause over these points of connection between film and culture in ways that an audience cannot easily do during an initial viewing. I often think of this process as working like a roller coaster. Looking at a coaster from a distance, from the safety and solidity of the ground, we can see all the mechanisms that cause us to flip, fly, and spin. When we're on the coaster we know these mechanisms exist, but if the coaster is successful we don't have time to reconcile that knowledge with our thrills and shrieks. Horror films, at least successful ones, operate in the same way. If we have the time and distance to see the artifice, then it doesn't work.

Of course, an awareness of audience is crucial. Our goal is not to look for any possible meaning but to seek those meanings that might resonate with a given audience. Despite the temptation to view films in the abstract as universal or transcendent symbols of some human impulse, we should never forget that they are shown in real space and time to real people who come for real reasons.[16] We cannot hope to know exactly what audiences made of each of these films, nor can we hope to gain that knowledge through interviews or archival research. Our hope, rather, is to offer an informed speculation about the possible relationship between these culturally significant films and the broader culture within which they became so meaningful and to ask the simple question, "Why?" Why did *Dracula* or *Halloween* or *The Silence of the Lambs* become so meaningful to their respective audiences? What in those films invited audiences to take them as so meaningful and important? We are, in essence, seeking to sit along-side those audiences in those darkened theaters of 1931 or 1960 or 1968 and, with the benefit of hindsight and critical distance, examine the complex relationship between film and culture, between fictional fear and cultural anxiety, between familiarity and shock.

My goal in the present book is to trace some of these points of resonant violation in those horror films that have defined and rede-fined the notion of horror in American culture. By focusing each chapter on one influential film, I hope to provide a specific and par-ticular reading of those films that have had an irrefutable impact on American culture and filmmaking. By pursuing these influential films in their chronological sequence, I hope to show the dynamic developments in the broader genre. By the end of this book, then, we should be able to trace the changes in America's notion of horror from *Dracula* to *The Sixth Sense*. By following the resonant viola-tion in these films, we should be able to examine the ways that our notion of horror adapts to the particular cultural environment in which we face very real fears and anxieties. Ultimately, we should gain some insight into the dynamic processes by which we project our collective fears onto the screen and by which these fears are projected back to us.

1 *Dracula* (1931)

"I am Dracula.... I bid you welcome."

The roots of the American horror film can be traced to turn of the century England. For it was in England in 1897 that Bram Stoker's *Dracula* first emerged from his crypt to frighten readers. Deeply influenced by classical Gothic texts such as Horace Waldpole's *The Castle Otranto* (1764) and following in the immediate footsteps of Mary Shelley's *Frankenstein* (1818) and Robert Louis Stevenson's *The Strange Case of Dr. Jekyll and Mr. Hyde* (1896), Stoker's novel was, as Rosemary Jackson explains, "the culmination of nineteenth-century English Gothic."[1]

Yet, despite its place in the literary canon and its popularity, Dracula was a surprising subject for a 1930s Hollywood film. The novel is a massive, labyrinthine tale with a large cast of characters and a plot that spans several countries. What's more, the novel oozes with violence, blood, and sexuality, all taboo during the restrictive reign of the Production Code. Paramount Studio's supervisor E. J. Montange reported the reaction of his reviewers to the prospect of a filmed version of *Dracula* in a company memo: "We did not receive one favorable reaction. The very things which made people gasp and talk about it, such as the blood-sucking scenes, would be prohibited by the Code and also by censors."[2] One reader for Universal Studios—which would, of course, go on to produce the film version—noted that the story "contained everything that would cause any average human being to revolt or seek a convenient railing."[3]

Despite the generally negative reaction of studio readers and over the objection of Universal's patriarch Carl Laemmle Sr., Carl Laemmle Jr. vigorously pursued a film version of the vampire's tale. Laemmle Jr. saw the film as a vehicle for Lon Chaney, the famous "Man of a Thousand Faces," who had already portrayed such villains as the title character in *The Phantom of the Opera* (1927) and the faux vampire of *London after Midnight* (1927). His enthusiasm was bolstered by the remarkable success of the Broadway play version of *Dracula*, which opened on October 5, 1927 and was a major success despite generally negative reviews. As Mark Viera reports, "The play ran for 261 performances and then went on tour, making a total of $2 million."[4]

Acquiring the rights to Stoker's novel, Laemmle Jr. brought established director Tod Browning in to helm the production. Browning, a carnival worker turned filmmaker, had successfully collaborated with Chaney on a number of silent films including *Outside the Law* (1920), *The Unholy Three* (1925), *The Black Bird* (1926), and *London After Midnight*. Interestingly, Browning had been contemplating adapting the successful stage play since shortly after its Broadway opening.[5] However, while Universal and Browning waited for Chaney to negotiate release from his contract with MGM, the legendary actor died from lung cancer.

Despite being battered by the stock market crash of 1929 and the loss of Chaney, Universal Studios went ahead with *Dracula*, which began filming on September 29, 1930. Assisting the sometimes unreliable Browning, who was a recovering alcoholic, were art director Charles D. Hall, the man responsible for much of the visual atmosphere of the film, and cinematographer Karl Freund, who had worked on F. W. Murnau's *The Golem* (1920) and Fritz Lang's *Metropolis* (1926) and is widely rumored to have directed several of the key scenes in *Dracula*. Replacing Chaney was the play's successful lead, Bela Lugosi, the Hungarian actor who had up to this point found only minimal success in Hollywood.

Browning's *Dracula* premiered in New York's Roxy Theatre on February 12, 1931, surrounded by studio anxiety and a minimal publicity campaign that emphasized the romantic angle in hopes of distracting from the more horrific elements. Contemporary critics echoed Universal's concerns. The film was criticized for its choppiness, for the discontinuity of its scenes, for its staginess, and for falling apart in the second half. Additionally, as the *Los Angeles Times* noted, it was considered "too extreme to provide entertainment that causes word-of-mouth advertising."[6]

These grim verdicts were, of course, staggeringly wrong. As Mark Viera reports, "The film sold 50,000 tickets in two days, building a momentum that culminated in a $700,000 profit, the largest of the studio's 1931 releases."[7] The film made Bela Lugosi a star and the character of Dracula one of the most filmed of all time. Perhaps of greater importance, as Joseph Maddrey notes, "*Dracula*'s success prompted the studio to rush more 'monster movies' into production." Dracula was soon joined at Universal by *Frankenstein* (1931), *The Mummy* (1932), and *The Invisible Man* (1933), and at Universal's rival, Paramount, by *Dr. Jekyll and Mr. Hyde* (1931).[8]

SYNOPSIS

The film opens with a dramatic carriage ride through some rugged, central European country. The coach contains a number of superstitious villagers and an English businessman. Over the objections of the frightened villagers, the Englishman, named Renfield, insists upon continuing his journey to Castle Dracula. Upon arriving at the castle, we learn that the villagers' fears were well founded, and the count is revealed to be a vampire. Renfield is subdued and, we learn later, turned into a raving mad servant of the undead count.

The vampire and Renfield make their way via a dramatic boat journey to London, where Dracula takes up residence in Carfax Abbey. The plot gains momentum as Dracula meets his neighbors: Dr. Seward, who runs an adjacent sanitarium where Renfield is confined; his daughter, Mina; her friend, Lucy Weston; and Mina's fiancé, John Harker. During the evening of their first meeting, the vampire attacks and kills Lucy and then it becomes clear that his attention is fixed on Mina.

All might be lost except for the intervention of Professor Van Helsing, a distinguished scientist who quickly realizes that the attack on Lucy and those on other women are the results of a vampire. Dracula and Van Helsing have a series of dramatic confrontations as the count, with the assistance of Renfield, seeks to turn Mina into his undead bride. Eventually, Van Helsing convinces the skeptical Dr. Seward and Harker that Dracula is the vampire and Mina's immortal soul is in danger.

In the film's climax, Van Helsing and Harker follow Renfield, who leads them to the vampire and Mina. The men arrive just as the sun begins rising and find Dracula in his coffin, where Van Helsing drives a stake through his heart. Mina is found, still among the living, and the film ends with Harker accompanying his beloved Mina up the stairs to the sound of bells. In the original version of the film, a brief curtain speech by Van Helsing alerted the audience that "when ... you dread to see a face appear at the window, why, just pull yourself together and remember that after all, there *are* such things." Interestingly, this curtain speech was cut from the negative in 1938 at the direction of the Production Code Association.[9]

Despite its place as the progenitor of the modern American horror film and the occasional gripping image or moment, Browning's *Dracula* is not a film of particular high quality. As contemporary reviewers noted, its dramatic opening is followed by a fairly static second and third act. Browning, as has been well noted, was uncomfortable with the relatively new technology of the "talkie" and, as such, the mix of visual and exposition is awkward.[10] As modern critics Alain Silver and James Ursini observe, "Throughout the narrative, the most extraordinary events are reported rather than visualized."[11] Additionally, the narrative itself is quite jumpy—due, in part, to a late studio-ordered reedit prior to release—and a number of loose ends continue to dangle (e.g., Lucy's fate and the resolution of Renfield's apparent attack on an unconscious maid).

These narrative and stylistic deficiencies have led some film historians to bestow the honor of "first American horror film" on James Whale's *Frankenstein*.[12] Released in the same year and vastly superior on almost all fronts, *Frankenstein* is a far more sophisticated and engaging text. Whale's film, however, owes much of its existence to the success of Browning's. As noted above, *Dracula's* dramatic and unexpected success motivated much of Universal's interest in Mary Shelley's tale of the reanimated dead. So, whatever the questions of quality and style, *Dracula* deserves to be recognized as the film that began America's love affair with horror.

Indeed, the popularity of this admittedly deficient tale of the macabre actually makes it theoretically more interesting. Given the various problems of *Dracula*—poor effects, staginess, narrative inconsistencies, and so on—the film's enormous popularity is a bit of a puzzle. Why would audiences flock to the film? What was going on in American culture to lead audiences to find this film so meaningful? To put this question in the theoretical language suggested in the Introduction, what aspects of the film resonated with broader cultural concerns and anxieties? Following the theory of resonant violation, an explanation for the film's popularity can be derived from (a) the ways that *Dracula* resonated with broader cultural anxieties and (b) the ways that *Dracula* violated the kinds of expectations audiences might have brought to the film.

CULTURAL CONTEXTS

The hypothesis that horror films attain popularity in times of cultural upheaval gains a great deal of credence from the rise of the horror film in the early 1930s. *Dracula* emerged onto the American screen just twelve years after the First World War, just three years after the stock market crash of 1929, and in the midst of the rise of fascism in central Europe, Communism in the East, and rampant anti-Semitism throughout the Western world. The America of 1931 was in the midst of one of its grimmest periods.

Culture, of course, is infinitely complex and, as such, any effort to offer a comprehensive description is doomed to fail. My goal in this section is not to offer an inclusive picture of American culture in 1931 so much as to sketch out some of the strands that, as I will suggest in the next section, are particularly relevant to *Dracula*: Politics/Nationalism, Economic Conditions, Cultural Knowledge, and Sexual Norms.

Politics/Nationalism

It is easy for us to forget the overwhelming trauma of the First World War. Contemporaries of that bloody and senseless war called it "the war to end all wars" for a reason. Those who survived the carnage of trench warfare, the introduction of aerial combat, and the use of chemical weapons surely believed—or at least deeply hoped—that this level of global savagery would never happen again. Yet, by the early 1930s, the rumbling tensions between democratic, fascist, and communist governments in Europe were already beginning to suggest the sound of war drums.

For American filmgoers in 1931, Europe was doubly vexing. Not only had hundreds of thousands of American men lost lives and limbs fighting a European conflict that now seemed to have accomplished little, but many Americans continued to feel threatened by European immigrants who had flooded into the country in the years prior to the First World War. While the war years had reduced the flow of immigrants into the United States, as Bill Hing notes, "At the conclusion of World War I, immigration again began to increase.

Widespread fear of inundation by a flood of immigrants from the war-devastated countries of Europe developed. The isolationist mood of the period and a severe postwar depression augmented the already strong sentiment for further restrictions."[13]

This fear of immigrants, particularly European immigrants, was fueled by more than just economic protectionism (i.e., the desire to reserve jobs for "Americans"). Interlocking cultural and racial concerns pushed many Americans to support the drastic immigration restrictions enacted into law in 1920, 1924, and 1929.[14] The cultural concern focused on the notion of assimilation, or "Americanization." European immigrants, it was feared, would not fully embrace their identity as "Americans," which would lead to a balkanization of America. This cultural concern was also underscored by racism. As Michael LeMay argues, "It was the triumph of racist ideas that provided the rationale for the restrictive immigration laws of the 1920s. 'Eugenics,' a pseudo-science that supposedly 'proved' that certain races were endowed with an hereditary superiority or inferiority, provided the basis of the quota system."[15] To a large extent both the cultural fear of balkanization and the "scientific" racism of eugenics were directed at eastern and southern Europeans.

The twin specters of cultural fear and racial hatred were also focused on people of Jewish descent. Writing in 1941, Donald Strong offered this insightful read of American anti-Semitism: "Anti-semitism in the United States may be considered as a phase of the anti-alien sentiment that has periodically manifested itself."[16] While anti-Semitism had long been part of American culture, Naomi Cohen contends,

> In the aftermath of World War I, the problems mushroomed. The Red Scare, the wide dissemination of the *Protocols of the Elders of Zion*, the fulminations of Henry Ford's *Dearborn Independent*, and the activities of a renascent Ku Klux Klan nurtured the popularity of a new anti-Christ, the "Bolshevik Jew," conspiring to overthrow Christian civilization. Hostility towards Jews—from discrimination in employment and universities to immigration restriction—rose to unprecedented heights. The decade of the 1930s was worse.[17]

Faced with unprecedented levels of global political turmoil, Americans became increasingly fearful of the "others" within their midst. As Cohen suggests, this increasing xenophobia became even more palpable with the onset of the global economic catastrophe of 1929.

Economic Conditions

Considering the cultural mood of 1931, David Skal writes,

> If not exactly crazy, the public mood had changed—and changed radically. The crack in the fabric of reality known politely as the year A.D. 1931 appeared to many Americans to be the end of all earthly possibilities. The economic free-fall that had begun in October 1929 was about to hit bottom. Within a year the industrialized world's unemployed population would reach an estimated 30 million people.[18]

The Great Depression had begun, and by 1931 even the Hoover administration could no longer deny its reality. Three years after the crash, there seemed little immediate possibility of a recovery, and the bread lines were growing longer.

While the devastating economic conditions greatly affected the film industry, audiences continued to flock to the cinema. Gangster films, with chaotic antiheroes like Dillinger and Capone, were remarkably popular, as were the physical comedies from the Marx Brothers and Laurel and Hardy. Films offered a refuge from the depressing conditions of the world. As John Flynn writes, "During the early part of the decade, the ravages of the depression ... and the winds of war in Europe caused many people to seek out the simple escapist fare of fantasy films."[19]

Cultural Knowledge

Amidst the wreckage of Industrial Age economics and the ominous threat of mechanized warfare, Americans were also struggling with the more abstract philosophical question of how they should understand the world. The heart of this struggle was between religion and science. The 1920s were a period of dramatic growth for science and technology. New technologies were being introduced into the marketplace on a regular basis, and the innovations of mass mechanization, such as the assembly line and the principles of Frederick Taylor's "scientific management," were making the American worker vastly more efficient. Increased efficiency, of course, helped to fuel growth in the economy and provided the average worker with more leisure time.

However, even before the Great Depression put an end to this technologically driven economic expansion, many Americans were conflicted about the growth of science and scientific reasoning in society. The spread of progressive philosophy—the abstract, intellectual theories of the avant-garde—was countered by a religious revival that swept through the American South in the 1920s. It is worth remembering that the infamous Scope's "monkey trial"—the legal battle over whether evolution could be taught in Kansas classrooms in place of religious creationism—had occurred in 1925. The dramatic clash between Clarence Darrow's defense of rationality and science and William Jennings Bryan's promotion of Biblical fundamentalism typified the broader cultural conflicts of the 1920s. While most popular accounts of the time paint Darrow as the clear winner in the battle of legal wits, the court's actual decision was in favor of the anti-evolution laws. The conviction was overturned a short time later, but only on a technicality. The national struggle between science and religion, between progressive and traditional ways of thinking, was far from over.

Ambivalence towards progressive, scientific approaches to life was also an important part of the broader cultural imaginary. Science's promise of a utopian life was viciously mocked in such films as Roland West's *The Monster*, a 1925 film starring Lon Chaney as a mad scientist seeking to transfer souls from body to body, and Fritz Lang's celebrated *Metropolis* (1926), and whatever remained of these hopes seemed largely dashed by Great Depression. As Paul Wells observes, "many horror films of the 1930s demonstrated a particular concern with science and its centrality in the context of social progress."[20] In the midst of global political and economic upheaval, the question of tradition versus progress became all the more pressing and poignant for those seeking a better life for themselves and their families.

Sexual Norms

Questions over cultural knowledge, naturally, correlated with struggles over social norms. The 1920s had, indeed, roared. It was a decade of jazz, illicit alcohol, sexual promiscuity, and gender confusion. The epitome of the Roaring Twenties was the "flapper"—a liberated woman of the jazz age who cut her hair short and began wearing trousers. An earlier generation of women had, ironically, been the principle proponents of the prohibition movement of the first decade of the twentieth century, but now, as George Mowrey notes, "The new woman of the post-war decade changed her attitude toward the consumption of alcoholic beverages, so she has also rapidly changed those pertaining to courtship, marriage, and the rearing of children."[21] While it is easy to overemphasize the progressive changes in a woman's place in the 1920s—the first decade of women's political enfranchisement through the vote—it is clear that this was a decade of dramatic changes. Angela Latham contends, "The 'flapper look' suggested far more than fashionable, if immodest, taste in clothing. It comprised a pose, a posturing, a contrived demeanor."[22] This posture entailed a more aggressive approach towards romantic relations, a more daring form of gender experimentation, and a more independent view of life.

As with other areas of culture, the 1920s represented a period of great moral experimentation within the seemingly secure envelope of American political and economic stability. The 1930s, on the other hand, brought this stability to a crashing end. As Skal observes, "The wreckage of the jazz age was a forbidding landscape." Americans sought out escape amidst the overarching confusion of the 1930s, which included the loss of global political and economic security, conflicts between science and religion, and confusion over gender and sexual norms.[23] For millions of these Americans, something about Tod Browning's tale of vampirism felt right or, in our terms, resonated with their concerns. Importantly, it resonated with these concerns in ways previous films had not.

SILENT SCREAMS

Of course, American audiences had encountered specters and ghouls in their theaters for years. The silent films were full of horrific elements. Indeed, many of the earliest filmmakers, including Georges Méliès, George Albert Smith, and Walter R. Booth, were magicians, and magic was a principal form of entertainment prior to the advent of the moving picture. For these early magicians cum filmmakers, images of ghosts, disappearing women, and horrific demons were part of the trade.

Most of the earliest films, such as Méliès's *The Haunted Castle* (1896) or Brown's *Chinese Magic* (1900), were shorts with limited narrative development or structure. Indeed, both Méliès's film and Brown's run approximately two minutes. It was only in the 1920s that films began to deal at greater length with tales of the horrific. The vast majority of these seemingly supernatural stories, especially the films produced in America, explained away their supernatural elements by the end. Films such as Rupert Julian's highly successful

The Phantom of the Opera (1925), starring Lon Chaney, or even Tod Browning's own *London after Midnight* revealed their monsters to be normal, albeit disfigured, men. Even the influential and celebrated German film *The Cabinet of Dr. Caligari* (directed by Robert Weine in 1919) explains away its macabre elements through mesmerism. As Roy Kinnard notes, "Before *Dracula*, horror films tended to veer away from the supernatural and offered 'logical' explanations for their fantastic onscreen events."[24]

There were, of course, notable exceptions to this rationality, particularly among German films of the 1920s. Two films by F. W. Murnau embraced the supernatural: *The Golem*, a tale of an inanimate sculpture brought to life through Jewish magic, and of most relevance here, *Nosferatu* (1922). Indeed, *Nosferatu* is an unauthorized adaptation of Stoker's novel—an adaptation vigorously opposed by Stoker's widow. Yet, while sharing the same source novel, albeit illicitly, Murnau's silent film is strikingly different from Browning's version. The vampire in *Nosferatu*, Graf Orlock, is a horrific, rat-like creature with long nose and protruding fangs. Additionally, while the film has some stunning stylistic moments, budgetary restrictions limited its overall visual quality.

These precursors, particularly the German films of the supernatural and uncanny, were highly influential on American filmmakers. American audiences, on the other hand, had only limited exposure to these films in their initial release. Many were considered more artistic than cinematic achievements—due in no small part to their heavy borrowing from cubism and other elements of modern art. Most of them received only limited American theatrical engagements—*Nosferatu*, as noted, was the subject of copyright litigation—and all of them faced the heat of anti-German sentiments in the aftermath of the First World War. The Los Angeles debut of *The Cabinet of Dr. Caligari*, for example, faced an anti-German riot so fierce that the owner of Miller's Theater pulled the film from its bill.[25] So, while studios studied these now-classic surreal films of the supernatural and the horrific, American audiences largely passed them by in favor of more rational American fare.

READING *DRACULA*

America's penchant for the cinema of the uncanny in which supernatural events were eventually explained away remained strong into the early years of the talkies. *The Terror* (1929), one of the first films to integrate sound and moving image, was a variation on *The Phantom of the Opera*, in which a maniac terrorizes those in an English mansion. This tendency towards the rational and natural is one of the things that make *Dracula's* popularity so surprising. Many of the classic silent horror films were billed as "melodramas," their horrific elements wrapped up in broader, often romantic, stories. Indeed, prior to 1931 there was no such thing as a "horror film"—a term coined after the success of *Dracula* and its successor, *Frankenstein*. Of course, after 1931, horror became a highly successful and enduring part of American film culture.

Browning's *Dracula*, in fairness, cannot be given all the credit for spawning the horror genre. This is surely due to the cumulative effect of a number of the early horror films. On the other hand, we cannot deny *Dracula*'s place in the history of the genre. *Dracula*'s box-office success opened the floodgates for the other films that would help create the genre and define the American notion of horror. We are left to wonder why this film, with all its flaws, so captured the public imagination that it almost single-handedly launched a new genre of film.

Appearing at a moment when virtually all the categories of American life were suddenly uncertain, *Dracula* and in particular, its titular character embodies this uncertainty—the chaos towards which the world seemed to be slipping. In so doing, *Dracula* poignantly resonates with the cultural upheaval of the early 1930s. Dracula clearly personifies this broader cultural turmoil for his very existence violates numerous core cultural categories: the distinction between living and dead, the separation of human and animal, and the division between past and present. The emergence of this ancient, undead, shape-shifting creature threatens the stability of both the natural and social world. For the characters in the film this threat is immediate; to reestablish normality, the count must be slain.

The violation of categories, as Noel Carroll observes in his insightful *The Philosophy of Horror*, is a crucial aspect of every monster. Monsters blur categorical separations like "living and dead" and "human and animal" and, therefore, threaten our basic understanding of ourselves and the world around us. Dracula, even in his initial literary characterization, is the embodiment of the violation. As Rosemary Jackson notes regarding Stoker's novel: "His appearance means that chaos is come again, for he is *before* good or evil, outside human categorization."[26] Within the film, Dracula embodies an almost primordial chaos—an ancient aporia in which all categories of civilization crumble and decay.

For the audiences of 1931, the existential horror of Dracula's status as ancient, undead, human/animal is magnified by the ways that the film resonates with the turmoil in more concrete aspects of culture. *Dracula*, as I'll try to read it, picks up on the broader cultural anxieties about National Identity, Economics/Class, Cultural Knowledge, and Sexuality and does so in ways that dramatically violated audiences' expectations. Importantly, the character Dracula embodies the violation of all these categories, and it is the intersection of these broad cultural anxieties that contributes to Dracula as embodied chaos. He represents a rupture in the fabric of civilization; precisely the kind of rupture that seemed increasingly likely in the darkest year of the interwar period.

National Identity

Dracula opens dramatically with a carriage speeding down a picturesque mountain pass. The first lines of dialogue describe the exotic nature of the wilds of central Europe. A young American woman reads from her guidebook: "Among the rugged peaks that frown down upon the Borgol Pass are found the crumbling castles of a bygone age." When the English passengers complain about the carriage's speed, the heavily accented locals explain: "We must reach the inn before sundown! It is Walpurgis Night, the night of evil Nosferatu! On this night, madame, the doors, they are barred and to the Virgin we pray." By the time the carriage stops in the village inn, there can be no doubt that the journey we are witnessing is through a largely uncivilized, or at the very least unsophisticated, land. The heavy accents, almost primitively superstitious Catholic gestures, and strange regional costumes make it fairly clear that the journey is passing through the dark wilds of central Europe.

Watching the film today, the setting, which we later learn is Transylvania, a region of Romania, seems naturally, almost inextricably, bound to the myth of the vampire. When Stoker first wrote *Dracula*, however, the setting was not necessarily linked with superstitious folklore and tales of vampirism. Stephen Arata notes: "Transylvania was known primarily as part of the vexed 'Eastern Question' that so obsessed British foreign policy in the 1880s and 90s. The region was first and foremost the site, not of superstition and Gothic romance, but of political turbulence and racial strife."[27]

Despite the popularity of Stoker's novel, there can be little doubt that audiences in 1931 had a similar sense of central and eastern Europe. Romania, it is worth recalling, sits on the eastern border of the Balkan region—a region prior to the First World War known as the "Balkan tinderbox" as a result of its turbulent politics. Hundreds of thousands of American men had gone to war because of, at least in part, events arising out of the turbulent politics of the Balkans. A horrific creature arising out of the Balkans must have made some sense to American audiences. Concerning Stoker's novel, Richard Wasson suggests that Dracula's invasion of Britain is a kind of grotesque caricature of British imperialism.[28] In a similar fashion, the 1931 film can be read as a caricature of America's political/military involvement in Europe. Dracula's invasion of America—via its fictional proxy England—can be seen as a kind of political consequence for America's abandonment of isolationist policies.

Dracula himself, of course, is dramatically foreign. His accent is extreme and his mannerisms peculiar. When we first meet the count his oddity is striking. He wears a cape and lives in a crumbling castle. His initial conversation with Renfield is filled with creepy non sequiturs interrupted by the howls of wolves and the movement of spiders.

Dracula's strangeness is made all the more disturbing when he arrives in London and is able to move without detection among the residents of the city. As Arata observes, "A large part of the terror he inspires originates in his ability to stroll, unrecognized and unhindered, through the streets of London."[29] With imagery reminiscent of Jack the Ripper—whose crimes occurred only thirty-two years earlier—Dracula moves through the streets. He passes through crowds on his way to his first onscreen victim, an impoverished flower girl. He enters the opera and interacts with the Seward party. Perhaps most striking, as Dracula approaches Lucy's apartment for the fatal attack, he passes a police officer. The officer nods and says, "Park seems to be closing down a bit, sir."

Van Helsing recognizes the danger. When his colleagues object that Dracula cannot be a vampire because such creatures do not exist, Van Helsing warns that this lack of belief will be shared by "your English doctors, your police. The strength of the vampire is that people will not believe in him." In this way Dracula's threatening otherness is far more frightening than Murnau's Nosferatu. His monstrousness is not immediately visible, the threat not immediately apparent. This fear of the unknown must have resonated deeply with an America that had grown increasingly fearful of others. The "war to end all wars" had clearly not lived up to its billing, and by 1931 the rumble of war was already audible across the Atlantic. Further, while the massive numbers of immigrants into the United States had been greatly reduced by quotas implemented in the 1920s, Dracula embodied American's greatest fear of eastern European immigrants—that they would bring their strange customs and political strife to American soil. In this way, Dracula represented a greatly magnified version of the underlying fear of the immigrant other.

One potential strain of this fear deserves special acknowledgment: anti-Semitism. While Dracula is certainly not designated as Jewish, certain aspects of his characterization suggest a potential resonance with Jewish stereotypes of the 1930s. With regards to Stoker's novel, Judith Halberstam writes, "Dracula ... resembles the Jew of anti-Semitic discourse in several ways: his appearance, his relation to money/gold, his parasitism, his degeneracy, his impermanence or lack of allegiance to a fatherland, and his femininity. Dracula's physical aspects, his physiognomy, is a particularly clear cipher for the specificity of his ethnic monstrosity."[30] Sadly, many of these characteristics continued in both anti-Semitic discourse of the 1930s and in the representation of the vampire in Browning's film. Perhaps most visibly, Dracula's medallion bears some resemblance to the Star of David. His origin in central Europe might also have cast him in broad anti-Semitic hues as well. If some members of the audience read Dracula within the discourse of anti-Semitism, then it is unfortunate that the vampire's portrayal would have fed the most vile of these stereotypes. Dracula is portrayed as a dangerous, rodent-like creature that threatens to infest Western Europe with his kind—precisely the kinds of horrid propaganda promoted by anti-Semitic and early Nazi literature. Read in this way, as perhaps some did in 1931, the scene in which Renfield reveals the promises Dracula has made becomes all the more chilling. Renfield describes an encounter with his vampire master:

> A red mist spread over the lawn, coming on like a flame of fire. And then he parted it and I could see that there were thousands of rats, with eyes blazing red, like his only smaller. And then he held up his hand and they all stopped and I thought he seemed to be saying, "Rats, rats, rats, thousands, millions of them, all red blood, all these will I give you if you obey me."

Read within the broader culture of American anti-Semitism, this scene bears a disturbing parallel with the Biblical story of the exodus from Egypt and the parting of the Red Sea, which enabled the children of Israel to escape the pharaoh's armies. While I am certainly not suggesting that the film intentionally casts Dracula or his promise to Renfield as anti-Jewish propaganda, given the prevalence of anti-Semitism in both Europe and America, it is possible that these elements of the story resonated with cultural prejudices. At the very least, it seems possible that some aspects of the film resonated with American xenophobia in general and, perhaps, anti-Semitism as well.

Economics/Class

Arguably, one of the most striking moments in the first reel is the conversation between Renfield and one of the frightened villagers who is seeking to dissuade him from going on with his journey. The villager warns Renfield, "We the people of the mountains believe at the Castle there are vampires. Dracula and his wives, they take the form of wolves and bats. They leave their coffins at night and they feed on the blood of the living." Renfield rebuffs these warnings, stating, "I've explained to the driver that it's *a matter of business with me.*" A matter of business. For audiences watching the film in the midst of the Great Depression, this explanation must have struck an odd chord. It had been "a matter of business" that led investors to carelessly speculate their money until the bottom fell out of the market, and it was a "matter of business" that led to massive unemployment and runs on the banks.

At its most basic level, Dracula's invasion of England is the result of a real estate deal gone bad. Renfield, the venture capitalist, travels to the chaotic regions of central Europe's wilderness in the pursuit of profit. His effort to extract profit from the most remote regions, however, backfires, and he falls victim to his own greed. There is more than a note of irony in the fact that the capitalist real estate broker is turned into a sniveling wretch who seeks to suck the blood from smaller, weaker creatures. The Great Depression had inflicted a similar fate on the venture capitalists in America. It was a great chaos that reduced businessmen to shadows of their former selves. The great capitalist "bloodsuckers," one might suggest, had fallen victim to the magnified embodiment of their own greed.

There is another interesting story of economic class underlying *Dracula*. After Renfield's enslavement, Dracula's first onscreen victim is an apparently poor flower peddler. Yet, there is little apparent reaction to this death within the film itself. The uproar over these attacks and, hence, the motivation that propels the plot occur only after the attack on Lucy. As we watch the autopsy of Lucy's body, we are told that she was "another victim." What then of these other victims? As far as we can tell from what we are shown, these other victims were from the lower classes and so were under the radar of the authorities. Just as Dracula's carnivorous hunger knows no national boundaries, so too it ignores class boundaries. Our protagonists, however, are not only clearly marked as members of the upper class, they only are motivated to destroy the vampire once he has crossed the class boundary and taken Lucy. There is an almost egalitarian simplicity in Dracula's feeding that, perhaps, helped to make him more intriguing to audiences in 1931. Perhaps, his seductiveness is, in part, a result of his flaunting of class and economic boundaries, his ability to cross these barriers with little regard to economic or cultural propriety.

Cultural Knowledge

The conflict between science and religion—two opposed ways of knowing the world—is most explicit in the films that followed *Dracula*. *Frankenstein* makes this its central theme, as do *Dr. Jekyll and Mr. Hyde* and *The Invisible Man*. However, the struggle between "rational" science and "superstitious" religion is also evident in the vampire's tale. Where *Frankenstein*, *Dr. Jekyll and Mr Hyde*, and *The Invisible Man* all offer cautionary tales of science pushed too far—a theme picked up more dramatically in the creature features of the 1950s—*Dracula* offers a much less clear sense of how we are to know the world or where the limits of our knowledge should lie. In the contest between science and religion, *Dracula* provides only uncertainty and doubt.

The villagers we meet early in *Dracula* are, with little doubt, only slightly more than objects of ridicule. Their heavy accents, strange local dress, and overly dramatic Catholic gestures seem almost comical. They certainly are treated that way by Renfield, who disregards their warnings, telling them "that's all superstition." The old woman who pushes him to wear a crucifix only persuades him by begging, "If you must go, wear this ... for your mother's sake." A few minutes later, we see the wisdom of these fearful peasants. As Renfield nurses a cut finger, the count's hunger overcomes his demeanor, and he stalks in to feed only to be driven back by the sight of the crucifix. The superstitious advice of the villagers, we quickly learn, is accurate.

This struggle between rationality and superstition continues to dominate the film's plot. The "rational" men, Dr. Seward and Harker, dismiss the possibility of a vampire in their midst. Dr. Seward exclaims, "Modern medical science does not admit of such a creature. The vampire is pure myth, superstition." Harker rebuffs Van Helsing, stating, "That's the sort of thing I'd expect one of the patients to say."

In a way, it is fitting that the third act of *Dracula* plays out mainly in the Seward Sanitarium. The question of sanity and insanity mingles with the broader questions of cultural knowledge. What are we to make of those superstitions that we carry along in our cultural memory—the ghosts and ghouls we now dismiss as unscientific? More pressing, what are we to make of those individuals who dismiss the rational scientific explanation in favor of the traditional or religious? As the plot of *Dracula* unfolds, an audience unfamiliar with tales of the genuinely supernatural, might well begin to question the sanity of all the players. As Martin, Dr. Seward's comical orderly, informs a maid in one of the film's moments of comic relief, "They're all crazy. They're all crazy except you and me. Sometimes I have me doubts about you." Harker's doubts about Van Helsing and his belief in vampires lead him to contend that it is the professor himself who is causing Mina's strange behavior, "Do you know what you're doing professor? You're driving her crazy!"

Caught between the incompatible claims of science and religion, the key players and, by proxy, the audience, are left to question their grip on the reality of their situation and, thus, their sanity. The reconciliation of this tension, to the extent there is one, comes in the person of Van Helsing, the famous scientist; Dracula has heard of him "even in the wilds of Transylvania." We first encounter Van Helsing as he examines blood in a test tube and is able, through some unexplained calculations, to determine that they are dealing with a vampire. Science and religion, as Van Helsing explains, are not necessarily incompatible. He counters Dr. Seward's incredulity towards vampirism by exclaiming, "But I may be able to bring you proof that the superstition of yesterday can become the scientific reality of today!"

If Van Helsing brought forward a scientific explanation of the vampire's existence, then the film could be said to have achieved some level of reconciliation between science and religion. Later vampire films, such as Kathryn Bigelow's *Near Dark* (1987) or Stephen Norrington's *Blade* (1998), provide this kind of scientific explanation—usually some kind of virus in the blood of the vampire. *Dracula* provides no such explanation, and in the end, Van Helsing, the scientist, employs only the elements of superstition—mirrors, a crucifix, wolfsbane, and a wooden stake—to vanquish the vampire. Rather than integrating science and religion, the conclusion of *Dracula* simply replaces one with the other without offering us any resolution to their conflict. Further, by replacing scientific certainty with the vagaries of superstition, *Dracula*'s conclusion leaves its audience no clearer about the foundations of the knowledge of the world. The only certainty we are given, at least in the original print prior to its 1938 reediting, is in the final curtain speech by Van Helsing: that the thing we dread is lurking behind our curtains or under our bed is, indeed, there! In other words, the only certainty we are provided is a foundation of uncertainty and fear.

Sexuality

Commenting on the enduring appeal of the vampire in American cinema, popular critic Roger Ebert notes, "The vampire Dracula has been the subject of more than thirty films; something deep within the legend is suited to cinema. Perhaps it is the joining of eroticism and terror."[31] Literary critics have long read Stoker's version in terms of its deeply sexual undertones, especially with regards to an underlying Freudian sensibility in the novel. Browning's *Dracula*, of course, also exhibits the kind of implicit and subtle sexuality allowed by the Production Code in the 1930s.

As with the other cultural strands, the sexuality of *Dracula* is one of transgression and boundary destabilization. Dracula's own sexuality is markedly unclear. At one level, he is a ravenous heterosexual with three brides and designs on two English women, Lucy and Mina. His power of seduction is overwhelming; all those we see him hypnotize are women, who immediately fall into his power. Yet, if we are to read Dracula's bite as somehow sexual—heavily suggested by Mina's recounting of his assault on her—then what are we to make of his attack on the prone Renfield? Carl Laemmle Jr. was so concerned about this he jotted a note in his copy of the final script reading, "Dracula should only go for women and not men!"[32] The potentially homoerotic nature of the vampire's attack, or kiss, has long been part of its literary tradition. Daryl Jones contends,

> From its very beginnings as a literary trope, vampirism has always been used as a vehicle for more-or-less encoded articulations of sexuality and desire (as a way of writing about sex without writing about sex), and importantly (though not exclusively) of articulating homosexual desire, thus operating on a dialectic of vampirism as dissident or deviant.[33]

While some critics choose to pursue this observation along more Freudian lines, with Dracula's penetrating kiss approximating the *vagina dentata* (the vagina with teeth) and thus operating as a kind of hermaphroditic sexual organ, it should suffice here to observe that by the standards of 1931 Dracula's escapades, including polygamy, sexual assault, and possibly, homosexuality, were wildly transgressive of existing norms.

Dracula's transgressions, moreover, are infectious. Consider the fate of his "surviving" victims. Renfield, the confident English businessman, becomes like a sniveling child—ranting and raving, spoiled and belligerent. He vacillates between loyalty and betrayal and looks up to the elder vampire almost as a child looks up to a father or as a younger lover admires an older man.

The fates of Lucy and Mina are equally instructive. Lucy and Mina both meet the count in the opera house early in the film's second act. Mina is shy and proper—almost clinging to her fiancé, Harker. Lucy, on the other hand, gives all the appearance of a more liberated woman. Her short-cropped blonde hair and more sexualized dress are reminiscent of the flappers of an earlier decade. When these two women meet Dracula, their reactions are diametrically opposed. Lucy is drawn to the count's exoticism. Mere moments before she is attacked she tells Mina, "I think he's fascinating." Mina, on the other hand, is repelled by the count's strange behavior. She tells Lucy that she desires someone "more normal."

After their respective encounters with the count each of these young women undergo a dramatic change in character. Lucy, of course, has become one of the living dead. The newspaper account that we hear of her nocturnal activities and our brief glimpse of her suggest her fate. Lucy, our liberated flapper, wears a gown of white and gathers small children to her. She has, in other words, become a vision—albeit a distorted one—of the traditional, maternal wife; a bride in white in pursuit of a child.

Mina's sexual transformation appears on screen and is, therefore, more dramatic. She describes her first encounter with Dracula in highly sexualized terms: "It came closer and closer. I felt its breath on my face, and then its lips, ohhh ... and then in the morning, I felt so weak. It seemed as if all the life had been drained out of me." Harker reacts to this erotic vision by urging her to "forget all about these dreams," but Dracula's attacks on Mina further open up her sexuality. When Dracula enters the room, just as she has finished recounting her "dream," Mina's face changes and her breathing becomes harder. At the sight of her vampire lover she exclaims, "I'm feeling quite well."

The sexual nature of Mina's encounters with the vampire is quite explicit. In a later scene, we observe Dracula embrace Mina, and she is enveloped in the blackness of his cloak. Of this attack she later explains: "Dracula, he ... he came to me. He opened his vein in his arm and he made me drink." The passing of fluids now complete, Mina has become a corrupted woman. As Harker seeks to comfort her, she rebuffs his pure advances, saying, "No, John. You mustn't touch me. And you mustn't kiss me, ever again.... It's all over John, our love, our life together." Mina's changed sexuality is also evident in the film's most sexually charged scene. Escaping her "vampire-proof" room, Mina escorts Harker onto the terrace and into the dark, foggy night. Dracula, in the form of a large vampire bat, hovers overhead, communicating to Mina through indecipherable squeaks. As Mina attempts to persuade Harker to help her thwart Van Helsing's plans, she begins to breathe heavily and fixes his neck with a ravenous look. Now Harker cannot ignore his beloved's overt sexuality, and he exclaims, "Mina, you're so like a ... changed girl!" It is only the intervention of Van Helsing and his crucifix that save Harker from Mina's ravenous appetites just as it is only the slaying of the sexually transgressive vampire that paves the way for a return to sexual normalcy for Mina and all concerned.

RESOLUTION?

American audiences in 1931 were facing a period of overwhelming cultural upheaval. The resolution of the First World War was rapidly sowing the seeds for the second. Global economic upheaval had sent millions to the bread lines, and the promise of a scientific utopia had, seemingly, vanished as Americans struggled to deter-mine how to live their lives, how to derive appropriate cultural val-ues, and how to protect their families. Americans, in other words, faced threats to their national, economic, cultural, and sexual iden-tity. Dracula emerged into this world of upheaval and uncertainty as the perfect embodiment of precisely the kind of chaos Americans most feared: an invasive, foreign creature of unnatural origins brought to their shores through greed and avarice and now threaten-ing the core values of their civilization.

Given the pervasiveness of the cultural anxiety and the perfec-tion with which the vampire resonated with those anxieties, one would suspect that *Dracula* ends with a reassuring sense of finality. At one level, the film does achieve a degree of resolution. The for-eign threat, at least we are told, is slain. The threatened upper class is again safe through the scientist's ability to use traditional reli-gious tools, and the sanctity of normal sexuality is reestablished. Indeed, the film's final narrative scene is Harker escorting Mina up the Abbey's crumbling stairwell to the sound of distant bells, per-haps suggesting a final, normalizing wedding between the two.

Upon closer examination, it is hard to see any resolution in the film's ending. While Dracula is slain, we experience the death off screen, watching Mina's almost erotic reaction to the vampire's death moans rather than the act itself. This offscreen death deprives us not only of the certainty that the vampire is dead, but also, as John Flynn observes, "robs the audience of the much needed cathar-sis."[34] Further, for audiences prior to 1938, the final curtain speech must have furthered this sense that the threatening chaos of the vampire was not ended but only held off for the moment. It is in this sense that the notion of violation becomes most poignant. The end-ing of *Dracula* provides it audience with no clear return to the nor-malcy and rationality of their "sane" lives. Rather, as audience members filed out of the auditorium, the threatening chaos embod-ied by the vampire lingered behind the curtains—both the curtains of the theater palace and of their own homes.

DRACULA'S LEGACY

Gothic fiction, of which *Dracula* is clearly a part, weaves tales in which something from the past returns. Out of those things we be-lieved we had left behind comes some thing to haunt our present and remind us that our confidence in our knowledge of the world is unfounded. Out of this distant past comes the chaos and savagery that we believed ourselves beyond.

Audiences sitting in the theater palaces of 1931 must surely have felt the resonance between the onscreen embodiment of amoral chaos and the offscreen whirlwinds of cultural, political and economic change. American culture was in the midst of widespread uncertainty, an uncertainty that encompassed moral, cultural, economic, and political facets of its national identity. At the heart of all these conflicts was a struggle between progress and tradition. As a nation, America struggled to forge an identity separate from its ties to Europe. As an economy, America sought to find a path out of the economic devastation of the Great Depression. As moral agents, Americans struggled to balance the progressive intellectual and moral experimentation of the twenties with the deeper traditions of their Judeo-Christian heritage. Read in this way, Dracula becomes an almost perfect embodiment of the underlying chaos threatening to unravel the thin fabric of American culture. Out of the distant, superstitious, European past came an entity of disorder and unrest whose hunger knows no political, class, moral, or natural boundaries.

Like the past itself, this embodiment of ancient chaos can never be fully vanquished but only momentarily overcome. The shadow of uncertainty that lingers in the final moments of Dracula parallels this general angst that the ghosts of our past can never be fully laid to rest. Dracula's seeming immortality may also stem from his underlying charisma. There is, after all, something seductive in this chaos from the past—the desire to succumb to our inner drives and urges and abandon the pretense of civilized society. This urge must have seemed particularly appealing in the midst of the apparent decay of modern society. If the vampire is indeed slain at the end of Browning's film we know that it is not final. Perhaps, it is only that we hope it is not final, that we hope the chaos embodied in the vampire continues to lurk in the shadows of our rationalized society. Caught between communism and fascism, between the dictates of science and the dogma of religion, Americans in 1931 may well have found in the voracious vampire count an appealing, if only momentary, liberator.

In terms of the cultural imaginary, Dracula was certainly a liberator of sorts—liberating a number of his fellow Gothic literary peers into the twentieth century world of film. The success of Dracula opened the floodgates of Gothic literature, and many of the horror films of the early 1930s continued to play out themes of national, economic, and cultural uncertainty. By the mid-1930s, however, the appeal of these Gothic creatures waned only to be renewed at the end of the decade. Sparked by the novelty of a *Dracula/Frankenstein* double bill in 1938, Universal and other studios returned to the Gothic in such films as *Son of Frankenstein* (1941), *The Wolf Man* (1941), and even *Frankenstein Meets the Wolf Man* (1943) and *Son of Dracula* (1943). Most of these films lacked the innovative punch of their predecessors, and by 1948 the death knell for these classic ghouls was rung by Charles T. Barton's *Abbott and Costello meet Frankenstein* (1948). While their legends endured and their films would continue to frighten children in midnight movies and television reruns, the age of the Gothic monster had come to an end.

2 *The Thing from Another World* (1951)

"Keep watching the skies!"

If the interwar years were haunted by legacies of the past, the post-war years were filled with uncertainties about the future. The end of the Second World War had left Americans in a decidedly unfamiliar world: a world of jet aircraft and atomic bombs and a world in which America was one of only two economic and military superpowers. The development of the atomic bomb by U.S. scientists in 1945 and the subsequent unveiling of a Soviet atomic weapon in 1949 heralded the beginning of a new American culture: a culture filled with television, "drop and cover" civil defense drills, rock and roll, and invaders from outer space.

In June 1947, Kenneth Arnold reported spotting a group of crescent-shaped objects flying in formation and at great speed near Mount Rainier, Washington. In 1948, newspapers around the world reported the crash landing of a flying saucer near an Air Force base in Roswell, New Mexico. By 1950, Americans had developed a cultural replacement for the Gothic ghouls from the crypt—little green men from flying saucers. As Richard Schwartz observes, "Despite an official U.S. Air Force investigation that concluded in 1949 that there was no evidence of their existence, the possibility of extraterrestrial visitations quickly caught the public imagination. It is within this context that the space invasion movies of the 1950s arose."[1]

Science fiction, of course, has a long history in literature dating back, at least, to writers such as H. G. Wells and Jules Verne who speculated about invasions from Mars, time machines, and journeys to the center of the earth. It is interesting to note that Cecil B. DeMille had plans to adapt H. G. Wells's *War of the Worlds* into an epic film as early as 1925.[2] However, it was not until the 1950s that American culture turned to the stars for its monsters. In the aftermath of the Second World War and the early years of the Cold War, American culture had changed so that it required new monsters, new horrors. While the Gothic creatures of old enjoyed reruns on television and at drive-in movies, their tales of the past no longer resonated with the fears of American filmgoers, and just as important, they were no longer able to offer shocks or surprises.

The 1950s was a new era and required a new monster—the invading alien creature. By the end of the 1950s, Americans would see literally hundreds of them: from body snatchers to robot monsters, from invisible "monsters from the id" to amorphous consuming blobs.[3] However, at the beginning of this alien onslaught there were two very different alien invaders. One was a philosophical messiah who came to invite the world into the broader galactic community and offer sage advice. *The Day the Earth Stood Still* offered a reflective vision of the future and the place of humanity in the broader cosmos, a future heralded by the messianic alien figure of Klaatu. The counterpoint to Klaatu's benevolence appeared in theaters about five months earlier and offered a much more horrific and disturbing vision of contact with other worlds. In April 1951, an "intellectual carrot," a kind of "vampire vegetable," arrived in the arctic wasteland to turn the human race into food for its offspring—Howard Hawks's *The Thing from Another World*.

While filming *I Was a Male War Bride* in Heidelberg, renowned American director Howard Hawks picked up a copy of *Astounding Science Fiction*. In the pages of this popular "pulp" magazine of science fiction stories, Hawks came across a short story titled "Who Goes There?" which was written by the magazine's editor, John Campbell, under the pseudonym "Don Stuart." Two years later and facing a three-picture obligation with RKO-Radio Studio, Hawks's independent production house, Winchester Pictures, optioned the story. As Hawks would later recall in an interview with Peter Bogdanovich, "I bought the story; it was just four pages long, and we took about a week to write it."[4] *The Thing* allowed Hawks, who had gained fame directing westerns and war films, to make an unexpected stretch into a new genre. His long-time script clerk, Richard Keinen would later recall, "We all thought it was the dumbest thing we'd ever heard of.

What is Howard Hawks doing making this stupid horror film."[5] *The Thing* also afforded Hawks an opportunity to repay a debt to editor Christian Nyby, who had helped salvage Hawks's *Red River* (1948), by making him the film's "director," although, by all accounts, Nyby's direction was in name only. As Robert Cornthwaite, who played Dr. Carrington, recalled, "On a Hawks picture, there was only one boss. He was an absolute autocrat."[6]

As with Gothic literature, elements of science fiction have been present in film since its earliest days. Early silent films derived from stories of science and outer space include Méliès iconic *A Trip to the Moon* (1902) as well as lesser known films such as Edison's 1910 *A Trip to Mars*. However, the birth of science fiction as a recognized genre of film would wait until the 1950s, and by 1951 almost all the major studios were pursuing science fiction projects. *The Thing* was not the first. It was preceded in 1950 by lower budget films such as Kurt Neumann's *Rocketship XM* and Mikel Conrad's *The Flying Saucer* and by Irving Pichel's more polished but less fantastic film about manned flight into space, *Destination Moon*. *The Thing*, however, had a number of advantages over these earlier films: it was well produced with a substantial budget, it incorporated a fantastic monster with realistic technical and military features, and of course, it was a "Howard Hawks Production." The film was heavily publicized and used the clever trick of keeping its plot largely a secret to pique audience interest. Hawks's film also received unexpected and inadvertent publicity from the popular—and completely unrelated—novelty song "The Thing" by Phil Harris.[7]

Released in April 1951, *The Thing from Another World* was enormously popular, and along with its counterpoint, *The Day the Earth Stood Still*, laid the foundation for the science fiction genre for decades to come. Released about five months ahead of *The Day the Earth Stood Still*, *The Thing* would also gross slightly more, with a box office of about $1.95 million. While the broader cultural hysteria over flying saucers and the growing space race made the growth of the science fiction film inevitable, the twin pillars of *The Thing* and *The Day* established the contour of the genre for decades to come.

SYNOPSIS

In Campbell's short story, "Who Goes There?" an alien has been buried in the arctic ice for 50,000 years. When it is uncovered, the alien "thing" is revealed to be a shape-shifting malevolent creature that assumes the form of his victims in order to kill more of the trapped explorers. Fortunately, the survivors find a means of discerning friend from alien foe in time to stop the creature before it escapes and spreads its kind across the planet. *The Thing from Another World* simplifies this plot and converts the doppelganger/identity plot into a more straightforward search-and-destroy mission. Hawks's Thing does not change shapes but does pursue a plan of reproduction, via seed pods nourished on human and animal blood, and eventual world conquest.

Hawks's film opens with the words "The Thing" melting or burning their way through the blackness of the screen. After the credits, the scene opens in a military officer's club where a close-knit group of soldiers accompanied by a newspaper reporter is sent to check on a scientific encampment on the North Pole. Upon arriving, the crew is alerted to a strange aircraft crash in the area, and upon traveling to the site, the soldiers and scientists find a flying saucer and its alien pilot encased in the arctic ice. While the ship is destroyed in the attempt to melt the ice, the creature is extracted and flown—still encased in a large block of ice—back to the camp.

While the military and scientific groups argue about whether or not to remove the body from the ice block, the creature is inadvertently thawed and escapes. The film continues with a progressively tense cat-and-mouse game between the creature and the humans. Unable to escape or make contact with the outside world because of inclement weather, the group bickers about how to handle the situation. The soldiers set about trying to capture and destroy the alien creature, the scientists insist it should be studied and communicated with.

Eventually, we learn that the creature is some kind of vegetable—an "intellectual carrot"—who lives on blood and is seeking to plant its seed. The scientists even speculate that it is emotionless, driven only by intellect and rationality, and is bent on conquering the planet with an army of similar plant things. While the cold does not affect the plant, the group reasons that it can be burned, and after trying to burn the Thing with kerosene, they devise a plan to use electricity. A trap is laid, and the group lures the creature to the appointed spot where it is burned by an electrical arc until nothing is left. The humans are left to care for the wounded and alert the world to "Keep watching the skies!"

Unlike *Dracula*, the success of *The Thing* is not entirely surprising. Where Browning was a director struggling to find his footing in the age of the "talking picture," Hawks—the authorial force behind the film—was a filmmaker at the height of his prowess and popularity. Additionally, where *Dracula* broke new Gothic ground and ushered in an unprecedented genre of horror, by 1951 it was clear that science fiction would become a major film genre. Almost every major studio had a science fiction film somewhere in development when *The Thing* was released, and science fiction would become a dominant genre of the decade. As Patrick Lucanio observes, "The proliferation of science fiction films is one of the most interesting developments in post–World War II film history. An estimated 500 film features and shorts made between 1948 and 1962 can be indexed under the broad heading of science fiction."[8]

What makes *The Thing* historically interesting is its position as the first film that effectively integrated science fiction and horror. Despite some efforts to distinguish the two genres, efforts I'll consider at more length below, *The Thing* succeeds by refashioning elements of Gothic horror within a broader cultural aesthetic of science fiction. In important ways, *The Thing* and *The Day the Earth Stood Still* provided a narrative foundation for the progress of science fiction. *The Day* paved the way for modern films such as *E.T.* (1982), *Close Encounters of the Third Kind* (1977), and *Starman* (1984), while *The Thing* opened the door for films such as *Alien* (1979), *Predator* (1987), and *Species* (1995). Critic Bill Warren considers *The Thing* one of the four most important science fiction films since 1950 and credits it with bringing "the idea of creatures from other planets coming here to vivid life."[9]

What makes *The Thing* theoretically interesting, especially in terms of the broader goals of this book, is the way that it picks up many of the broad issues we found in Browning's *Dracula*. However, Hawks's film constructs these same broad cultural anxieties in very different ways. In other words, Hawks's film resonates with these cultural anxieties in a way unique to 1950s America. Read in this way, *The Thing* can be compared to *Dracula* to suggest the ways American culture had changed in the years following the Second World War.

To accentuate this notion, I will analyze *The Thing* along the same lines as we previously used to examined *Dracula*. *The Thing*, I will contend, is also a film that engages a widespread American fear of upheaval and chaos. Further, I will seek to articulate the points of resonance between elements in the film and the same broad categories of cultural anxiety as were found in Chapter One: National Identity, Economics, Cultural Knowledge, and Sexuality. What I hope to show through this exercise is not that *The Thing* is a rehash of its predecessor but that the changes in American culture in combination with the overfamiliarity of the Gothic tales created a space in the cultural imagination where Hawks's invading alien could achieve a high level of resonant violation.

CULTURAL CONTEXT

In the 1930s, Americans feared they were being dragged into chaos by outside forces they could not control. By the 1950s, America found itself in a position of leadership—one of only two major global superpowers. Americans shouldered the leadership of the "free world" in a conflict with the communist world led by the Soviet Union. In a way, the Second World War had a familiar hue for those who had survived the first—a conflict drawn out of German aggression and central European politics. The Cold War, on the other hand, with its global scope and horrific weaponry, was an uncharted terrain—a terrain into which America was to lead its allies and the world.

National Identity

Arguably, the Second World War didn't end in 1945 but merely transformed into a second phase. Fascism had been the first enemy, an enemy engaged through direct combat. Communism was the second enemy. With the introduction of atomic weapons, this was an enemy that could not be engaged directly but rather, through a series of indirect clashes. The Cold War began almost immediately after the defeat of the Axis powers. The Soviet blockade of Berlin began in 1948 but was defeated within a year by an allied airlift of supplies into the besieged city. By 1949, the Soviet Union had exploded its own atomic bomb, and both countries were soon pushing to develop more powerful weapons such as the hydrogen bomb.

By 1950, the first of the Cold War skirmishes began as U.S. forces were officially committed to the "police action" known as the Korean War. Unlike the conflicts of the previous decades, the invasion of South Korea by the North and the subsequent commitment of U.S. troops came as an almost complete surprise to most Americans, including the Truman administration.[10] The undeclared war in Korea lasted only three years but would be America's fourth bloodiest war—more than 50,000 Americans lost their lives in the fighting.

Reactions to the war at home reveal an interesting contradiction emerging within America's Cold War cultural logic. On the one hand, with the entry of China into the conflict and the looming possibility of Soviet involvement, the Korean War represented the very real possibility of a Third World War and the widespread use of atomic weapons. Speaker of the House Sam Rayburn warned in early 1951 that the nation may be facing "the beginning of World War III," and war correspondent Hanson W. Baldwin declared that the Korean conflict represented "the greatest danger in our history."[11] While initially a popular conflict, Americans began to turn away from the conflict as early as 1951. As historian Stanley Sandler observes, "As the war degenerated into weary stalemate, however, the American public, according to practically all indicators, continued to accept the war with a sullen resignation, and the conflict faded, if not from the front pages, at least out of the headlines. Americans picked up the thread of what would distinguish the decade of the 1950s: the motorized flight to suburbia amidst a prospering economy, punctuated only occasionally by a brief notice in a hometown newspaper of a local boy's death in Korea."[12]

Perhaps unable to sustain the unified effort of the Second World War, even in the face of a potentially greater threat, Americans effectively turned the problem over to a technically sophisticated and increasingly professional military. The postwar period maintained a combat and military orientation. As Russell Shain notes, "Since 1939, the country has sustained an efficiency of war alertness—economically, militarily, and emotionally."

The prominence of the military and war readiness in American culture was also reflected in the films of the period. While war-related films were most dominant during the early 1940s, averaging more than 25 percent of the total film output between 1942 and 1944, the 1950s saw a substantial number of war-related films, averaging almost 10 percent of the total American film output between 1951 and 1959.[13] The 1950s were also a time when, as Per Schelde notes, "portraying the military in heroic terms was still the norm."[14] Indeed, many critics of early science fiction films focus on the influence of the military and Cold War ideology on these films. Peter Biskind, for example, attends to the way the science fiction invasion films create a national emergency that "dramatised the need of consensus, of pulling together."[15] This consensus was often towards acquiescence to the authority of the state, usually represented by military officials. Andrew Tudor argues that the science fiction films of the 1950s taught Americans, paraphrasing Stanley Kubrick's *Dr. Strangelove*, "to keep worrying and love the state."[16]

If Cold War ideology suggested a reliance on authorities, it also suggested a keen-eyed watchfulness over those authorities. The spy scandals of the early 1950s paved the way for the surreal paranoia of the McCarthy era. Joseph McCarthy, a junior senator from Wisconsin, rose to remarkable prominence based on his increasingly outlandish claims to have evidence of high-level communist infiltration into the U.S. government. While his paranoid reign would eventually collapse under its own weight in 1953, in the early years of the 1950s he held the country in the grip of a paranoid nightmare. As James Darsey reflects on the period, "In emphasizing the darkness of the postwar world, McCarthy concentrated on what was unseeable and thereby unknowable. His promises notwithstanding, he never turned on the light. Rather he insinuated the lurking presence of 'things that go bump in the night.' There is no salvation here, only the articulation of anxiety."[17]

Behind the paranoia about infiltrating communist spies and the on-again, off-again military clashes, lay the most potent of 1950's America's anxieties. As Joseph Maddrey puts it, "The threat of an impending atomic war was the ultimate collective nightmare."[18] Americans were deeply conflicted about the bomb. On the one hand, many Americans considered it the greatest scientific invention of the century. On the other hand, it was also clear that Pandora's box had been opened, and as the country began the atomic arms race with the Soviet Union, the deadly possibility of the bomb became all the more palpable. The proliferation of atomic weapons made the metaphorical "doomsday clock" all the more literal. Picking up this notion, Hannah Arendt labeled the generation of the fifties, "those who hear the ticking."[19]

Economics

America's economic revival, sparked largely by the growing military-industrial complex, led to a return of the scientific-efficiency efforts from the 1920s. By the 1950s, America's economy was largely organized by the principles of "Fordism." Derived largely from the assembly-line logic of Henry Ford, the system of Fordism expanded to encompass the relationship between corporations, labor, governments, and eventually, the broader culture. As Mark Jancovich explains, "Fordism was a system of centrally ordered administration which relied on an elite of experts. It was their task to regulate social, political, economic and cultural life, and they did so through the use of scientific-technical rationality."[20]

While Fordism proved effective in revitalizing America's postwar economy, it carried with it a number of questionable cultural tendencies. First, Fordism relied heavily on a cadre of elite experts, preferring the opinions of experts to the deliberation of the average citizen. Second, corporate and governmental systems were organized through a kind of cold, scientific rationality as opposed to traditional or sentimental principles. The underlying principle of cultural development became "progress." In his 1953 book *The Ethics of Rhetoric*, Richard Weaver explored the cultural power of the term: "'Progress' becomes the salvation man is placed on earth to work out; and just as there can be no achievement more important than salvation, so there can be no activity more justified in enlisting our sympathy and support than 'progress.'"[21]

Underlying the emphasis on progress was a belief in efficiency as a chief cultural goal. This version of efficiency, however, came into stark conflict with the traditional American value of individualism. Fordism insisted that individuals subjugate themselves to processes dictated by experts. Each member of the organization essentially functioned as a disconnected, unthinking cog in an increasingly distant and complicated machine. The interconnection between a culture of expertise, the rise of scientific rationality, and the emphasis on efficiency made the American worker both increasingly productive and increasingly alienated.

Cultural Knowledge

The Fordist economic system pervaded the broader culture, and science became a central cultural value. However, the rise of scientific expertise and experts was not unambiguous. Just as Americans became increasingly dependent on a cadre of experts to direct their economic, political, and cultural life, they were growing more and more suspicious of these expert elites. The products of science had certainly given warrant to many of these fears. Nazi medical experiments and the pseudo-science of eugenics provided one nightmarish vision of science gone too far, and the aftermath of the American bombing of Hiroshima and Nagasaki had provided another. Indeed, the atomic bomb had gone from celebrated weapon of victory to harbinger of global doom in just a few short years. The horrific images of fallout victims in Japan left an indelible impression on the American public, an impression of both guilt for the victims of the bomb and fear for the fate of the world.

Perhaps the most spectacular examples of the underlying fear of science and scientists gone awry were the spy scandals of the 1950s. A prominent political bureaucrat, Alger Hiss, was among the first of the communist spies to be convicted, in February 1950. In the same month, a prominent scientist, Klaus Fuchs, admitted under questioning to have passed on atomic secrets to the Soviet Union. Fuchs was convicted one month later, and his conviction would lead to the arrest and conviction of the most notorious atomic spies in the early 1950s—Julius and Ethel Rosenberg. The couple was indicted in January 1951, and their trial would fill newspaper headlines for weeks. The Rosenbergs were found guilty of conspiracy to transmit secrets to the Soviet Union on March 28, 1951, and sentenced to death (interestingly, only a few days before Hawks's *The Thing* would premiere).

A contradiction emerged in 1950s cultural logic. On the one hand, efficiency and stability demanded a reliance on experts and subservience to organizational processes. On the other hand, the paranoia created by the Cold War and McCarthyism suggested a deep-seated suspicion of those who claimed authority and expertise. Americans in the 1950s, in other words, were asked to place their security and prosperity in the hands of those they were told, implicitly, not to trust. Alan Nadel labels this point of tension "containment." While containment was the official U.S. foreign policy during the Cold War in the sense of containing communist expansion, Nadel observes its larger cultural meaning, "If containment thus names a foreign and domestic policy, it also names the rhetorical strategy that functioned to foreclose dissent, preempt dialogue, and preclude contradiction."[22] Americans were, in essence, guaranteed the security necessary for personal liberty only on the condition that they conform to the will of the expert authorities.

Sexuality

Another holdover from the Second World War was the ambivalent position of women in American society. The simultaneous need for men and new equipment in the European and Pacific battlefields required the mobilization of a vast female workforce—the rise of Rosie the Riveter. Nancy Nichols recalls the heroic figure, "Rosie the Riveter is both a romantic and a heroic figure from the World War II era. A former housewife turned war hero, Rosie emerged from the kitchen and built the machinery necessary to fight and win World War II. Posters emblazoned with her picture became a symbol of wartime courage and patriotism."[23]

The fate of Rosie, however, was far from noble. As Nancy and Christy Wise note, "When the war ended, factories and shipyards devoted to wartime manufacturing shut down immediately, some in midshift.... This abrupt change in circumstances was a jolt for many women, bordering on insulting. For several years, they had proven they could successfully perform work formerly considered too difficult, dangerous, or complex for women, and now they were loath to leave."[24]

Women in the 1950s were largely returned to the domestic roles, a role made all the more important by the increasingly dehumanized world of the expert-driven Fordist society. As Mary Ryan notes, "A new definition of the family was constructed out of an absorption of all emotional satisfaction into the home.... The domestic unit was an emotional refuge in a bureaucratized and routinized society."[25] On its surface, at least as it is often represented, the return of women to the domestic realm resulted in a harmonious, picket-fenced American culture—the kind depicted in television shows such as *Father Knows Best* and *Leave It to Beaver*. Upon closer examination, the return of women to domestic duty opened an increasingly tense point of cultural contradiction. In the face of the heroic production efforts of American women during the war, patriarchal culture could not easily dismiss women's intelligence or capability. This cultural contradiction became increasingly evident in the popular culture of the early 1950s. As Brandon French explains, "On the surface, fifties films promoted women's domesticity and inequality and sought easy, optimistic conclusions to any problems their fictions treated. But a significant number of movies simultaneously reflected, unconsciously or otherwise, the malaise of domesticity and the untenably narrow boundaries of the female role."[26]

In the early years of the 1950s, Americans sought to move on from the past. Of this attitude, W. T. Lhaman Jr. writes, "Without denying or forgetting their agonies, Americans were distinctly more optimistic following World War II, after taking a decade to think it all over, than during the wallows of despair that followed the trench warfare of the first war and the dislocation of the Depression."[27] Borrowing Alan Nadel's helpful term, 1950s America attempted to "contain" the threat of communism at home and abroad, the increasingly impersonal structure of Fordist work, the side effects of science and scientists gone amok, and the cultural contradictions surrounding the place of women. If such containment could be achieved, the cultural logic suggested, the problems of the past might also be contained and a bright new future attained.

THE BIRTH OF SCIENCE FICTION

The horrors of the past, of course, could not be contained. Within popular film, science fiction emerged from remnants of the earlier generation's Gothic horror. Indeed, a cursory glance at the two most prominent harbingers of science fiction reveals their reliance on the conventions of Gothic horror. The sympathetic alien Klaatu in *The Day the Earth Stood Still* parallels important elements of James Whale's *Frankenstein* (1931). Both films utilize a mix of fear and sympathy, and indeed, the relationship between the intelligent Klaatu and his powerful robot Gort is reminiscent of Dr. Frankenstein and his creature. Also evident is the parallel between *Dracula* and *The Thing*. Both involve monstrous blood-sucking creatures bent on destroying civilization, and both involve a small group of people who must harness their expertise and will to overcome the threat.

There are, of course, substantial and important generic differences between the Gothic horror of the 1930s and the science fiction films of the 1950s. Patrick Lucanio argues that these two genres differ in the kinds of worlds they present. Gothic horror presents an alternate world, often drawn from the past, filled with crumbling castles, foggy forests, and arcane superstitious practices. This is an almost mystical realm in which forces of evil and good meet in some transcendent, eternal conflict. To the contrary, science fiction presents either our existing world—as in films such as *The Thing*—or a "continuous world" where the developments of the future can be logically derived from our existing world. As Lucanio argues, "The horror film offers a supernatural force grounded in a theological, closed world; the science fiction film offers a natural force grounded in a physical, historical context."[28]

Lucanio's observation is productive, though perhaps a bit rigid in its attempt to differentiate horror from science fiction. Perhaps it is more appropriate to argue that the distinction between "alternate world of the past" and "continuous world of the future" marks an important point of change in the development of the horror genre broadly conceived. This is not to suggest that all science fiction is essentially horror, but to note the way that the underlying impulse of the horror genre was reconceived in relation to the same cultural changes that prompted the birth of science fiction. Thus, it can be argued that the two films that mark the emergence of the science fiction genre—*The Thing* and *The Day the Earth Stood Still*—represent the two sides of the cultural contradiction at the heart of 1950s America. *The Day* presents the optimistic belief that, despite our human failings, we might someday achieve a scientifically derived utopian life of peace and prosperity, and as such, it is not a horror film.

More to the present point, the rebirth of the horror genre occurs in Hawks's film. Unlike the potential utopia of *The Day*, *The Thing* presents the fearful paranoia of the 1950s, and it is this representation of our broader cultural fears that allows *The Thing* to successful draw on the generic elements of horror while simultaneously transforming them.

Howard Hawks was well aware of the need to transform the elements of the familiar Gothic horror tale. In making *The Thing*, he noted, "It is important that we don't confuse the *Frankenstein* type of picture with the science fiction picture. The first is an out-and-out horror thriller based on that which is impossible. The science fiction film is based on that which is unknown, but is given credibility by the use of science fiction facts which parallel that which the viewer is asked to believe."[29] It is clear that Hawks's intent is to create a new sense of horror.

In thinking about the ways that *The Thing* utilized and transformed the cultural notions of horror, it is important to also consider the impact the phrase "Howard Hawks Production" must have had on audiences. With little doubt, audiences flocked to the mysterious science fiction adventure in part because of the association of Hawks's name. By 1951, Hawks was already one of America's most prominent filmmakers. His resume already included an impressive list of classic films: *The Dawn Patrol* (1930), *Scarface* (1932), *The Road to Glory* (1936), *Bringing Up Baby* (1938), *Sergeant York* (1941), *Red River* (1948), and *I Was a Male War Bride* (1949).

A considerable amount of critical attention has been paid to the films of Howard Hawks, and it is worth drawing on these studies to gain some general sense of Hawks's style as an auteur. For, just as Hawks's name likely drew audiences to *The Thing,* it also likely created some expectations for those familiar with his previous films. There are three broad tendencies that seem relevant in examining Hawks's science fiction / horror film: his emphasis on group collaboration, the relationship between the group and the encroaching "other," and his use of humor.

A number of critics note Hawks's tendency to engage the problematic relationship between the individual and the community. While many films depict the struggle of individuals against communities, it was Hawks's tendency to place a kind of idealized community at the center of his films. Robert Ray, discussing Hawks's *Only Angels Have Wings* (1939), describes these groups, "In fact, his groups are very special, capable of accommodating individualism without devouring it, relying as much on personal acts of heroism as on teamwork. The members of these groups were carefully particularized: Hawks's ideal world was a melting pot full of distinctly different individuals. Thus, his films represented a mythic solution to the individual—community opposition central to American culture."[30]

Hawks's groups are typically heterogeneous, at times even contentious.[31] Whatever their differences, they are bonded together in common cause and by a deep and abiding affection. As Robin Wood observes this tendency in *The Thing*, "What makes the characters live is the human values they embody. The affection of the characters for each other reflects that which Hawks feels for them: an affection warm but unidealising, dignified by respect."[32]

What motivates Hawks's groups into action, and also the plot of his films, is the encounter of some "other," some entity that disrupts the functioning of the group and obstructs their progress. In the combat films, the other is, obviously, the enemy—usually depicted as faceless, deceitful, and ruthless. The tendency to explore the encroachment of some other is pervasive. As Jacques Rivette observes, "Whether he opposes old to new; the sum of the world's knowledge of the past to one of the degraded forms of modern life (*Balls of Fire, A Song Is Born*); or man to beast (*Bringing Up Baby*), he sticks to the same story—the intrusion of the inhuman, or the crudest avatar of humanity, into civilized society."[33] In many of Hawks's films, these intrusions represent a playful reversal of roles—adults act like children, men like women, humans like animals, and so on—though in *The Thing* and the various combat films, the encroachment of the other is of a more grave and threatening nature.

One of the central ways that the gravity of the danger is contained even in Hawks's most serious films is through his characteristic use of rapid-fire, overlapping, humorous dialogue. Gerald Mast contends that Hawks uses dialogue as a soundtrack, the speed and rhythm of the speech creating the broader tone of the film. Indeed, in later films, Hawks developed the technique of having pointless lines of dialogue that could be "stepped over," or interrupted, by other lines of dialogue, thus crafting, particularly in the comedies and combat films, a kind of natural buzz of conversation and comments. This buzz of conversation helps craft not only the overall tone of the film but also suggests the relaxed and natural relationship between the members of Hawks's groups. The banter is filled with light-hearted ribbing, references to past adventures, and allusions to inside jokes. Additionally, and perhaps most importantly, Hawks's humor functions to buffer the group from the hardships of horrors they encounter. Mast observes this juxtaposition of violence and humor in films such as *Scarface*, in which acts of brutality are followed by lines of witty banter. Robin Wood notes this tendency in Hawks's use of banter in *The Thing*, "The banter and the joke *contain* the brief, central moment of terror, providing a means of either denying or distancing the threat of the unknown ('chaos')."[34]

Entering the theater in April of 1951, audiences knew very little about *The Thing* they were about to encounter. The details of the plot were kept intentionally secret. Still, they knew a great deal about Hawks and his style of storytelling, and they were well acquainted with the Gothic monsters of the 1930s and 1940s. They also knew perhaps more than they wanted to know about the Cold War and its odd mix of dependence and paranoia, science and militarism, hopefulness and despair.

READING *THE THING FROM ANOTHER WORLD*

In approaching *The Thing*, the points of resonance between broader cultural issues of national identity, economics, cultural knowledge, and sexuality become readily apparent. The invading creature lands in the North Pole, a place where American and Soviet forces played a complex chess game for supremacy. Our heroes must struggle not only against the invading alien but also against the bureaucratic regulations of the Army and against the overly rational notions of the group of scientists. The leader of the military group, Captain Hendry, must also struggle to negotiate an ambiguous romantic relationship with the masculine "pin-up girl," Nikki. Even a cursory viewing of the film suggests the ways that broader cultural anxieties resonate within the film.

Of greater interest are the ways that *The Thing* violates audience expectations and the ways that the film deals with this violation. At its heart, the violation embodied in *The Thing* is the shifting of horror from the alternate world of the past—as in Gothic horror—to the continuous world of the present. In Gothic horror, our past returns to haunt our present by drawing us into an alternate world of castles and forests and myths. The advent of science fiction horror, on the other hand, confronts its audience with the uncertainties of the future. Given the cultural contradictions of the 1950s and the sense of impending atomic doom, the parallel between the real horror and the fictional horror could be too close.

Following the broader cultural logic of the 1950s, the film works to simultaneously present its audience's worst real-world fears and to contain these fears within a confident and reassuring aesthetic. This becomes the most interesting aspect of *The Thing*, the way it functions to contain the horror of the continuous world, and it is this observation that drives my reading of the film. The containment of the "realistic" horror of *The Thing* is effected through the stylistic devices common to the films of Howard Hawks: his depiction of the professional, inclusive combat group; his confrontation of this group with threatening others, and his use of humor and light-hearted banter to distance the audience from the horrors depicted on screen. Read in this way, *The Thing* brings its monster significantly closer to the audience than the films of the Gothic tradition but does so safely by maintaining a tight, stylistic containment of its threatening invader.

The Group

As with many of Hawks's films, at the core of *The Thing* is the bond of camaraderie among members of "the group." Hawks's groups are often hodge-podge mixes of men who work together, joke together, and evidence a great affection for each other. It is this core group that must face the challenge of the threatening other and overcome it without falling into fractiousness or conflict. The group becomes, for Hawks, a metaphor for the American dream—a nation capable of facing the challenge of the unknown and facing its own diversity and division, not through strength or knowledge alone, but through an abiding affection that bonds it together.

As audience members, we enter into the film in the company of newspaper reporter Scotty, and in the officer's club we encounter the members of this core group for the first time, enjoying a poker game. Our initial encounter with Captain Hendry provides an interesting example of the ways the Hawksian group leader differs from the typical heroic figure. Hendry is clearly the group's leader—his rank and bearing indicate his role—but he is not above the group or even removed from it. The other group members, Lieutenant Eddie and the navigator, McPherson, joke about the captain's romantic misadventures, and all three engage in a kind of playful back and forth. The equal exchange of light-hearted insults avoids straying into the territory of disrespect because it is both reciprocal and founded on mutual affection.

It is also telling how quickly Scotty, and by proxy the audience, are absorbed into the group. After a discussion of a past meeting between Scotty and Eddie, the group accepts the newspaper reporter. Indeed, when Captain Hendry is called away for duty, he leaves his card hand with Scotty. From this moment on, Scotty becomes a part of this tight-knit group. He helps the crew chop the frozen alien out of the ice, and he assists with bringing supplies in from the plane. On two occasions, as the danger becomes intense, Hendry orders Scotty to "get back with the rest," but on both occasions Scotty is allowed to stay for he is now a part of the core group that must overcome the threat of the Thing.

The group is both tight-knit and open to new members, but it also embodies a unique blend of professionalism and independence. On a number of occasions, the members of the group cease their banter and play and almost instantly fall into their professional role of soldiers. They follow "standard operating procedure" for removing the saucer from ice with thermite bombs with all the speed and efficiency of a well-oiled machine. They quickly assemble to pursue the creature as it races off into the frozen night. They fight the creature with a well-trained and professional precision and quickly move to care for their own once the skirmishes are over.

This professionalism, however, is not a blind obedience to the rules and regulations of standard operating procedure or to hierarchy. The group openly ridicules Army regulations and eventually chooses to disobey direct orders from their superiors regarding the alien invader. The same disregard for regulations and hierarchy is evident within the group itself. On a number of occasions, the members of the group suggest alternatives to Captain Hendry's orders, and their suggestions are quickly taken up. For example, after setting guard duty at four-hour intervals, Captain Hendry is approached by Bob, who observes that the current guard is "having kittens" from being in such close confinement with the frozen alien. Bob suggests they change the rotation intervals to two hours, and the captain agrees. "I think you're right, sir," Bob says, almost winking. "I think *you're* right," the captain replies. Indeed, the final plan to kill the beast—running electrical wires along a hallway to create the trap—is devised by Bob and one of the scientists. Captain Hendry, clearly, only barely grasps the mechanics of the trap and has no sense of the reasons it will work. He has no objection, however, relying in good faith on the ideas of his team members. It is clear that among the military men (and Scotty), the whole is greater than the sum of its parts.

The synergy of the group is based largely on bonds of mutual respect and affection. Even the cinematography indicates their closeness. The film is filled with tight shots, focusing on the men in close proximity to each other, for example, sitting in the plane's cockpit or making their way into the encampment for the first time. It is clear, though never explicit, that these men have a history together. They share inside jokes, they care for each other, and they bond together in the face of adversity.

These deep bonds of affection also create perhaps the most important though understated aspect of the group—they forgive each other. The escape of the alien Thing from the ice block is, clearly, due to the incompetence and inattention of one of the crew, Barnes, who throws the warm electrical blanket onto the block and fails to notice it melting. Yet Barnes faces no rebuke or censure. More explicitly, after Bob fires indiscriminately into a room where the Thing is trapped, McPherson, who was on the other side of the room, says, "And Bob, next time you use that canon, raise the sights a little." Bob replies, "I'm sorry sir, I was too busy to think about that," and with a laugh the hasty action is forgiven.

The group's capacity to maintain integrity in the face of internal conflict is most evident on the issue of whether or not Scotty will be allowed to send his report without Army clearance. The argument is ongoing, and Scotty is clearly frustrated with the gag order, but the argument maintains a light tone and never threatens the group.

The ease with which Scotty enters the group and maintains his affiliation despite disagreements suggests that the strong bonds that hold them together do not function to exclude others. Indeed, in addition to Scotty, one of the scientists, Dr. Chapman, clearly becomes more affiliated with the military group than with his fellow scientists. Additionally, and perhaps more importantly, by the end of the film Nikki, Captain Hendry's love interest, transfers her allegiance from Dr. Carrington, her employer, to not just Hendry but the entire group. It is their capacity to engage these others, including reporters, scientists, and (even) women, that marks the group as something special.

The Others

There are three prominent others the group encounters: Nikki, the scientists, and, of course, the Thing. These three others exist along a continuum of acceptance in which Nikki is sought out by the group, the scientists are accepted but largely not incorporated, and the Thing must be destroyed entirely.

Nikki is, in many respects, a very typical "Hawksian woman." She is not the kind of female heroine typical of the period. We learn that in her previous "date" with Captain Hendry she outdrank him and left him passed out on a bed with a note that his "legs aren't very pretty." In their onscreen courtship, she ties his hands behind his back and pours him drinks. It is Nikki who grabs Captain Hendry's head and pulls it forward for a kiss and, while Hendry pulls the same move after untying himself, there is clearly a kind of gender reversal game being played out between the two. When Nikki wants to pass on Dr. Carrington's secret and dangerous experiments, she hands Hendry the notes and says, "You'd better take a swing at my chin." Indeed, the very name "Nikki" is, at least, gender neutral.

Taking on these masculine characteristics does not mark Nikki as undesirable. On the contrary, her competence and toughness seem to make her more desirable to both Captain Hendry and the group. As Naomi Wise puts it, "Hawks's films frequently show a merging of sexual roles for the benefit of both sexes—the women learn certain 'masculine' values while men become 'feminized.' Frequently the men have more to learn (and to gain) than the women, who are already mature at each film's beginning."[35] Indeed, as the men struggle to devise a plan to kill the Thing, it is Nikki who suggests the way to destroy a vegetable is to "boil it ... fry it." It is Nikki's ability to comfortably accept both her feminine and masculine traits that makes her an invaluable addition to the group.

A more ambivalent relationship exists between the group and the scientists, the group of researchers led by Dr. Carrington who insist on researching the alien rather than destroying it. If Nikki can be seen to offer an optimistic affirmation of the "post–Rosie the Riveter" woman of the 1950s, the scientists suggest a negative vision of the decade's Fordist expert culture. Carrington clearly leads and represents the scientists, and from his first appearance on the screen he is marked as odd. His clothes, facial hair, and demeanor suggest a snobbish intellectualism and, possibly, a disregard for humanity. It is Carrington who asserts the superiority of science in dealing with the problem of the Thing, an insistence that hampers and endangers the military group.

It is clear from very early in the film that the military group and the scientists will be in conflict. Carrington openly questions Hendry's competence and authority—even questioning how the captain can navigate in the magnetic interference—and effectively establishes a second hierarchy of command. Carrington also develops an ongoing hostility with Scotty, bristling under the reporter's questions. When the conflict becomes intractable, the scientists seek higher authorities, relying on the military officials in Alaska to countermand Captain Hendry and his men. It is this arrogant reliance on their own expertise and the bureaucratic structure that most clearly distinguishes the scientists from Captain Hendry's group. As we watch the interaction among the scientists it becomes clear that they are held together by authority and expertise, not by affection and respect.

The degree to which the scientists disregard human sentiment is made most evident by the admiration Dr. Carrington has for the invading Thing. Dr. Carrington describes the creature by stating, "On the planet from which our visitor came vegetable life underwent an evolution similar to our own animal life, which would account for the superiority of its brain. Its development was not handicapped by emotional or sexual factors."

Upon discovering the creature's seedpod, he adds, "The neat and unconfused reproductive technique of vegetation. No pain or pleasure as we know it. No emotions, no heart. Our superior. Our superior in every way. Gentlemen do you realize what we've found? A being from another world as different from us as one pole from the other."

The Thing, in other words, is the perfect embodiment of the corporate / bureaucratic entity—inhuman and dispassionate, driven by rationality alone. On one level, perhaps the more obvious, this unfeeling, unsentimental being resembles the American stereotype of the Soviets. On another level, the description also fits the "organizational man" of the American Fordist economy, and it is interesting how this notion of the superior alien as emotionless has endured.

The invading alien creature, we are led to believe, seeks to spread its seed and create a "horrible army" and conquer the planet. Like the Soviets—or American capitalist corporations—the Thing is driven not by passion or sentiment but by the desire to expand and conquer. Of course, all the conjecture about an emotionless and highly rational creature with the same attitude towards humans "as we have toward a field of cabbages" is undercut by what we see of the creature. While the Thing is never clearly visible, it seems a hideous creature, reminiscent of Frankenstein's monster, with thorns on its fingers and a high, bald head. Its actions are also far from rational or superior. We see it tearing away at the camp's dogs; we hear of how it slaughters some of the scientists. Perhaps most dramatically, as Dr. Carrington pleads with the Thing—"Listen, I'm your friend, look I have no weapons. I'm your friend. You're wiser than I, you must understand what I'm trying to tell you"—it brushes him aside with a violent blow and continues to advance on the military group. In a way the Thing represents the savage inhumanity at the heart of all attempts, communist or capitalist, to regulate human life based solely on rationality and expertise.

Humor

Read in this way, the horror of *The Thing* resonates strongly with the cultural concerns of 1950s Americans. The horror of the invading menace from outer space and the hindrance of the scientific experts strikes particularly close to the reality of the contemporary American situation. Further, by bringing this horror out of the alternative world of the past and placing it in the continuous world of the near-present, *The Thing* substantially violates the audience's sense of security. Hawks manages this violation both through the strength of his military group and by containing the horror with humor.

The first and most indicative use of humor to encapsulate horror occurs as the frozen alien is being flown back to the camp. As McPherson reads the text of an Air Force memo dismissing the existence of flying saucers, the crew members take turns poking fun at the memo's "reasons" for dismissing UFO sightings. In the midst of this revelry, McPherson turns back to see the block of ice and a look of horror comes over his face. His comrades break the tension. "What are the other reasons?" one asks, and the joking continues. The horror of the menace is encapsulated within the humorous bonds of the group's camaraderie, and this is one way that humor functions as containment within *The Thing*. A similar example occurs in the film's dramatic conclusion. As the group waits for the creature to appear, McPherson asks urgently, "What if he can read our minds?" Amidst the growing tension, Eddie replies, "He's gonna be real mad when he gets to me."

A second function of humor is to contain the horror through reconciliation. The earlier example of Bob's reckless firing into a room is one example of this function. Another example is the way that humor resolves the conflict between Hendry and Scotty over the news report in the preceding scene. In one of the more startling scenes, the group opens the door to the greenhouse as they search for the Thing. With no warning, the creature is at the door and violently swings outward. As Hendry slams the door shut he asks Scotty if he was able to snap a picture. Scotty replies that the captain was in the way and the door wasn't open long enough. Hendry asks, "Do you want me to open it again?" "No!" the reporter replies.

Indeed, humorous banter and camaraderie encapsulates every scene of horror and tension. The affectionate bonds of the group work to contain the menace and no matter how horrific the experience, the rapid banter soon brings each member back into the security of the group.

RESOLUTION

In a way, the ending of *The Thing* is more open-ended than that of *Dracula*. Where the count was apparently staked and his reign of evil forever ended, the dramatic final speech of *The Thing* describes it as "the first battle" and urges us to "keep watching the skies." Yet, just as a close reading of *Dracula*'s ending suggests it was more open and uncertain than at first glance, so too the ending of *The Thing* can be seen as more closed and comforting. In his final speech, Scotty—our companion from the start of the film—reveals the way that each of the antagonistic relationships is resolved. In other words, by the end of the film the group has effectively managed its encounter with each of the threatening others it has faced.

Nikki, the most appealing of the others, becomes a member of the group. Not only does the ending suggest that she and Captain Hendry will marry, but the discussion that leads to this conclusion involves the playful banter of Nikki, Eddie, Bob, and McPherson as they team up on the agreeable captain. "See, they know what's best for you," Nikki concludes. As he makes his final speech, Scotty explains that he would bring the senior Air Force officer to the microphone but that "Captain Hendry is attending to demands over and above the call of duty." The happy couple is shown embracing in the background.

If it is almost inevitable that Nikki will be absorbed by the group, the fate of the scientists is less clear. Carrington survives the attack by the Thing, suffering only a broken collarbone, but his reputation and judgment could clearly be in jeopardy. Ultimately, he was as much the villain of the film as the alien menace. However, as Scotty continues his speech he explains that he would bring the scientific expert to the microphone except that he "is recovering from wounds received in the battle." In the background Eddie pats the reporter on the shoulder, saying "Good for you Scotty." Clearly, the group could have rejected the misguided scientist, held him up for public scrutiny and ridicule. However, the underlying ethic of respect and mutual affection embraces even the obnoxious arrogance of Dr. Carrington.

The only other the group is unable, and indeed unwilling, to embrace is the Thing, which, in essence, embodies the exact opposite of the group. Where the group is based on affiliation and respect, the alien evidences no such capacity for the warmth of human affection. As such, the creature is destroyed. While the film leaves open the possibility that this is only the first of many encounters to come, it is clear that we can take some comfort. This comfort does not come from a reliance on scientific expertise or military bureaucracy, but it comes from an underlying faith in the good judgment of people of good character and strong bonds. Ultimately, it is our faith in each other that will allow us to weather whatever invasive forces the uncertain future threatens.

THE THING FROM ANOTHER WORLD'S LEGACY

The Thing brought horror out of the Gothic past and placed it squarely into the continuous world of the near-future. The monster was not some creature of lore and superstition but one based, however loosely, on the possibilities afforded by science. By bringing the monster into the more realistic realm of the continuous world, the points of resonance between the elements in the film and broader cultural anxieties seem to become more acute. Wrapped up in the fantastic horror of *The Thing* were American fears of invasion, communism, Fordism, science, authority, expertise, and gender displacement. The intensity of the resonance may be part of the reason that critic Bill Warren contends, "*The Thing* must have been overwhelming in 1951. Certainly there had never been a previous horror movie that was such a relentless assault on people's sensibilities."[36]

For Americans in 1951, of course, much of their daily life could have been considered overwhelming. The Cold War was settling into a grim reality accompanied by paranoia, suspicion, and betrayal at all levels. At the end of all these struggles, conflicts, and witch hunts lay the finality of atomic warfare and apocalypse. Of course, even if spared this fate, American prosperity was being purchased largely through American humanity. Men had replaced women in the workforce leaving neither in a better position. The workingman faced an increasingly regulated, technological, and inhuman workplace, while women struggled to gain some sense of their place in a society they had effectively managed during wartime.

The Thing, then, might be said to run the risk of having too much resonance and too much violation. The horror resonates too closely to the real world fears and is presented too directly—no longer removed to the Gothic world of the past but placed squarely into the continuous world of the present. Confronted too directly with their real cultural concerns, audiences might have turned away from the horror of the continuous world. However, as with all the cultural contradictions of the 1950s, the operative term was containment. Hawks's masterfully contains the horror within the reliable bonds of communal affection. In the end, audiences were asked to put their faith not in the military or in science, but in the good character and mutual affection of their fellow citizens. Such good character could, the film suggests, overcome any invading threat.

Of course, the invasion continued. Throughout the fifties, American filmgoers faced an amazing onslaught of alien invaders. The science fiction craze would last for the majority of the decade, and while the creatures would get progressively bigger—such as the giant ants of *Them!* (1954) and *Godzilla* (1956)—the basics of the Hawksian formula would remain. Whatever their shape or size, the horrors of the future would be contained within the bonds of human courage and affection.

The invading creatures would also get progressively cheaper. The court-ordered demise of the studio monopoly on distribution and theaters in 1948 would significantly change the way movies were made and exhibited. Additionally, the rapid growth of television in the 1950s would dramatically impact movie attendance. As the studios focused more and more attention on the big blockbuster, the door was opened for independent distributors to push more and more inventive but cheaply made products into neighborhood theaters. Producers like William Castle and, later, Roger Corman would begin to fill these empty theaters with countless B-movies, often featuring wobbly cardboard spaceships and Styrofoam-headed creatures with visible zippers. The proliferation of these "creature features" slowly ebbed away the potency of the alien invader, and by 1959, the science fiction horror film had become so tame it no longer needed the kind of careful containment erected by filmmakers like Howard Hawks. By the end of the decade, Americans found they no longer needed to "keep watching the skies," and on June 16, 1960, Americans would learn to turn their eyes away from the skies and place them firmly on the horrors lurking next door.

3 *Psycho* (1960)

"We're all in our private traps."

What more can be said about *Psycho*? With little doubt, Alfred Hitchcock's *Psycho* is the most heavily analyzed film in the long career of the most investigated director in the history of American film. Raymond Durgnat estimates that the number of published criticisms has reached "well into three figures."[1] The film has been the subject of numerous books, hundreds of essays, and indeed, the critical and academic attention to Hitchcock and *Psycho* played an integral part in the development of film studies. While many of its contemporary critics dismissed it as "low culture," in the intervening four decades *Psycho* has become one of America's most celebrated and influential films. Most relevant to the present work, it is a film that both resonated with and violated American cultural norms.

Very few people wanted Hitchcock to make the twisted tale of a transvestite, a shower, and a motel. As Robert Bloch, author of the novel *Psycho*, recalls, "Paramount absolutely didn't want to make it. They didn't like the title, the story, or anything about it at all."[2] By 1959, however, Alfred Hitchcock was one of if not the most important filmmakers in Hollywood. Hitchcock had already directed forty-six films, including classics such as *The Lodger* (1927), *The 39 Steps* (1935), *Rebecca* (1940), *Shadow of a Doubt* (1943), *Strangers on a Train* (1951), *Rear Window* (1954), and *North by Northwest* (1959), and he had spent three highly successful seasons on television as the face—and occasionally the creative mind—of *Alfred Hitchcock*

Presents. Despite these formidable achievements, Paramount placed numerous obstacles in the way of this, Hitchcock's forty-seventh film, including setting a miniscule budget of $800,000—compared to the $3.3 million for *North by Northwest*—and refusing to let Hitchcock use the Paramount lot for filming. Still, the strong-willed British director outmaneuvered his studio bosses, using the Universal Studio's production facilities and much of the crew from his successful television show to shoot *Psycho* quickly and cheaply.

Hitchcock's strong commitment to the project came in part, undoubtedly, from his stubborn independence. The film also presented a much-needed challenge to the director, who greatly feared repeating himself or becoming too predictable. There is also some reason to believe that Hitchcock was wary of being upstaged by other directors who were straying into the thriller/suspense genre. In particular, the French film *Les Diaboliques* (1954) seems to have aroused Hitchcock's interest with its dark black-and-white cinematography, gritty locations, bathroom murder, and twist ending. Some critics were already dubbing its director, Henri-Georges Clouzot, the "French Hitchcock."[3] Hitchcock was apparently being replaced as the master of suspense and thrills, a title he did not intend to relinquish quietly.

If Hitchcock set out to shock his audience, he clearly succeeded, though not to everyone's approval. Numerous contemporary critics blasted *Psycho*. *Time* magazine called it "a spectacle of stomach-churning horror," *Esquire* called it "a reflection of a most unpleasant mind, a mean, sly sadistic little mind," and the *New York Times* dubbed the film "a blot on an honorable career."[4] The film reviewer for *The Nation* was "offended and disgusted."[5] The film was censored in a number of countries, and calls to boycott the film echoed from various religious leaders and psychiatrists.

Despite the controversy and a smattering of negative reviews, the reaction of audiences was undeniable. Huge lines met the movie's premieres in major cities; audiences howled, screamed, and threw popcorn into the air. Audiences reacted so loudly, in fact, that Hitchcock reportedly wanted to reedit the film so that dialogue would not be so drowned out by the audience's screams.[6] By the end of its first year of domestic release, Hitchcock's sordid, low budget picture had grossed $15 million.

SYNOPSIS

Hitchcock's forty-seventh film begins dramatically. Bernard Herrmann's score screeches with strings as the screen is filled with moving vertical and horizontal lines. The opening credits fade into a high crane shot over Phoenix, Arizona. A series of crane shots move in slowly, almost randomly, to a building, then to a window, and then into a hotel room where we find a half-dressed man and woman. The woman is Marion Crane, and the man is her boyfriend, Sam Loomis. As they prepare to leave their afternoon rendezvous, Marion makes it clear that she wants a more normal, "respectable" relationship. However, it is also clear that Sam's financial problems present an insurmountable obstacle.

Marion returns to her job as a secretary at a real estate office where she is given $40,000 in cash to drop off at the bank. We next see Marion at her home, packing a suitcase and still carrying the money. Soon we learn that she has stolen the money and is planning to meet up with her lover, Sam, in secret at his Fairvale, California home. After a harrowing encounter with a highway patrol officer and switching cars at a used car dealer, heavy rains and darkness force Marion to stop at the Bates Motel.

At the motel, Marion meets Norman Bates, the hotel's manager, and in a long and intense conversation, she learns of his isolation, loneliness, and strained relationship with his mother. Unaware that Norman is spying on her through a peephole in the wall, Marion returns to her room where she prepares for a shower and makes plans to return to Phoenix and make reparations for her crime.

Marion enters the shower and is murdered in the most famous sequence in the history of American cinema. A shadowy figure, apparently an older woman with her hair in a bun, pulls back the shower curtain and proceeds to stab the naked Marion Crane repeatedly with a butcher knife. The sequence is made all the more shocking because of its montage style—thirty-four segments in rapid succession punctuated by staccato strings, the sound of a knife piercing flesh, and a woman's scream. Norman arrives soon after and cleans up what appears to be his mother's crime.

The film then dramatically shifts to the story of Marion's sister, Lila Crane, who is searching for Marion with the help of Sam and a detective named Arbogast. The detective eventually traces Marion to the Bates Motel, but as he seeks to question the mother he is murdered, apparently by the old woman. Lila and Sam eventually go to the hotel where Lila sneaks into the Bates home and eventually finds the mother in the fruit cellar. Here the film's final twist is revealed: the mother is a preserved corpse, and the murderer has been Norman Bates—dressed as his mother.

The film concludes with a lengthy exposition on the murder by a psychiatrist, who explains that Norman had killed his mother and her lover and then, overcome by guilt, taken on her personality. The final word goes to Mother/Norman who professes her innocence. The final shot is a scene of Marion's car being pulled up from the swamp.

The impact of *Psycho* can hardly be overestimated. For one, the film began a trend that would dramatically change the way that American audiences attended the movies. As Amanda Sheahan Wells notes, in the late 1950s, "Cinemas usually played main features, B-movies, and shorts in a loop and people wandered in and out of the cinema whenever they felt like it. People would often come in midway through a film and then sit through everything until they got back to the point where they had started."[7] In an inspired promotional move, Hitchcock insisted that audiences not be allowed into the film after its beginning. Despite resistance from theater managers and from crowds, audiences were forced to line up, enter the theater prior to the film's beginning, and remain until its end.

More importantly, *Psycho*, like *Dracula* and *The Thing*, changed the way Americans understood horror. The film spawned innumerable immediate imitators—films such as William Castle's *Homicidal* (1961), Francis Ford Coppola's *Dementia 13* (1963), and Roman Polanski's *Repulsion* (1965)—and inspired a generation of American directors such as Brian De Palma, John Carpenter, and Jonathan Demme. For numerous film critics, *Psycho* represents a fundamental shift in the American notion of horror. With *Psycho*, American horror turned inwards. On one level, the horror of *Psycho* is found in the psychological rather than physiological. On another level, the monster comes not from beyond the grave or the stars, but from right next door. As Robin Wood contends, "Since *Psycho*, the Hollywood cinema has implicitly recognised Horror as both American and familial."[8]

Undoubtedly, part of *Psycho*'s impact comes from its quality. The film is remarkably well designed, an elegant and complex puzzle. Even after its initial shocking twists are known, the film bears up well under repeated viewing. Repeat viewers can enjoy tracing any number of subtle clues such as the ways that early dialogue prefigures the twist endings as well as the many recurrent motifs in the film—water redeems, mirrors reveal inner crimes, birds represent women, and so on.

For the present purpose, what is most interesting about *Psycho* is the way that the film resonates with cultural anxieties and violates audience expectations. The end of the 1950s was a time of both optimism and narcissism. While the Cold War still simmered under the surface, America was finally free from military conflicts, the economy was booming, and Americans were increasingly able to pursue their own individual pleasures. This cultural comfort and security was bought, in part, by the cultural logic of containment exemplified by *The Thing*: cultural and, indeed, global anxieties were contained within an optimistic veil of ignorance. As the 1950s turned into the 1960s, Americans turned away from the cultural problems rife in their society: racial injustice and unrest, the continuing danger of the Cold War, and a growing teenage rock and roll culture that was challenging notions of family and morality. In *Psycho*, Hitchcock revealed this thin veil of optimistic normalcy and then violently tore it open.

CULTURAL CONTEXTS

For many Americans—particularly those who were white and middle class—the cultural means of escaping their problems and anxieties involved retreating to the suburbs. While Americans had been drifting out to the regions surrounding their major urban areas since the late nineteenth century, in the 1950s the move to the suburbs became a flood.[9] Motivated by a complex mixture of upward economic mobility, fear of minorities and immigrants, and a pervasive cultural sense of the wickedness of cities, American families were creating a new culture of automobiles, commuters, and "bedroom communities." The birth of suburbia had begun.[10]

As suggested above, *Psycho* can be read as a critique of the veil of normalcy drawn around American suburban culture. In particular, *Psycho* resonates with many of the prominent characteristics of suburbia and suggests a deep anxiety underlying America's apparent confidence and progress.

Prosperity

At its roots, the cultural move from urban/rural life to the suburban life was the result of a booming U.S. economy. The end of the Second World War saw America at the top of global politics and economics. As American GIs returned to civilian life, the population of workers and, more importantly, consumers exploded. Adding to this renewed American economy were the enormous needs for goods and services from war-ravaged European and Pacific countries.

By the end of the 1950s, America's economic boom had become less about production and more about consumption. Americans increasingly defined their success by what they bought rather than the objects they made. Indeed, American workers were less likely to make anything, as the economy began the slow and difficult shift away from production and towards the service and information economy. Suburban Americans spent their days in urban office buildings where they made enough money to afford their suburban homes and the automobiles that took them back and forth. David Reisman, writing in 1958, called this a "revolt against industry," a cultural shift away from factory and industrial life and towards the emerging "leisure class"—a shift integral to the new suburban culture.[11]

With the diminishing importance of work, at least the traditional notions of industrial work, suburban culture defined itself through conspicuous consumption, the purchase of large, flashy, new products as a means of defining cultural status. Roger Silverstone puts it simply, "Suburban culture is a consuming culture."[12] Suburban Americans wanted the newest, largest, and most advanced products: new cars, new gadgets, and new fashions.

Family Home

The shift from work to consumption as the defining element of cultural worth also led to a shift in the location of cultural meaning. The workplace faded from cultural importance, and suburban culture focused its energy on the family home as the center of life. While the home had always been an important concept in American culture, the suburban home was unique. Unlike either the urban neighborhood or the rural farm, the suburban home was founded on its separation from both the world of work and from the world of others. The underlying motive of suburbanization, as Gary Cross observes, was "the desire for domestic seclusion."[13] Removed from the hustle and bustle of the urban neighborhood, the suburban home became a private island that turned increasingly inward.

Having achieved domestic seclusion, however, the suburbanite was seen as both isolated and confined. The weekends were spent working on the yard or garden, the weekdays filled with work and child care; the suburban home was, potentially, a trap and one particularly dangerous for women.[14] Reisman voiced the general concern, "When the husband goes off with the car to work (and often, in the vicious circle created by the car, there is no other way for him to travel), the wife is frequently either privatized at home or must herself, to escape isolation, take a job which will help support her own car, as well as the baby-sitter."[15]

As Reisman suggests, suburban life substantially affected gender and familial relations. On the one hand, the suburban home was a space of women's domestication where women were, by and large, left alone in their isolated home with a variety of domestic duties. This pressure was particularly difficult in terms of child care where women could no longer rely on close neighbors or members of an extended family. Even during the 1950s and early 1960s, the frustrated and lonely mother became a dominant image of the suburbs. Cross summarizes this impression, "A well-known, mostly American literature portrayed suburbs as producing rootless, transitory, upwardly mobile 'status seekers' and hypersocial communities of conformists. There, children were smothered by Momism and fathers were absent. Suburban women were characterized as lonely while men felt used as mere providers."[16]

On the other hand, social isolation and the financial burden of maintaining conspicuously ostentatious homes eventually pushed many women into jobs, and the burden of maintaining larger homes with yards and gardens meant that more men were being pulled into domestic chores.[17] As Americans settled into the new suburban landscape, they found that the vision of domestic bliss and the clear separation of male and female duties were untenable. Thus, much of the late 1950s and early 1960s was marked by increasing confusion over the relationship between the sexes and the propriety of gender roles. Eventually, this tension would lead to the explosive rise of feminism and the women's rights movement of the 1970s and early 1980s, but in the early 1960s the tension mainly simmered beneath the apparently blissful surface of suburbia.

The idealized suburban home embodied the paradox of the prosperous late fifties. Technological innovations—freezers, washers, dryers, televisions, and automobiles—freed the homemaker from the daily grind of shopping, washing, and seeking information or entertainment, but the freedom from daily necessities was limited by the overall sense of isolation wrapped up in the suburban vision.

Families achieved their dream of conspicuous consumption—a gorgeous showcase home in an affluent suburb—but the dark underside was a sense of confinement, isolation, and confusion.

Television

Another peculiar development of American culture in the late 1950s was the relationship between suburbia and television. Both achieved prominence at roughly the same time. Americans were heading to the suburbs at about the same time that television was becoming the country's dominant form of media. More importantly, television was a crucial dynamic in shaping the suburban vision.

Suburban homes, as Lynn Spigel has observed, were built and decorated with the theatrical space of television in mind—the home, in essence, was a space of display. As she notes, "Home manuals, magazines, and advertisements extended this emphasis on the home as showcase, recommending ways to create glamorous backgrounds on which to enact spectacular scenes."[18] The suburban home of the 1950s expanded the space of display—rooms such as the living room, dining room, family room, and so on—always with a mind towards the home as a place for enacting a particular vision of suburban domesticity.

The template for this vision of suburbia was also provided by television. Television in the 1950s was dominated by the family situation comedy, a form of entertainment largely set within the suburban domestic space. Shows such as *I Love Lucy* (1951–1957), *The Burns and Allen Show* (1950–1958), and *The Adventures of Ozzie and Harriet* (1952–1966) set most of the action within the family home in which a particular vision of affluent American domesticity was enacted for the consumption of American families aspiring to affluence. The situation comedy not only established the home as a space for theatrical display but also a tone of optimistic harmony. Any problem was resolved within thirty minutes, and family relations and hierarchies were always reinforced.

There was also a deeply narcissistic aspect to the correlation between the television sitcom and the rise of suburbia. Increasingly isolated in the suburban domestic space, Americans spent more and more time watching television, and they saw idealized images of themselves on these televisions. Television functioned as a kind of mirror—albeit an unrealistically positive and optimistic mirror—into which suburban Americans could spend hours gazing. The narcissism of television was also, of course, voyeuristic. Television allowed families to spy through the window of other people's lives, seeing their dramas and tragedies, their foibles and follies. Supported by this narcissistic voyeurism, Americans were able to take comfort from their isolation and withdraw further into the optimistic self-gaze of their televised normalcy.

Mobility

The rapid growth of American suburban culture necessitated a great movement of people. While the move to the suburbs often involved a flight from the perceived dangers of urban areas, the suburban destination was far less defined. For this reason, some critics have called suburbia "rootless" and "aimless."[19] This lack of clarity or tradition may be part of why Americans were so interested in watching television shows about suburban culture in an attempt to gain some insight into the norms and directions for suburban life.

Such lack of clarity also led many Americans to become disillusioned with suburbia and to dream of escape.[20] These fantasies were largely fixated on the most prominent form of transportation: the car. Of course, the automobile had been part of American culture since the 1920s. However, the expansion of the suburbs was heavily dependent on massive investments into new highways, freeways, and the growing interstate highway system.[21] More highways provided for more cars on the road and more Americans moving back and forth from work.

In a way, the commuter automobile was a perfect model of suburban life. The automobile, especially in the ostentatious period of the late 1950s, was a prime example of conspicuous consumption—the cars were bigger and covered with tail fins and chrome. The automobile also emphasized the seclusion of suburban life. Unlike mass transit, automobile commuters spent their time alone, protected from interaction with strangers and enclosed by their own property.

As the daily grind of suburban life wore on, Americans dreamed of using their vehicles to escape. While the car facilitated suburban commuter life, it increasingly became a symbol of freedom as well. Indeed, this liberating potential of the automobile made it alluring to American youth, who saw in the car the means for independence and maturation. Cynthia Golomb Dettelbach captures the cultural importance of the automobile, "For youth, cars open up the physical spaces beyond the neighborhood and metaphorical places beyond childish concerns and pastimes. In pursuing a dream of freedom, Americans look to the car as a practical means of finding the (impractical) liberation they seek. Freedom is the road beyond the last stop sign ... and before the next one."[22]

The contradiction underlying much of suburban culture is embodied in both the television and the automobile. It is the dream of private mobility—to be elsewhere without the danger of being exposed to others. It is, as Lynn Spigel characterizes it, the fantasy "of being somewhere else while in the comforts of one's own home."[23] Watching television allowed suburbanites to observe other places from the safety of the home, and the automobile provided a means of moving through other places while being protected in a homelike environment. In essence, having escaped from urban life, suburbanites sought to escape suburban life without actually leaving their prosperous and secure isolation.

ALFRED HITCHCOCK PRESENTS

Audiences lining up to see *Psycho* in 1960 were undoubtedly drawn by one overwhelming figure—Alfred Hitchcock. By 1960, the fastidious British director had become a ubiquitous icon in American popular culture. His films had garnered remarkable popular and critical acclaim, his name was associated with a popular mystery magazine, and his television program was a Nielsen success. If Mr. Hitchcock insisted that the audience arrive on time for his film or not at all, American audiences were willing to comply.

Of course, it is easy in the post-*Psycho* age to forget that while Hitchcock was a major cultural figure, he was not actually associated with horror. Hitchcock's previous forty-six films were largely films of suspense, often based on mistaken identity, and while they may have contained some moments of shock or fright, they were not considered horror films. Indeed, by 1960, Hitchcock was becoming increasingly associated with big, Technicolor adventures with beautiful stars in exotic locations in films such as *To Catch a Thief* (1955) and *Psycho*'s immediate predecessor, *North by Northwest*.

Psycho, as noted earlier, marked a dramatic departure for Hitchcock, and while it would become a major part of his legacy, it was effectively his first horror film.[24] This is, of course, not to say that *Psycho* was utterly dissimilar to his previous films. Indeed, many of Hitchcock's typical motifs and elements are prominent in

Psycho: the seemingly fated meeting of antagonist and protagonist, the way the camera acts as an explicit narrator, the inevitable Hitchcock cameo, the often harsh treatment of beautiful women, the use of stairs and banisters, and so on. *Psycho* is replete with these and other typical Hitchcock themes and images. Readers interested in pursuing these various directorial tendencies in *Psycho* would do well to consider some of the many detailed readings of Hitchcock's oeuvre.[25]

For present purposes, the complex relationship between Hitchcock's directorial style and *Psycho* are of only occasional interest. I set these relationships aside, in part, because they have been so thoroughly—perhaps too thoroughly—discussed by others and, in part, because the overall thesis of the present book recommends a more careful attention to the relationship between *Psycho* and the cultural contexts surrounding its reception. Hitchcock, therefore, is more interesting as an element of popular culture than as an artist expressing his unique vision.

In particular, Hitchcock's ubiquity led audiences to enter *Psycho* with an assumption of safety. Americans flocked to his comfortable and safe form of suspense in movie theaters, and they allowed him into their homes via his television show. Hitchcock had become the things he seemed to fear most, safe and predictable. With *Psycho*, Hitchcock achieved his desire to shock audiences and, in the process, redefine himself and, ultimately, his legacy.

Hitchcock's maneuver is the reverse of Howard Hawks's in *The Thing*. Hawks brought horror closer to audiences by removing it from the supernatural Gothic realm of the past and placing it into the continuous world of the present. However, he achieved this move by containing the horror within his typical tight veil of human affection and humorous banter. Hitchcock also relied on audience's assumption that he, like Hawks, would provide for their safety as he had previously. Yet, as Hitchcock brought his monster even closer than the alien menace of *The Thing*, literally housing Norman Bates on a familiar American highway, he violated the perceived promise of safety and left his audience shocked and hysterical. The shock of *Psycho*'s major twists is made all the more disturbing because it is, in essence, a kind of betrayal.

This sense of betrayal is evident in some of the reactions to the film. Renee MacCall reported in the *Daily Express*, "I have just seen the most vile and disgusting film ever made. It is titled *Psycho* and is showing at the de Mille Theatre on Broadway. The shocking thing is not only its repulsive contents but the fact that it was made by, of all people, Alfred Hitchcock."[26] Alexander Walker recalls a similar response, "'Who does he think he is!' Caroline Lejeune [a British film critic] repeated as we left shaken and shocked—and she promptly handed in her resignation from the *Observer*. If that's the way films were going, she wanted none of it."[27]

Not only is *Psycho* made to appear safe through the established credibility of Hitchcock as popular figure, but it is also wrapped within its own veil of security: the aesthetics of suburban American life. While not explicitly engaged with the issue of suburbia, *Psycho* seems to resonate with a number of the broad cultural shifts that accompanied America's move to and growing disillusionment with the suburbs. The violation of our trust, thus, not only redefines Hitchcock as an artist but also undermines American confidence in the suburban vision.

READING *PSYCHO*

Psycho can easily be read as two interrelated stories. The film's first half is Marion's story—her flight from Phoenix, her sympathetic encounter with Norman Bates, and her brutal murder. The second half is Norman's story as he is pursued by Lila, Sam, Arbogast, and ultimately, the psychiatrist. The two halves are separated by the brutal shower scene and Norman's tedious cleanup.

In my reading of the film, I find that the first half seems to resonate most dramatically with America's vision of suburbia. In this first half, elements of conspicuous consumption and prosperity, the idealized family home, the narcissistic voyeurism of television, and the fantasy of safe mobility all intermingle. The resonance between the film's first half and suburbia helped to draw audiences into Marion's story, to sympathize with her crimes and desires, and then to have this sympathy brutally exploited in the disconcerting suddenness of the shower murder. The second half of the film, in essence, rips through the veil of suburban desires that engulf the film's first half and, after the tearing shock of the shower murder, slowly strips off the illusions of America's suburban fantasies.

Prosperity

One of Hitchcock's most well-known tendencies is his use of what he called a "MacGuffin," which is a plot element that seems to motivate the plot but, eventually, becomes irrelevant. Jimmy Stewart's broken leg in *Rear Window* is an example of a MacGuffin, as is Ivor Novello's need for a room in *The Lodger*. While each of these elements is important for getting the plot rolling, ultimately they are irrelevant to the film's core. In *Psycho*, importantly, the MacGuffin is Marion's theft of the $40,000. This act starts her flight from the city and her eventual intersection with the nightmarish world of Norman Bates. While in the end, the money is superfluous to the drama that unfolds, it is the pursuit of money that starts the seemingly inevitable chain of unfortunate events.

Hitchcock is careful to emphasize the centrality of money in the early moments of the film. The opening conversation between Marion and Sam in the hotel room is filled with allusions to the potential liberation provided by money. Sam cannot commit to a relationship to Marion because of what he owes—his late father's debts and alimony for his ex-wife. Sam describes his vision of matrimony without prosperity, "Live with me behind the hardware store in Fairvale? I tell you what, when I send my ex-wife her alimony, you can lick the stamps." While Marion is less concerned about accumulating wealth—"I'll lick the stamps" she insists—it is clear that wedded bliss and a normal life are attainable only through the accumulation of money.

The temptation of money and what it can bring to her is too great for Marion. Presented with an opportunity to achieve her dream of a "respectable" life, Marion is willing to risk violating her boss's trust and breaking the law. Hitchcock makes the temptation of money and the lure of prosperity visually clear. As Marion changes her clothes to prepare to flee with the ill-gotten gains, her lingerie has changed from white to black, visually denoting her choice of an evil act. As we watch her preparing for her escape, the money is tightly framed at the bottom of the shot. In *Psycho*, the love of money is the root of Marion's evil decision.

The freedom afforded by prosperity and conspicuous consumption is represented by the wealthy southern gentleman, Tom Cassidy. It is Cassidy's apparently flippant attitude towards money that most embodies the ethic of conspicuous consumption—that despite the desperate pursuit of money, it is to be treated as if it was irrelevant. Flipping through the stack of bills, Cassidy dismisses the amount, "I never carry more than I can afford to lose." It is Cassidy who most clearly articulates the suburban approach to money, "You know what I do with unhappiness? I buy it off." Marion's flight from her unhappy urban life is motivated by and facilitated by money. She even trades in her car and uses cash to buy a new vehicle.

Still, the MacGuffin of money is soon revealed for what it is—utterly irrelevant. In her conversation with Norman, Marion realizes that the happiness offered by prosperity is illusory. In important ways, Norman Bates is a clear example of the emptiness of prosperity. Norman has achieved the kind of isolated, protected life recommended by the suburban vision, and he is a clear example of the postindustrial man. His work is empty and meaningless, his life is confined to his private property, and he spends his time pursuing leisure. Norman articulates the empty moments lying beneath the life of leisure, "A hobby's supposed to pass the time, not fill it."

If Marion is drawn into her crime by the dream of prosperity proffered by the suburban vision, Hitchcock judges this dream harshly. It is telling that Marion flushes the sheet of paper with her financial figures down the toilet; the figure of $40,000 is later discovered by Lila and Sam as they search for the murdered girl.[28] More telling, in the moment between the dramatic shower murder and Norman's cleaning up, the camera makes a very explicit move to point out the stolen money, still in its hiding place. The money, Hitchcock seems intent on making clear, is ultimately irrelevant.

Family Home

While Marion's flight may be facilitated by money, it is clear from the beginning that the prosperity is only a means to an end. Marion insists that her relationship with Sam can only continue if it leads towards matrimony. "We can see each other," she tells him at the beginning of the film, "we can even have dinner, but respectably." Despite the banal tedium of married life portrayed by her married coworker—"Teddy called me. My mother called to see if Teddy had called"—Marion longs for the security, stability, and respectability bestowed by family life.

What she finds at the Bates Motel is a version of the suburban family home. Secluded on a seldom-used highway, Norman lives in perfect isolation with only his mother for company. His time is spent in the pursuit of leisure, with the absence of meaningful work, and in the absence of friends or a father. His only meaningful relationship is with his mother: "A boy's best friend is his mother."

The Bates family and their creepy Gothic home suggest the reality lying behind the optimistic veneer of suburbia. The family, left in isolation, becomes twisted and distorted. As the psychiatrist explains during the film's final moments, Mrs. Bates "was a clinging, demanding woman, and for years the two of them [Norman and his mother] lived as if there were no one else in the world." Mrs. Bates becomes an extreme version of suburbia's fear of the "smothering mother." It is the smothering mother that becomes the root cause of Norman's psychosis and his crimes. In becoming completely isolated from the world of others, Norman and his mother turn increasingly towards each other, and after Norman kills his mother and her lover, this introverted seclusion becomes entirely narcissistic. After killing his mother, the psychiatrist explains, Norman "began to speak and think for her, give her half of his life so to speak. At times he could be both personalities, carry on a conversation."

Norman's gender confusion is mirrored by the "masculine" behavior of both Marion and Lila Crane. Marion, while more obviously sexual and feminine, displays bold initiative in stealing the money and remarkable assertiveness in the face of the various leering males she encounters. When the inquisitive highway patrolman asks if everything is all right, she defiantly states, "I've told you there's nothing wrong except that I'm in a hurry and you're taking up my time." Lila is even more obvious in her gender bending. She is largely asexual, and even when forced to play the part of Sam's wife, it is Lila who is the more assertive and aggressive in their investigation.

Interestingly, it seems that all three of these gender-confused characters—Norman, Marion, and Lila—share one relevant characteristic. They have all lost their mothers. While the death of Norman's mother is an integral part of the plot, in the opening scene of the film it is suggested that Marion (and presumably her sister Lila) have also lost their mother. She invites Sam to dinner but only at her home and with her "mother's picture on the mantle." Both Norman and Marion are dominated by a departed maternal figure, and both seem to be seeking some kind of vision of familial comfort—a pursuit that puts them on a tragic collision course.

Television

One of the most prominent trailers promoting *Psycho* featured a guided tour of the set by Hitchcock himself. The tour focused on the Bates home and the motel and cleverly reveals more than it seems to while simultaneously providing misleading cues. What is interesting about this trailer, likely seen by many of the patrons of the film itself, was how much it parallels Hitchcock's popular television show. Each episode of *Alfred Hitchcock Presents* opened with an introductory monologue by the director filled with his uniquely dark sense of humor.

The prominence of this theatrical trailer suggests the way that audiences viewed *Psycho* in terms of the broader impact of television. As James Naremore notes, "Audiences were given every reason to believe that *Psycho* would be something like the macabre little stories they had been watching at home on Sunday nights."[29] While no television sets appear in the film, *Psycho* did play on the expectation of its audience by commenting on the underlying nature of America's new "televisual" aesthetic. In particular, as numerous other commentators have noted, *Psycho* seems to be a kind of meditation on the act of viewing and the kind of narcissistic voyeurism characteristic of suburbia.[30]

The opening sequence suggests this meditation on voyeurism. The camera swoops down to peek through a hotel window and then slips through to join the two lovers. Later, the audience watches Norman peek through his peephole to observe Marion as she disrobes, and almost instantly, we share Norman's point of view as we also peer in at the unaware young woman. In the subsequent shower scene, the audience is provided an even greater voyeuristic thrill as we observe Marion in the shower, presumably washing away the sin of her crimes and seeking redemption. While the scene undoubtedly plays up the possibility of redemption, it also clearly plays to the audience's own voyeuristic tendencies. The voyeuristic enjoyment, of course, is quickly punished, but I'll focus more on the sudden shift from pleasure to terror in the discussion of the violation below.

Cinema, of course, is by nature a voyeuristic medium.[31] What makes Hitchcock's attention to voyeurism all the more provocative is the way that the camera acts as a kind of conscious narrator. The most obvious moment of this display of narrative intent occurs in the immediate aftermath of the shower murder. As noted, the camera explicitly "points" to the money still hidden in a copy of the *Los Angeles Times*. This is not a simple pan across the room but a complicated maneuver designed to direct the audience's attention to the hidden money as if to say "Look, you thought it was about money but now you know its not." The camera then pans over to the window where it directs our attention to the Bates house and we hear Norman's cry at the revelation of his mother's crime.

While the camera provides us with a means of peeking into the lives of others and voyeuristic pleasure, Hitchcock reminds us in this and other sequences that he controls our view. At times this control is almost mischievous, as in the almost humorous gesture towards the money after Marion's murder. At other times it is in the service of the grander misdirection—for instance, the torturous over-head, or God's eye, shot that allows us to see "Mother" murder the detective without revealing the killer's true identity. Of course, at other times Hitchcock uses his control to punish us for what we have seen. In all these instances, *Psycho* continually reminds its audience of their own status as voyeurs and, perhaps, suggests the potential dangers of unrestrained looking. As J. P. Tellotte reads the film, "What we witness through much of *Psycho*, then, is a failure of that vital participation, the transformation of the human into object—of visual pleasure, sexual desire, and finally homicidal mania. The potential consequences of this human failing are manifest. Once a person is shorn of his humanity and reduced to nothing more than an object, he is hardly still alive. Looks, perhaps, can kill after all."[32]

Mobility

If the opening series of crane shots over the Phoenix skyline suggests the film's attention to voyeurism, it also draws attention to the sense of aimlessness of American suburban culture. As others have noted, the camera seems to move in an almost random fashion. For some, this aimless floating suggests the flight of a bird, and as noted, the film is replete with a bird motif.[33] However, the seeming uncertainty in the camera's flight also suggests the anonymity of urban and suburban life—the sense that the camera might choose any window to peer through and any person to visit its horrors upon. Marion is simply the one chosen. As Norman says later to the detective, "People just come and go, y'know."

At the root of this anonymous coming and going is the suburban fantasy of mobility, a fantasy Hitchcock exploits ruthlessly in *Psycho*. The first half of the film is, essentially, Marion's fantasy of anony-mous mobility—the desire to flee her urban, family-less life for a new future of wedded bliss in Fairvale with Sam. That the automo-bile is a space of fantasy is made apparent as Marion escapes Phoenix and fantasizes about the reactions to her crime. "Marion, what in the world—what are you doing here?" Sam intones in her fantasy. Her boss exclaims in frustration, "Oh for heaven's sake, a girl works for you for ten years, you trust her." She grins mischievously as she imagines the way her crimes will be received—for she is safe and secure, escaping the danger in the private space of her automobile.

Read in this way, the changing of automobiles at California Charlie's is less about covering her tracks—indeed, it draws more suspicion to her than anything else—than about forwarding this fantasy of flight. Choosing a new vehicle cuts any ties to her past and pushes her over the horizon of her urban life and into the limitless freedom promised by the automobile and endless highways. The sheriff's later explanation, in the film's second half, that "she's not so much missing as run away," is largely true. She is, as she explains to Norman, just "looking for a private island."

The suburban home was envisioned as just this kind of private island as was, in its own way, the automobile. Marion's flight to freedom, perhaps foreshadowed by the floating camera in the opening scene, is emboldened by her dream of an idyllic life: a life of comfort and prosperity, a home and family away from the urban life of work. Marion's dream must have resonated with audiences in 1960, most of whom were either dreaming of such a suburban fantasy or trying to live up to it.

Violation

Psycho represents a dramatic shift in the nature of American horror films. Not only had Hitchcock brought horror into the "house next door," but he had cloaked it in all the apparent trappings of normal American suburban life. Anthony Perkins, it is worth noting, was a budding matinee heartthrob before his dramatic turn as Norman Bates. Janet Leigh was a major star, and audiences, drawn by the publicity posters that featured her prominently, would have expected her to be their primary focal point throughout the film. In shattering these expectations by casting Perkins as a gender-confused homicidal killer who murders Janet Leigh and eliminating Leigh in the first half of the film, Hitchcock left audiences with no way of knowing what to expect next.

The shower murder has received considerable attention by innumerable film critics. For the present purpose, it is worth observing the way it shatters the expectations established in the first half of the film—killing off our protagonist, revealing the money as irrelevant, and leaving us with no immediate sense of the movie's ultimate direction. From the moment the camera spirals down the shower's drain, the audience passes into another world, one without any sense of security or direction. The sequence itself, as others have noted, is a series of cuts between each montage image, and each cut seems punctuated by the sound of shrieking, staccato strings. The knife itself, the film editing, and the music all cut through our understanding of the film and leave us stunned and uncertain.[34]

The remainder of the film, however, is charged with much less energy. Sam Loomis is, for the most part, a cardboard cut-out caricature of the handsome leading man, and while Lila Crane is confident, assertive, and capable, she has little do to except bring us, almost inevitably, to the fruit cellar and a final confrontation with Mother. If there is any dramatic crackle in the film's second half, it is in the conversation between Norman and Arbogast where cracks in Norman's innocent veneer begin to show most dramatically and in the psychiatrist's dramatic—perhaps overly dramatic—explanation of Norman's psychosis.

The real function of the second half of *Psycho* is to pick up the pieces of our shattered expectations and reveal to us just how dramatically wrong we were. It is, in other words, a careful explanation of the violation. Hitchcock was notorious for wanting to avoid loose ends, and the second half of *Psycho* carefully weaves together each remaining thread of the mystery, all the way down to showing us the removal of Marion's car from the swamp.

On a rhetorical level, in the second half of *Psycho* Hitchcock reveals, almost methodically, the emptiness of the suburban vision with which the first half had so deeply resonated. Wrapped up in their own assumptions about prosperity, Lila and Sam pursue Norman Bates based on their erroneous belief that he has killed Marion for the money. The point is raised again at the end. As the sheriff asks who got the money, the psychiatrist explains, "The swamp. These were crimes of passion, not profit."

The suburban dream of a secluded and private family home is revealed as a sterile and claustrophobic environment where the human spirit becomes twisted and distorted. The images from Norman's bedroom, with its child's bed, stuffed bunny, and classical music, suggest the disturbing results of a "smothering mother." Indeed, up until the dramatic fruit-cellar revelation, Lila, Sam, and the audience are still conceiving of the Bates home in terms of an overly protective mother—another expectation Hitchcock takes pains to undermine.

The audience, like Marion, has fantasized about this prosperous family home or, conversely, dreamed of escaping this suburban life in fantasies of flight and, so, takes pleasure in gazing on as Marion enacts these fantasies. However, Hitchcock is quick to punish this desiring gaze. The shower scene is, in this way, as much an attack on the audience as it is an assault on Marion.[35] The second half of the film takes great pains to show the audience just how dangerous their voyeuristic gaze can be. Hitchcock's *Psycho* suggests that at the end of that fantasy of flight lies the ugly truth—the swamp behind the Bates Motel. So, as Marion's car is dragged out of the swamp so too were audience members dragged out of the film's narrative and returned, perhaps shaky and disturbed, to the gleaming surfaces of the American dream. *Psycho* had, in effect, revealed just how thin and misleading the surfaces of that dream were and suggested, brutally, just the kinds of things lying beneath.

PSYCHO'S LEGACY

In his forty-seventh film, Hitchcock meticulously laid out the American dream of prosperous, suburban family dwellings and liberating mobility—a dream disseminated in movies and television—and then proceeded to savagely tear it in half. Beyond *Psycho*'s popularity, its impact on Hitchcock's reputation, and its many imitators, the film dramatically upped the ante for future horror films. As Paul Wells notes, "*Psycho* works as an act of permission for filmmakers in the genre to further expose the illusory securities and limited rationales of contemporary life to reveal the chaos that underpins modern existence and constantly threatens to ensure its collapse."[36] After *Psycho*, filmmakers pursued the horror that dwells in the human psyche and within the presumably safe bonds of family, depicting it in increasingly savage and confrontational ways.

While *Psycho* did not herald the end of suburbia or American dreams of prosperity, seclusion, and mobility, the film does seem a kind of landmark of the changing American attitude. The dreams of domestic bliss promoted in the 1950s faded during the 1960s, a decade dominated by youthful dreams of peace and played out against the backdrop of one of the most spectacularly bloody and divisive wars in American history. The hippies of the late 1960s sought to turn away from the private illusions of greed and family and forge a new world of harmony and community. The rise of the "flower power" generation was, in a way, as much a revolt against the American dream of suburbia as it was against the war in Vietnam.

4 *Night of the Living Dead* (1968)

"But we'll have to work together. You'll have to help me."

As a climax to their successful 1969 North American tour, the Rolling Stones staged a final concert at the Altamont Speedway in Livermore, California. The free concert was designed as a West Coast answer to the already legendary upstate New York Woodstock music festival held five months earlier. Yet, where Woodstock reportedly embodied all the utopian dreams of the flower power generation, Altamont embodied all its nightmares. The poorly planned concert devolved into an increasingly violent confrontation between the audience and the Hell's Angels gang members who had been brought in as "security guards." The conflict led to hundreds of injuries and one horrifying murder of a young African American man, all caught on film in what would become the documentary *Gimme Shelter* (1970). For many critics, both at the time and for years to come, Altamont represented the end of the "Age of Aquarius." Todd Gitlin recalls, "The effect was to burst the bubble of the youth culture's illusions about itself.... We had witnessed the famous collectivity of a generation cracking into thousands of shards."[1]

Of course, in fairness, the dreams of a youth revolution—motivated by opposition to the war in Vietnam and embracing tolerance, free love, and common property—had already been coming apart. The assassination of the Reverend Dr. Martin Luther King Jr., perhaps the most authoritative voice for change during the turbulent decade of the sixties, on April 14, 1968, was followed just a few months later by the assassination of the heir to the decade's optimistic beginning. The death of Senator Robert Kennedy, the brother and close ally of slain President John Kennedy, seemed to sum up the rapid and violent dissolution of the decade's movements toward peaceful cultural revolution. At Altamont, the brutal violence of this unraveling was visited upon the last refuge of the sixties' utopian dream, music.

The ugliness unraveling the sixties counterculture was paralleled by the growing prominence of a film *Variety* called an "unrelieved orgy of sadism."[2] George Romero's *Night of the Living Dead* premiered in Pittsburgh, Pennsylvania, in October 1968 and went on to a limited but controversial release in cities along the East Coast. Just after the film had faded from American theaters, it found strong success in Europe where critics championed it as an important film. *Night* returned to America in 1970, and its controversial reputation grew rapidly in drive-ins and midnight movies across the country.

Of all the films in this book, *Night* was the least profitable in its initial release; it did not gross more than $1 million in 1968. It was not even that year's most prominent horror film, a title certainly taken by Roman Polanski's highly successful *Rosemary's Baby*. Where Polanski's film was, largely, overshadowed by *The Exorcist*, *Night of the Living Dead*'s legacy—despite numerous imitators and sequels—cannot be questioned. As Kevin Heffernan observes, "*Night of the Living Dead*'s influence on the horror genre was incalculable."[3]

Unlike the previous films in this book, *Night* was the product of a group of independent filmmakers. Image Ten consisted largely of people who worked together in a commercial and industrial film company in Pittsburgh. With no studio backing and a very limited budget of $114,000, the group chose horror because of its potential profitability. Romero, one of the group's more prominent and committed members, was chosen to helm the production. Despite these inauspicious beginnings, *Night of the Living Dead* successfully took up the challenge of Hitchcock's *Psycho* and pushed the boundaries of shock and gore to new heights.

Night creates an interesting contrast to *Psycho*. Where Hitchcock was already a well-established director with studio backing, Romero came to *Night* with little experience in feature-length films.[4] This lack of experience and funding shows throughout the film. Although such crude quality was the cause of derisive laughter at many of the other cheaply made B-movies flooding into neighborhood theaters in the late 1950s and 1960s, the almost-documentary style of filming in *Night* made the horror all the more graphic and immediate.

Hitchcock's *Psycho* may have been startling and shocking, but it was always filtered through Hitchcock's narrative style. *Night of the Living Dead* appears so stark and minimal—its graveyard an actual graveyard, its farmhouse an actual farmhouse—that audiences had difficulty finding a safe distance from which to enjoy the film.

The graphic directness brought about much of the controversy that surrounded the film in America, as did the nature of its distribution. The distributor hoped to maximize profit by marketing the film for both adult evening showings and for children's matinee double features, where many of the cheaply made creature features appeared. In a famous condemnation of the film, Roger Ebert wrote about his experience watching *Night* during one such matinee in Chicago. As the film reaches it nihilistic ending, Ebert recalls, "The kids in the audience were stunned. There was almost complete silence. The movie had long ago stopped being delightfully scary and had become unexpectedly terrifying. A little girl across the aisle from me, maybe nine years old, was sitting very still in her seat and crying."[5]

In *Psycho*, Hitchcock had torn the veil of decency and safety audiences expected from horror films. In *Night*, Romero's zombies slowly and disturbingly shredded the last vestiges of American hope and optimism. The 1968 film would lead to an even more successful and graphic sequel, *Dawn of the Dead* (1978), and a third, though less successful, chapter, *Day of the Dead* (1985).[6] With these and a number of other films, Romero has produced not only a body of interesting films but also a provocative argument about the nature of the American dream in the postcounterculture age. As Reynold Humphries observes, "*The Living Dead* trilogy constitutes a full-scale criticism of American values."[7]

SYNOPSIS

Night of the Living Dead opens with an apparently banal conversation between a brother, Johnny, and sister, Barbara, as they drive to a remote cemetery to visit their father's grave. Despite a disruption with the car radio, they travel on without incident to the gravesite and observe their annual ritual of leaving flowers. As they depart the gravesite, a rambling, disheveled, and ghoulish man attacks the sister. The brother attempts to fight the ghoul off but is knocked unconscious and Barbara is forced to flee.

Her flight takes her, eventually, to an old farmhouse where she discovers a decomposing body and realizes that the ghoul is not alone. The yard surrounding the farmhouse soon fills up with shuffling ghouls. After a few moments, an African American man named Ben joins Barbara. By now, Barbara has gone into a state of shock, and she is either catatonic or rambling hysterically.

Ben secures the windows and doors with wood and eventually finds a radio from which they learn that the dead have returned to life and begun feeding on the living. The sound of the radio brings out two other couples who had been hiding in the basement for all this time: a young couple, Judy and Tom, and an older couple, Harry and Helen Cooper, who also have a little girl who has become ill after being bitten by one of the ghouls. The appearance of the other couples provokes an ongoing power struggle principally between Ben and Harry over how the group will survive the siege from the growing army of the living dead.

An escape plan is devised, and Ben, Tom, and Judy race out in a truck to get gas from an old pump. As the dead surround the group, a torch is dropped near the gas tank and the truck explodes—killing Tom and Judy whose bodies are soon devoured, graphically, by the hordes of living dead. Ben fights his way back to the farmhouse, but Harry, who has been left inside, refuses to let him back into the house. Ben forces his way in, and in the midst of the ghouls' assault, he struggles with and fatally shoots Harry, who stumbles back into the basement.

The attack of the living dead becomes more intense. Barbara is pulled out of the house by her now-living-dead brother, and Helen retreats back to the basement where she finds her daughter, now turned into a ghoul from a bite, feasting on Harry's arm. The daughter kills her mother with a garden spade. The scene then shifts back to Ben, the only survivor, who fends off the dead, including Harry and Helen's daughter. Eventually, he is able to barricade himself into the basement.

The scene next shifts to an armed posse of men who are moving through the countryside shooting and burning the living dead. They soon arrive at the farmhouse, and Ben comes tentatively to the window to see if rescuers have, indeed, arrived. Seeing a body moving in the house, one of the posse members shoots Ben in the head. The film ends with disturbing and grainy photographs of the posse disposing of Ben's body in an enormous bonfire. The callous voices of the posse echo over these final images.

Like the living dead of the title, Romero's film also conquered the American horror audience with slow and steady progress. It became one of those "forbidden" films that grew in popularity based on word of mouth and controversy. The film opened sporadically in the United States in late 1968 and early 1969 to harsh controversy but limited audiences. It then traveled to Europe where it met with remarkable critical and popular acclaim. Indeed, the *Wall Street Journal* reported it was the top-grossing film in Europe in 1969. *Night* returned to the United States to much more interest and critical acclaim. Ebert reconsidered his earlier condemnation, and the film was showcased at the Museum of Modern Art.[8]

Night of the Living Dead, of course, was not the first film to focus on graphic violence. Respected directors such as Arthur Penn had already begun to traffic in violence, as in his controversial but successful *Bonnie and Clyde* (1967). Graphic horror films had also appeared, particularly the campy and colorful films of Herschell Gordon Lewis, *Blood Feast* (1963) for example, and the popular British horror films from Hammer Film Productions, Ltd. *Night*, however, removed the campy and overly colorful silliness of previous graphic violence and presented it instead within a stark and harsh realism.[9] The documentary-style filmmaking removed the distance between the audience and the savage cannibalism portrayed on the film.

In addition to these stylistic elements, it is hard to ignore the obvious points of resonance between *Night of the Living Dead* and the social upheaval occurring in the final years of the 1960s. In this regard, it makes some sense that the film would connect to European audiences before it would connect to Americans. The dreams of a youth revolution and the utopian culture they would create were, after all, global. The European efforts to enact this revolution reached their culmination in 1968. In France, for example, students and workers united in the streets of Paris in May and seemed on the verge of pushing the conservative de Gaulle government out of power. The European revolution was even moving behind the Iron Curtain. In Czechoslovakia, the "velvet revolution" had begun in April as the Czechs decided to refuse Soviet hegemony and take up self-rule, but these dreams were quickly suppressed. By the end of 1968, the student/worker revolt in Paris had been silenced by the arrival of French tanks, and back-room political negotiations and Soviet tanks were preparing to put an end to the "Prague spring."

As *Night* opened in theaters across Europe, the continent was pervaded with the sense that the dreams of revolution had dissipated under the pressure of governmental force. By the end of 1968, the same kind of dissipation was occurring in the United States. The counterculture movement was becoming fragmented and divisive, the peace movement was becoming increasingly violent, and the hope of a peaceful future seemed lost. As *Night* returned to American theaters in 1970, its popularity was bolstered not only by its European success but also by the way it resonated with a new, more cynical American youth.

CULTURAL CONTEXTS

The sixties have become more about mythology than reality. In reality, the majority of American citizens, even of American youth, did not "tune in, turn on, and drop out." They did not, at least in the first six years of the decade, oppose the presence of the U.S. military in Vietnam, and they did not embrace the use of marijuana, LSD, or the practice of "free love." Popular claims to the contrary, they were not all at Woodstock. However, despite its numerical limitations, the youth counterculture would become a prominent and important movement in American culture—the consequences of which are still being felt.

Flower Children

The young people who became flower children were largely the product of the American suburbia of the 1950s. They were, as Tom Shachtman observes, "children of the bomb, children of prosperity, and children of television."[10] The return of massive numbers of American GIs at the end of the Second World War led to an enormous number of weddings and, within a few years, a massive "baby boom."[11] This sudden explosion in the population led to a bubble of young people who began graduating high school around 1963 and, for many, soon entering colleges and universities across the country.

For this generation that grew up, largely, in the protected and isolated environment of 1950s suburban culture, the desire for liberation and experimentation became almost an obsession. Traditional rock and roll music melded with more politically progressive folk music to spawn a series of increasingly experimental and psychedelic music subgenres. Drugs became prevalent as young people pushed the envelope of their experiences further and further.

Sociologist Lauren Langman examined the identity of the budding counterculture in the mid-1960s and found it almost diametrically opposed to the 1950s suburban "industrial man" of the fifties who had faith in rationality, self-reliance, hard work, technological control, and progress towards the future. The flower children of the counterculture distrusted rational systems, preferring spontaneous self-expression. They embraced community and communal living. Indeed, the commune would become one of the typical social structures for those who truly embraced the counterculture's ethics. Dedication to hard work was replaced by a hedonistic ethic of enjoyment and freedom. Nature was preferred to technology, and the children of the counterculture embraced the moment, often expressing doubt that there would be any future.[12]

A sense of fatalism underscored the counterculture's almost childish hedonism. Members of the counterculture played in the parks, ran through the streets engaging in pranks and parties, and sought to drop entirely out of the mainstream responsibilities of American economic and political life. However, the specter of nuclear war became overshadowed by a more immediate threat. The war in Vietnam was always unpopular among members of the counterculture, but the war was demanding more and more troops, and changes to the draft laws in 1966 allowed draft boards to consider a student's class standing in their decisions. College students were in growing danger of being drafted into the war in Vietnam.

Changes in the draft laws were certainly not the only motivation for the counterculture to take on a political hue. Resistance to the draft and to the war in general was certainly a substantial motivation for the merging of hippie counterculture and progressive New Left politics. Additionally, the espoused values of freedom and community helped to forge alliances between counterculture hippies, the long-struggling civil rights movement, and the newly emerging feminist movement. Increasingly, the counterculture began to embrace a wider and wider array of political liberation movements: liberation for the oppressed peoples of the third world (including Vietnam), liberation for American people of color, liberation for women, liberation for the poor, and more. Groups such as Students for a Democratic Society, the Student Nonviolent Coordinating Committee, the Black Panthers, and the newly emerging National Organization for Women were becoming interconnected with the counterculture. Forged within the optimistic hedonism of the counterculture, these various movements seemed to coalesce into an overarching "youth revolution," which aspired to overturning the institutions of their parents' society and forging something new, a culture founded on freedom, enjoyment, and love.

The movement reached its height in the "summer of love" of 1967 as the music of *Sgt. Pepper's Lonely Hearts Club Band* wafted from vans and tents in Greenwich Village, People's Park, and the San Francisco Bay. In the midst of this musical, drug-induced party, tensions were beginning to emerge between the loose coalition's politics and its hedonism. Gitlin recalls, "There were tensions galore between the radical idea of political strategy—with discipline, organization, commitment to results out *there* in the distance— and the countercultural idea of living life to the fullest, *right here*, for oneself."[13] These tensions would become dramatically evident in 1968.

1968

As Irwin and Debi Unger observe, "The 1967 Summer of Love ended with a cosmic letdown followed by ugly incidents of murder and mass flight."[14] 1968 was the beginning of the end for the counterculture and New Left revolutionaries. The year saw an increase in violence, divisiveness, and an increasingly bitter and cynical sense that all the dreams of revolution were dissipating.

Part of this frustration must have come from the failure of the movement to halt the war in Vietnam. While public opinion was, increasingly, against the war, 1968 saw a major expansion of U.S. involvement. On January 31, the war took a dramatic and bloody turn as the North Vietnamese launched the Tet offensive, which would push U.S. and South Vietnamese forces to their limits and see the U.S. embassy in Saigon briefly occupied. During 1968, U.S. troop numbers in Vietnam would peak at 541,000, and the death toll was dramatic. In one week in February, 543 Americans were killed, and on February 27, even venerable news broadcaster Walter Cronkite was suggesting the war effort was failing.

A mere list of the horrible events that occurred in 1968 is enough to recommend it as one of the darkest years in U.S. history. On January 23, the USS *Pueblo* was captured by North Korean forces. On April 4, Martin Luther King Jr. was assassinated, sparking violent riots in cities across the country. On June 4, Robert Kennedy was shot and killed during a campaign stop in California. Protestors and police engaged in a series of violent, televised clashes during the Democratic National Convention in Chicago in August. On November 5, Richard Nixon would be elected president on a platform of victory in Vietnam and law and order at home.

The counterculture revolutionaries struggled against these discouraging and infuriating developments. Unfortunately, in the face of the long list of assassinations and escalations, the movement became violent and divisive. Violence, indeed, became an almost defining characteristic of what had been a largely peaceful cultural revolution. Civil unrest had been a fairly consistent aspect of the civil rights movement, though usually in the unorganized form of riots in major urban areas. By 1968, more and more organized movements were embracing violence as a means of social change.[15] The nonviolence championed by the assassinated Martin Luther King Jr. was slowly being replaced by the militant violence of groups such as the Black Panters. As Gitlin notes, "The rhetoric of showdown and recklessness prevailed."[16]

For many of the counterculture leaders, "the system" was inundated with violence—the economic violence of capitalism, military action around the world, the brutal police response to protestors—and the only fitting response was more violence. Ultimately, violent actions became a sign of authentic commitment to progressive politics and social justice.[17] Groups such as the Weathermen embraced an agenda of domestic bombings and assassinations, and the cycle of violent clashes between government forces and counterculture movements escalated. In 1970 alone, for example, the FBI reported more than 3,000 domestic bombings and more than 50,000 bomb threats.[18]

Perhaps part of what stimulated this increasingly violent decade was the degree to which this violence was disseminated in television and newspapers. The American television news was bloodier and more graphic than ever before, and citizens were confronted with the horrific images of war as never before. Images of war dead, bombings, napalm, political assassinations, and violent protests filled the American media, promoting the view that America was on the edge of a violent cultural civil war.

The End of the Counterculture

After the traumatic events of 1968, the counterculture became increasingly divided and divisive. In part, this division was motivated by broader ideological and identity issues. Some feminists, for example, found it difficult to embrace the apparently misogynist views of radical "Black Power" groups, and members of civil rights groups felt conflicted over association with student rights groups made up, largely, of privileged white college students. It was, as Unger and Unger observe, "the year that the liberal consensus fell apart and was replaced by rancorous resistance to further social change."[19]

The divisions were also driven by more personal, petty political maneuverings. As David Rossinow observes, movement leaders "fused their desire for individual empowerment with their dissident cultural politics."[20] Egos and dogma began to replace unity, and the various members of the counterculture coalition began a series of rancorous splits. The Students for a Democratic Society split into warring factions over who should lead the coming revolution, and the civil rights movement would fragment over questions of methods—whether to work inside or outside the political system—and of militancy.

By the time the Altamont concert erupted into violence and murder, these events were a tragically familiar aspect of the decade. The counterculture movement had begun based, in part, on a general lack of faith in the official institutions of America—government, corporations, leaders, and so on—but it ended with a divisive mistrust of almost everyone.[21]

The End of the Studio System

Hitchcock's *Psycho* cast a large shadow over 1960s cinema. Even Hitchcock himself could not live up to its reputation. His follow-up film, *The Birds* (1963), seemed an attempt to hold onto the mantle of "master of horror" and to demonstrate that he was the kind of genius academic and intellectual film critics had dubbed him. The film, while interesting, could not live up to the performances and shock value of *Psycho* and, ultimately, collapsed under the weight of its own pretensions. While Hitchcock continued to make films into the late 1970s, *Psycho* would serve, for many, as the denouement of his long career.

Psycho's lingering impact on film was due, in large part, to its own quality but it was also due to some substantial changes occurring in the nature and business of cinema. Many of these changes would open the doors for an independent, low-budget film such as *Night of the Living Dead* to create such an international sensation.

From the 1920s through to the mid-1960s, the Hollywood studio system existed with a fairly rigid hierarchy. At the top were the big five studios: MGM, Paramount, Twentieth Century Fox, RKO, and Warner Brothers. These studios not only produced many of the more expensive and heavily publicized blockbuster films, they also maintained distribution networks and, importantly, ownership over lucrative, regional chains of theaters. Below the big five were the three smaller studios that could not afford to compete directly with their virtual monopoly over distribution and theaters: Columbia, Universal, and United Artists. Beneath these two tiers existed a host of smaller studios that produced B-movies to appear on the bottom half of double bills: companies such as Republic and Grand National.[22]

The end of the Hollywood studio system began in 1938 when the U.S. Department of Justice filed suit claiming the big five held an illegal monopoly. The case wound its way through the court system for most of the next decade until the U.S. Supreme Court ruled that the big five would have to sell off their theater chains in 1948. The repercussions of this decision would greatly affect filmmaking in the 1950s and 1960s as the major studios, no longer assured of profitable theater space, focused on making fewer and "bigger" pictures. The sudden shift in the way films were made and distributed substantially reduced the number of films available, thus opening the door for numerous independent filmmakers who began pushing lower-quality, though more daring, films into American theaters.

These structural changes, of course, also occurred as televisions were achieving almost complete penetration into American society. Theater attendance plummeted as Americans found they could access entertainment, including older films, from the comfort of their own homes. With the major studio's restrictions on the number of high-quality pictures and the competition created by the spread of television, theaters and independent producers became more and more innovative in their efforts to attract audiences. William Castle became famous for his pioneering antics to promote low-quality horror films with gimmicks such as "the tingler," a motor that shook certain theater seats during the film, and even the major studios picked up on innovations such as 3-D. Indeed, Hitchcock's edict that no one shall be seated after the start of *Psycho* was part and parcel of these desperate marketing times.

By the mid-1960s, the movie industry was increasingly aware that the landscape had changed, and part of this change was the increasingly diverse movie-going audience. So, marketing and production efforts began to focus more and more on these diverse audiences. Many independent theaters focused on two major audiences, "kiddie" matinees and adult films in the evening. Many inner-city theaters began to focus more on films reflecting African American issues, even to the point of marketing films such as *The Greatest Story Ever Told* as "featuring Sydney Portier."[23] Other theaters transformed themselves into "art-house" theaters, a trend beginning in the postwar period, and featured foreign and quirky independent films.

Interestingly, in the midst of these dramatic changes to the Hollywood system, films were finally being taken seriously by intellectuals and, more slowly, academics. Beginning in France and slowly spreading to America, films were increasingly embraced as their own form of literature. Prior to the 1950s and 1960s, films were largely conceived as low culture, but on both sides of the Atlantic, intellectuals were beginning to champion the medium of film, or at least certain films. The writers of France's *Cahiers du Cinema* and the American critic Andrew Sarris argued persuasively that certain filmmakers transcended this low-culture label and ought to be considered, following the French, auteurs. Among those directors championed by these critics were the likes of John Ford, Howard Hawks, and Hitchcock. Throughout the 1960s, the criticism of film moved from newspaper reviews to intellectual and literary journals and eventually found its way into the formal structures of academic research. By the end of the 1960s, students were being taught to think of films as more than mere entertainment and to seek in them intellectual and political stimulation.

These changes in the film industry were particularly relevant to understanding how *Night of the Living Dead* achieved prominence in American culture. As indicated in Ebert's condemnation of the film, part of its initial controversy was provoked by the attempt to market it as a kiddie matinee film. The film's reemergence at the end of the 1960s was also the result of the broader changes in the American film culture. *Night's* success in Europe provided the film a level of intellectual and cultural validation that brought it to the attention of American intellectuals and students. It is also interesting to note that, because of its African American protagonist, the film was prominently marketed in the inner-city theaters that catered chiefly to African American patrons. It seems, therefore, that as *Night of the Living Dead* returned to American theaters in 1970, its audience consisted of many of those students, intellectuals, and African Americans who had been, and some who still were, involved in the youth revolution of the late 1960s. It is within this context that Romero's low-budget horror film resonated so profoundly with American culture.

READING *NIGHT OF THE LIVING DEAD*

There is, of course, a certain irony in a horror film achieving such cultural success during a period of such unrelenting real-world horrors. For many contemporary critics, the film was "cathartic for us, who forget about the horrors around us that aren't, alas, movies."[24] It is, however, difficult to imagine the film's success solely in terms of catharsis, if for no other reason than the fact that the ending is quite the opposite of a cathartic victory. The protagonist, with whom we've spent most of the film, is unceremoniously shot in the head by those who should be rescuing him, which hardly feels like a moment of great emotional release.

Critics picked up on the obvious resonance between the film and the broader social upheaval that was engulfing American at the end of the 1960s.[25] Clearly, both the film and the surrounding culture were awash in violence, division, distrust of authority, and a sense of social chaos gnawing at the edges of civilization. Added to this are a young, female protagonist and a resourceful, African American male. Whatever Romero's objections that he did not intend *Night of the Living Dead* as a cultural critique,[26] it is clear that the film rakes up many contemporary cultural issues and anxieties.

Rather than simply add to the consensus about *Night*'s relationship to its culture, I want to add another level to this cultural resonance. Not only does *Night* draw on the political images and concerns relevant to the counterculture of the 1960s, but also its narrative structure parallels the emergence and dissolution of the counterculture's political aspirations. It is the narrative parallel that created the potent resonance with its audience at the beginning of the 1970s. *Night of the Living Dead*, in other words, acted as a kind of eulogy to the revolutionary spirit that had mobilized, unified, and ultimately divided a generation of Americans.

A New American Generation

A sense that the film is engaged with the broader American question is presented visually during the opening credits. As Johnny and Barbara's car makes its way up the lonely Pennsylvania road and into the cemetery, one shot frames the car with an American flag, which dominates most of the screen. The shot lingers, and the flag waves across the screen for a few seconds after the car has left. Not to push this visual metaphor too far, but it is interesting that the symbol of America is so prominently framed in a shot that also establishes the scene in a cemetery, perhaps suggesting the death of America—at least the old, optimistic sense of the American dream.

Of course, it is also possible to read the connection between flag and cemetery in terms of a place of transition—moving, ostensibly, from the old life into some new realm. In this regard, it is interesting that the first line of dialogue in the film refers to the time change, which we are informed is occurring on this day. "They ought to make the day the time changes the first day of summer," Barbara says to her brother. The times, to paraphrase, are changing.

It is also interesting that this time change is linked, at least in Barbara's wishes, to summer. The height, at least symbolically, of the counterculture revolution had been the summer of 1967, and continuing to push this time change metaphor, it seems as though Barbara wishes that the times had changed in accordance with the utopian dreaming of that summer. However, the time change is not occurring in summer. While it is possible that it is the spring time change, the dead trees and overcoats suggest it is the fall change. Fall, of course, is the time of death. The plants lose their leaves, and the green grass turns to brown in preparation for the long sleep of winter. The fall time change is also a period when the hour goes back or, in the common parlance, the hour "falls back." The sense of death and of retrograde motion seems to prefigure the narrative structure of the film.

Barbara and Johnny, to be sure, are not stereotypical flower children or hippies. They are, however, young and immature. Johnny complains about having to drive out at such a late hour to visit their father's grave and resents their mother's demands. He asks Barbara if there is any candy remaining and, later, plays the same kind of prank he recalls being scolded for as a child.[27] As a figure lumbers up the path towards the siblings, Johnny taunts his sister, "They're coming to get you Barbara." Little does he know in his childish prank that the figure is, indeed, coming to get them. Soon the ghoul kills Johnny and begins chasing Barbara. Their innocent play has been brought to an abrupt halt by an encroaching, lethal danger.

A Militant Response

Barbara's flight from the ghoul is harrowing, but she holds her wits together long enough to lock herself into an old farmhouse she runs across. Beyond that, however, she is incapable of much. Barbara, ostensibly our protagonist, fluctuates between a catatonic stupor and hysterics for the rest of the film. Interestingly, her reactions—raving about going out to get Johnny or staring blankly at a music box—mirror the stereotypical reactions of those tripping on LSD or other hallucinogens. If Barbara stands in for the innocent and childlike dreams of the hippie culture, her catatonic state resembles the decade's stereotype of the drugged-out shell of that innocence.

Much as in *Psycho*, our first protagonist does not last very long. While she only meets her end in the last few minutes of the film, she is no longer an effective point of identification for the audience and becomes more of a burden to be carried. Fortunately, the narrative supplies an energetic and effective protagonist with which the audience can identify, Ben. Obviously, the most striking aspect of Ben is that he is an African American, and to emphasize the point, one can imagine few other films that would encourage a 1968 American audience to cheer along as an African American male beat a white man, even a dead white man, in the head with a lug wrench. If such an image seems unlikely, we might be even more shocked to see Ben punch Barbara in the mouth to end one of her hysterical fits or, perhaps most shocking, to shoot one of the living whites trapped with him in the farmhouse.

What is it about Ben that draws audiences to identify with him, even root for him, in the face of these various transgressions of racist norms in the 1960s? At one level, the degree to which audiences identified with Ben may have depended on the makeup of that audience. African American audiences living in inner-cities would, likely, have found Ben's direct and aggressive response to oppressive whites a refreshing change of pace. Even for audiences not directly identified with the racial frustrations implicit in Ben's actions, Ben is an attractive protagonist because he embodies a pragmatic militancy.

From the moment Ben appears he is a figure of action. He beats down a group of zombies who are surrounding the hysterical Barbara. He kills a few of them and sets one of the corpses on fire to frighten the others away. He quickly begins searching for boards and tools to secure the doors and windows. Unlike Barbara, Ben seems largely unfazed by the horrors going on around them, save for a brief monologue describing how he escaped from a horde of the ghouls. He does not seek explanation or offer sentiment but immediately recognizes the need for action and, therefore, acts. Even when the others arrive, drawn from their hiding place in the basement by the sounds of a radio, Ben continues his unrelenting pursuit of action. In this regard, the debate concerning whether to stay on the first floor and protect the house or to barricade into the basement shows Ben's true nature. Hiding in the basement is a "death trap" but staying on the first floor provides a means of fighting. "If you box yourself in the cellar and those things get in the house, you've had it. At least up here you have a fighting chance," Ben insists.

The fact that, by the end of the film, Ben himself has retreated into the barricaded basement and, thus, had to rely on the death trap promoted by others does little to undermine our connection to Ben. He survives the attack of the living dead based not on superior intellect or planning but based on his unrelenting commitment to acting with increasing violence in the face of the growing danger.

Violent Divisions

Graphic violence, of course, fills *Night of the Living Dead*: A decomposing corpse is glimpsed upstairs in the farmhouse; skulls are crushed; and entrails, arms, and legs are devoured. The violence encompasses the entire film, particularly as the living people in the house turn violently on each other, and the film describes a world awash in violence. The situation is, as a newscast reports, one of "wholesale murder engulfing much of the nation."

Most of the violence is perpetrated by either the slow, shuffling living dead or by Ben, the militant actor. While the dead are clearly the villainous monsters of the piece—a bit of a contrast to their almost sympathetic portrayal in *Dawn of the Dead* and *Day of the Dead*—it is Ben's violence that becomes increasingly disturbing. Punching Barbara is, obviously, an excessive response to her angry slap. His later running conflict with Harry, one of the basement dwellers, only exacerbates the growing tension in the house.

Ultimately, the real threat to the survival of the nine humans in the farmhouse is not the growing army of living dead outside but the tenuous relationships inside. It is clear from their first meeting that Ben and Harry will struggle for dominance. Helen criticizes her husband, insisting that he is only concerned "to be right and everyone else to be wrong." Ben, of course, is equally insistent. If the group stays on the first floor, "You'll take orders from me!" While the group is able to hold their fragile alliance together at the beginning of their escape plan—Tom pleads for the group to "stick together"—as things fall apart so goes the group. Tom and Judy die during the escape plan as the truck catches fire and explodes. Ben fights his way back to the house, but now it is Harry who has the upper hand and refuses to unlock the door. Ben kicks in the door and then threatens Harry, "I ought to drag you out there and feed you to those things!"

Mounting tension among those trapped is nothing new. Even in *The Thing* it is clear that the threatening, claustrophobic environment strains the cohesion of the group. As Wells observes, "*Night of the Living Dead* suggests that all of the consensual bonding that was possible in previous models of 'community-under-threat' has now dissipated into petty feuding and almost willful misunderstanding predicated on each person's belief in their own intrinsic 'rightness.'"[28]

It is worth noting that during the film's final, dramatic assault, the humans might have survived if they had worked together and fallen back into the barricaded basement. By this point, however, it has become more about being "right" than surviving together. Harry foolishly tries to steal the rifle away from Ben, who retrieves the firearm and shoots Harry. Ben refuses to leave the first floor despite being overwhelmed by the living dead. Barbara is dragged from the house by her now-living-dead brother Johnny. Helen does manage to retreat to the basement only to find her sick daughter, now a ghoul, devouring her husband. She, too, is killed by the child. Only Ben survives the final assault.

Distrusting Authority

Throughout the duration of their siege in the farmhouse, the nine survivors pin their real hopes on the authorities. "They'll tell us what to do," Ben says. Instead, the portrayal of these authorities provides anything but assurance. Military and scientific officials seem more interested in bickering about explanations—arguing over whether the mutations were caused by radiation from a space probe—than providing for the survival of the citizenry.

In the midst of the growing danger, the news reports that the situation is growing and engulfing the eastern third of the country. The only constructive advice given is for survivors to find their way to central locations, but even this advice only leads our protagonists to the ill-fated attempt at escape. "Everything is being done that can be done," the television reports as the living dead threaten from outside.

The only constructive action comes from a heavyset rural sheriff and his posse of gun-toting rednecks—a sight disturbingly reminiscent of southern lynchings and police brutality. The posse moves through the countryside, systematically and brutally shooting the living dead and burning their bodies. The members come, as Wood notes, "to restore the social order that has been destroyed."[29] In a way, the posse is similar to Ben in that both choose action as their means of survival. What differentiates these to me, however, is the cold and systematic brutality of the posse, devoid of passion or desperation. The posse members kill because they have been ordered to. They perform their lethal duties without remorse or hesitation. It is this systematic extermination that ultimately kills Ben.

The film's final moments, as the closing credits roll, consist of a series of grainy still photographs of the disposal of Ben's body on a bonfire filled with the now dead living dead. The sequence is made all the more disturbing as the photographs seem so realistic, reminiscent of the innumerable newspaper photographs from the war in Vietnam and domestic civil unrest. As meat hooks pierce Ben's flesh and he is dragged out to the bonfire, it is interesting to note that his body is placed directly beside that of the ghoul who attacked Barbara and Johnny in the cemetery. Whatever Ben's pragmatism, whatever his dynamic militant action, he ends up amidst those he was fighting.

Violation

Night of the Living Dead violates many of our generic expectations. On the most obvious level, the film is an ode to Hitchcock. It uses *Psycho*'s trick of switching protagonist early in the film and *The Birds*'s motif of a dysfunctional group trapped in an old house. However, where these tricks are unsettling in Hitchcock, in *Night* they are disturbing. Romero's film lacks the sense of a narrator—the presence of the authorial camera—that pervades Hitchcock's films. Romero's film feels more like cinema verité in that the camera is almost always still and the film is grainy and dark. *Night* fails to give its audience the kind of aesthetic distance Hitchcock's intricate tales involve. We are not separated from the violence and mayhem by artistry but, to the contrary, directly confronted with graphic images and chaos.

Beyond the structural and aesthetic aspects, *Night* is disturbing because of how ordinary its characters are. These are not glamorous or exotic figures but the kind of hodgepodge of humanity we encounter in city streets on a daily basis. Their reactions are not especially

superhuman; they, like us, bicker, cower, and take desperate mea-
sures. Watching the film, we know that these nine could survive the
night if they could band together, but the film avoids the sentimen-
tality of a communal bonding moment and leaves us with only the
basic human qualities of fear, hatred, and arrogance.

In *Night*, as Jane Caputi notes, "the world turns upside down."
The dead return to devour the living. Racial power relations are
inverted, structures of authority and power crumble, and in the
midst of this chaos, the farmhouse group has the potential to overcome and survive. They are, however, unable to overcome their own
divisive desire to be right and, thus, fall apart and do not survive.
Our desire to see the group, at least one representative of it, survive
and smuggle some inkling of optimism out of the *Night* is, ultimately, thwarted. We leave *Night* with nothing but an overwhelming
sense that the oppressive, chaotic world around us may be insurmountable. As R. H. W. Dillard observes, *Night of the Living Dead*,
"as a whole undercuts most of the cherished values of our whole
civilization."[30]

Of course, "undercutting the values of civilization" was the aim
of the countercultural revolution—to tear down the oppressive
structures of western civilization and build a more equitable, just,
and free society in its place. The dream moved dramatically forward
as various factions sought a unified framework for action. In the
end, they could not overcome their own individual aspirations, and
their divisiveness tore this dream to pieces. Sitting in movie theaters in inner-cities and near college campuses in the immediate
aftermath of this dissolution, the resonance with the desperate and
divisive group surrounded by chaos and violence must have been
palpable.

NIGHT OF THE LIVING DEAD'S LEGACY

Slowly but surely between 1968 and the early 1970s, Romero's
Night of the Living Dead found its way into the American consciousness. While it is difficult to trace exactly how much the film made at
the box office—the strange relationship between distributor and
producers has been mired in numerous lawsuits—Paul Gagne estimates that the film has grossed in excess of $30 million.

More importantly, *Night* became one of the forbidden midnight
films that teenagers would flock to throughout the 1970s and 1980s.
The success of *Night* would spawn both a new tone in horror films

and an entirely new subgenre. The new tone led to numerous films that, as Andrew Tudor explains, collectively crafted, "a world of mass psychosis in which we are doomed to decline into a subhuman state."[31] Horror films moved beyond death and defilement and towards the apocalypse.[32]

Many films approached this end of the world, or at least end of humanity and civilization, with a sense of foreboding. Others embraced the end. Beginning with Romero's successful sequel, *Dawn of the Dead*, a subgenre of films emphasizing gore and anarchic humor emerged. The "splatter" subgenre reveled in special effects and psychotic senses of humor. These increasingly postmodern films often lack any clear sense of narrative coherence or resolution. Examples of splatter films include Sam Raimi's *Evil Dead Trilogy*, the *Return of the Living Dead* series of films, and virtually any of the films from Troma Entertainment. Additionally, the splatter aesthetic became an integral part of nonsplatter films such as the *Nightmare on Elm Street* films and the *Friday the 13th* series.[33]

1968 was an important turning point in American culture and in the history of the horror genre. The American horror film had long been threatening its audiences with the sense that something dark and deadly was lurking at the edges of modern life. *Dracula* threatened defiling chaos, *The Thing* initiated an invasion of inhuman monsters, and *Psycho* unraveled the illusions of the American dream. In those films, the threat was always something that was on its way. With *Night of the Living Dead*, the threat to American security and optimism was over. The end had begun.

5 *The Exorcist* (1973) and *The Texas Chainsaw Massacre* (1974)

"I think I've lost my faith."

"My family's always been in meat."

If there is a pinnacle year in the history of the American horror film, it is 1974. Some might argue for 1968, the year both *Night of the Living Dead* and Roman Polanski's *Rosemary's Baby* arrived on American screens, or perhaps 1978, which saw both *Dawn of the Dead* and John Carpenter's *Halloween*. In 1974, audiences could, conceivably, arrange for themselves a double feature of two of the most notorious and influential films in the history of American cinema: William Friedkin's *The Exorcist*, which opened on December 26, 1973, and Tobe Hooper's *The Texas Chainsaw Massacre*, which premiered October 11, 1974.

While these two films share important places in the pantheon of American horror films, on the surface they share little else. *The Exorcist* was a major Hollywood movie event. Based on a best-selling novel by William Peter Blatty, who also wrote the screenplay, and directed by the Academy Award-winning director of *The French Connection* (1971), William Friedkin, *The Exorcist* is a film of amazing quality and production value. To the contrary, *Texas Chainsaw* was based on a jumble of memories and childhood stories in the mind of Hooper, an unknown filmmaker living in Austin, Texas. Produced with money from various sources, including the production company behind *Deep Throat* and, reportedly, the mob,

Texas Chainsaw is a low-budget shocker more in the vein of *Night of the Living Dead*. *The Exorcist* was nominated for a number of Academy Awards, including best picture, director, leading actress, and supporting actor and actress, and won awards for adapted screenplay and sound. *Texas Chainsaw* received some accolades in Europe—playing the London Film Festival and at Cannes in 1975— but was generally reviled by the American mainstream. *Harper's Magazine* called it a "vile piece of sick crap with literally nothing to recommend it."[1] Friedkin's film had a budget, from Warner Brothers, of $12 million; Hooper's had a budget of $125,000.

The films do share a few important characteristics. They were both remarkably successful. *The Exorcist* grossed around $128 million in its initial release, a figure that, when adjusted for inflation, would make it the most successful R-rated film in American history.[2] Like *Night of the Living Dead*, the various dealings and double-dealings behind the scenes of the release of *Texas Chainsaw* make its exact gross impossible to determine, but estimates range between $30 million and $100 million in its first seven years.[3]

Additionally, both films developed a complicated kind of apocrypha. *The Exorcist* was supposedly based on an actual exorcism in the Washington, DC area. *Texas Chainsaw* presented itself as "based on actual events," a reference to its very loose association with the story of Ed Gein, whose crimes also inspired *Psycho*. Legend has it that the set of *The Exorcist* was haunted and that the sites of its filming in Georgetown are still visited by demonic spirits. A woman reportedly had a miscarriage while viewing *The Exorcist*, and people supposedly stumbled out of *Texas Chainsaw* in a state of psychological shock.

More importantly, in this chapter I will argue that *The Exorcist* and *The Texas Chainsaw Massacre* share a crucial apocalyptic tone. Following from the kind of horror narrative popularized in *Night of the Living Dead*, both these films engage the question of the end of humanity as we know it. Apocalypse has at least three broad senses: First, in its literal sense it is about the end of the world, a notion influentially depicted in the Biblical book of *The Revelation of Saint John the Devine*. Second, apocalypse evokes a sense of catastrophe that, if not literally the end of the world, resembles this kind of final moment and a sense that the world can never be the same. Third, and finally, apocalypse involves a revelation—a pulling back the curtain of illusion and uncovering of the underlying truth. While neither of these films deals with the end of the world in as explicit terms as Romero's films do, both *The Exorcist* and *Texas Chainsaw* approach the broader struggle between good and evil, the edges of civilization, and ultimately, the things that lie beneath, albeit, in instructively different ways. In this regard, these two films can be constructively read against each other—to read, in other words, the dialectic tension between the ways these two films engage the apocalypse.

SYNOPSES

Friedkin's *The Exorcist* opens in Northern Iraq, where Father Lancaster Merrin (Max von Sydow) attends to an archaeological dig. In one of these digs a demonic talisman is discovered along with a medal of Saint Joseph. It soon becomes clear that this discovery portends a major struggle between the powers of good and the forces of evil, dramatically symbolized in an image of Father Merrin facing the enormous statue of a winged demon.

The scene shifts to Georgetown in the District of Columbia where the film follows three converging storylines. In the first, famous actress Chris MacNeil (Ellen Burstyn) is completing a movie and enjoying a comfortable life in a townhouse she shares with her daughter, Regan (Linda Blair), and various servants. Strange events soon begin around Regan. Strange noises emanate from the attic, a Ouija board moves dramatically when the daughter plays with it, and the young girl complains of her bed shaking. When young Regan disrupts a dinner party by urinating in the middle of the floor and telling an astronaut, "You're going to die up there," she is taken to medical doctors.

Various painful medical procedures, including two spinal taps, reveal nothing, but Regan's behavior becomes more and more bizarre. She curses viciously, is violent, and flies up and off of her bed in unnatural ways. Her appearance also begins to change dramatically. Her eyes are often yellowish, and her face puffs out and begins to display large gashes. Soon the only way to control her is through physical restraints and heavy doses of sedatives. Eventually, after more dramatic and increasingly unnatural behavior, the medical doctors suggest consulting psychiatric care. The psychiatrists, however, are equally at a loss. They suggest that Regan is suffering from a delusion that she is possessed by some "alien intelligence" and that the only slim possibility would be to perform an actual exorcism as a kind of "shock treatment."

Interspersed through the story of Regan's possession and the failure of medicine is the story of Father Damien Karras (Jason Miller), a priest and psychiatrist working for the Jesuit order. In Father Karras's story we learn of his ailing mother, who eventually dies alone in New York, and his frustration at being unable to help her financially. Father Karras confesses that he fears he is losing his faith and is therefore unfit to counsel other priests.

The third storyline attends to the director of Chris MacNeil's movie, Burke Demmings, a stereotypically drunken British director. Burke is, we are told, left alone to watch Regan one evening as her possession becomes more and more violent and is later found dead at the bottom of a long flight of stairs with his neck broken and his head turned backwards. A police detective, who appears intermittently in the film, begins investigating the possibility that this crime is somehow linked to a series of church desecrations and interviews both Father Karras and MacNeil in his investigation.

Father Karras is eventually asked to see Regan, and while he is skeptical that she is actually possessed, he asks the church for permission to perform an exorcism. Father Merrin, who has returned from Iraq and has, we are told, experience with exorcism, is called in to perform the exorcism with Father Karras's assistance. The two priests perform the rite of exorcism amidst a maelstrom of supernatural incidents: the bed levitates, walls crack, objects fly across the room, and the young girl's head makes a full rotation. Eventually, Father Merrin dies from what appears to be a heart attack, and Father Karras cries out for the demon to come out of the young girl and into him. For a moment he is visibly possessed by the evil entity before regaining his senses and hurling himself out of the window and down the same stairs where the director had died.

The film ends with the actress and her daughter, who now remembers nothing, departing Georgetown. As they leave, MacNeil gives one of Father Karras's friends his St. Joseph's medallion, which had fallen to the floor during the climactic struggle. The screen then quickly turns black and the red lettering of the title appears.

Not since *Psycho* had a film provoked the kind of hysteria that accompanied Friedkin's tale of possession. Around the world, the appearance of the film was accompanied by long lines, vomiting, and claims of supernatural events.[4] In some ways, *The Exorcist* followed a long line of increasingly grotesque shock films in the vein of *Night of the Living Dead*, but what Friedkin and his major studio budget added to this tradition was a technical production value that raised the horror genre to a level of cultural respectability. As Mark Kermode observes, *The Exorcist* provided an unprecedented "visceral visual onslaught."[5] The technical skill and excellent pacing of the film attracted not only enormous popularity but also unprecedented critical acclaim for a horror film, acclaim that opened the door for a number of big budget, high-quality horror films, which sought the same kind of success.[6] As Tudor contends, "It is widely agreed that *The Exorcist* marks a crucial transition in the modern horror movie."[7]

If *The Exorcist* borrowed obliquely from Romero's 1968 shocker, the true heir to his gory legacy was another low-budget film put together by another group of inexperienced friends, this time from Texas. Hooper's *The Texas Chainsaw Massacre* seems to open precisely where Romero's film ends, with a series of photographs of decomposing bodies. The camera soon reveals a hideous sculpture of decomposing body parts arranged on a tombstone. The credits roll across a strange series of almost psychedelic images that, upon closer inspection, are solar flares on the surface of the sun. Accompanying these images are a series of disturbing radio news reports—first of a series of grave robberies in Texas and then of other equally grizzly crimes and catastrophes.

The story itself begins with a group of young people traveling in a van through Texas: Sally (Marilyn Burns); her disabled brother, Franklin (Paul Partain); her boyfriend, Jerry (Allen Danziger); and another couple of friends, Kirk (William Vail) and Pam (Teri McMinn). Hearing of the grave desecration, they travel to Sally and Franklin's ancestral home to check on the fate of their grandfather's grave. As they depart the cemetery, assured their grandfather has been undisturbed, they pick up a hitchhiker. The unnamed hitchhiker (Edwin Neal) begins acting strangely—cutting his own hand with a knife, burning a picture he has taken of Franklin, describing the process for making headcheese in graphic detail—and then cuts Franklin's arm with a straight razor before being kicked out of the van.

As they travel on to the abandoned home of their grandparents, the young people stop for gas only to learn that the station is out of gas. They decide to wait at their grandparents' old farmhouse until the next tanker truck arrives. At the farmhouse, the group splits up. Kirk and Pam head off to a swimming hole but take a detour to another old house. In the old house, Kirk encounters Leatherface (Gunnar Hansen), an enormous man wearing a mask of human skin, and is killed. Pam later enters the house looking for Kirk and is captured by the inarticulate Leatherface.

After waiting for Pam and Kirk to return, Jerry decides to go looking for them. He also ends up in the house, where he discovers the barely alive Pam, but he also is killed by Leatherface. As night falls, Sally, pushing the uncooperative Franklin in his wheelchair, goes looking for her friends. Leatherface kills Franklin with his chainsaw and then chases Sally into the old house, out of the house, and to the gas station. At the gas station, Sally solicits help from the station's owner (Jim Siedow), only to have him take her captive and return her to the old house. At the old house, Sally is subjected to torment and torture at the hands of the strange family made up of the station owner, called the Cook; Leatherface; the Hitchhiker; and a wrinkled, nearly dead grandfather.

As the group decides to kill Sally, she escapes and runs out into the road where the pursuing Hitchhiker is run over by a tractor-trailer truck. Leatherface pursues Sally until she jumps into the back of a passing pickup truck. The film ends abruptly with a hysterical, blood-covered Sally laughing and Leatherface spinning and swinging his chainsaw.

While nowhere near as financially or critically successful as *The Exorcist*, *Texas Chainsaw* was, in many ways, far more influential. *Texas Chainsaw* became a kind of taboo film—horrifying and condemned for its graphic brutality and, of course, irresistible to young audiences seeking to break taboos. *Texas Chainsaw* took the familiar tale of the psychotic killer and simultaneously distorted and amplified it. As Carol Clover notes, Hooper's film provided a crucial bridge between Hitchcock's *Psycho*—the insane killer, the remote location, and the confusing issues of gender and sexuality—and the slasher films of the 1980s, films such as *Halloween* and *Friday the Thirteenth*.[8] Indeed, Jones, in his survey of horror in film and literature, declares *Texas Chainsaw* "the greatest of all modern horror movies," and Christopher Sharrett argues that the film "represents a crucial moment in the history of the horror genre."[9]

CULTURAL CONTEXTS

It is interesting that critics read both *The Exorcist* and *Texas Chainsaw* as important turning points in the history of the modern horror film, and in a way, this lends credence to exploring the films' apocalyptic tones. Taken together these two films not only dramatically extended the brutal and graphic nature of modern horror films but also ushered in an increasingly urgent and pessimistic tone. Following in the footsteps of *Psycho* and *Night of the Living Dead,* both Friedkin's and Hooper's films suggested that the world as we know it is ending and that behind the layers of cultural illusion lies a deep, inner truth about our nature.

This sense that the hopes and aspirations of the American dream had ended, of course, was pervasive in 1970s America. As detailed in the previous chapter, the youthful optimism and utopian dreams of the 1960s had fallen into increasingly divisive fragments by the beginning of the 1970s. The collapse of the counterculture had left only the promises of the official authorities and, within months, even those guarantees were unraveling. In contrast to the hopefulness of the 1960s, the 1970s began, as Slocum-Schaffer notes, "like a pounding hangover."[10]

An Age of Paranoia

If there is a clear epitome of the paranoid fragmentation affecting America in the early seventies, it is the presidency of Richard Nixon. After a tight campaign against Hubert Humphrey, Nixon won the 1968 presidential election with a margin of only about 500,000 votes. He had campaigned with a series of optimistic promises: to end the conflict in Vietnam quickly and with honor, to restore law and order to the increasingly chaotic and violent America, and to restore confidence and openness in the federal government.

As history has well recorded, Nixon not only failed to achieve these promises but he also fundamentally eroded American faith in the presidency and the federal government. Only a few months after taking office, he reneged on his promise to withdraw from the conflict in Vietnam by beginning a campaign of bombing in Cambodia. The antiwar protests became larger and even more vocal across the country, adding to Nixon's frustration and fear that his presidency would be undone by the conflict in the same way that President Lyndon Johnson's had been. The murder of four students during an antiwar protest at Kent State in 1970 added even more fuel to the antiwar protests.

Nixon was eventually able to end the Vietnam war, suspending offensive actions in January of 1973 and withdrawing the last American troops by March. The end of the war, however, was anything but honorable as veterans returned to indifference by some and condemnation for atrocities by others. South Vietnam fell just twenty-seven months after the peace treaty was signed and, for the first time in its history, the United States tasted military defeat. After almost a decade of conflict, 1.3 million Vietnamese deaths and 56,000 American losses, there was little that was honorable about the end of the war in Vietnam.

The end of the war, however, was, partially overshadowed by another disturbing development in the Nixon White House. On June 17, 1972, security guard Frank Wills called the D.C. police about a piece of tape covering the lock on an office door at the Watergate complex. Police arrested five men inside the Democratic national headquarters who were attempting to place surveillance equipment into the offices. Ultimately, this attempt to sabotage the Democratic presidential campaign of George McGovern was pointless. Nixon won the 1972 election with an enormous majority, winning every state except Massachusetts. However, the foiled break-in would bring an end to Nixon's presidency, as various attempts at covering up the connection to the White House failed, and the investigative work of the *Washington Post* and later the U.S. Congress would lead to formal House hearings on impeachment beginning May 9, 1974. On August 8, 1974, President Richard Milhouse Nixon became the first U.S. president to resign.

The failed war in Vietnam and the Watergate scandal further reduced Americans' trust in their government. As Slocum-Schaffer concludes:

> Perhaps the most heart-wrenching aspect of Richard Nixon's betrayal was the hope and promise that he had conveyed. He had been elected in 1968 on the strength of promises to heal and unite America.... But instead, Nixon became the president who destroyed American notions of true leadership; he was the one who betrayed America's trust. That betrayal rocked the nation. It was to have a profound impact on the American people, shaping not only the rest of the decade but also the conduct of politics in America for the foreseeable future.[11]

The legacy of paranoia from the Nixon administration pervaded American culture in the 1970s. Conspiracy theories, given new credence by the clandestine complexity of the Watergate scandal, circulated with explanations for many of the events of the tumultuous 1960s: John Kennedy was assassinated by the CIA, Martin Luther King Jr. by the FBI, and so on. American cinema also embraced this paranoia with numerous films focused on government conspiracies, films such as *Parallax View* (1974) and *Three Days of the Condor* (1975).[12] Where the 1960s had revealed the failures of antiestablishment forces, the 1970s revealed the corruption at the heart of the establishment.

Decline of the American Family

If broad social structures seemed to have failed, there was little solace to be found in the most intimate structure of social life, the family. Beginning in the late 1960s, the American divorce rate increased dramatically at the same time as birthrates dropped to historic lows.[13] This trend accelerated in the early 1970s as Americans turned away from the traditional models of family life. As the flower power generation entered adulthood, their suspicion of suburban American values remained, and they continued to explore new forms of intimacy. Their explorations were greatly facilitated by the expansion of contraceptive technology and the legalized right to abortion—*Roe v. Wade* was decided in January of 1973, guaranteeing a woman's right to choose an abortion.

The dramatic decline in the number of American families was symptomatic of a broader change in the concept of both marriage and children. Where children had been at the center of the suburban family of the 1950s and 1960s, Americans in the 1970s held an uneasy view of children. On the one hand, traditional marriage and the responsibilities of children infringed on the new self-oriented middle class ethic. Having developed a deep distrust of traditional institutions, the now-adult former flower children seemed reluctant to relinquish their hedonistic impulses for the difficulties of raising children. It is telling, as David Frum observes, that almost all the popular television sitcoms of the 1970s featured childless protagonists, for example, *The Mary Tyler Moore Show*, *The Bob Newhart Show, Rhoda,* and *The Jeffersons.*

In a way, there seemed a growing fear of children, not only as limitations upon individual freedom but also a fear of children themselves. The films of this period seemed to pick up on this fear— films such as *Rosemary's Baby*, in which Satan's child is born, and Larry Cohen's *It's Alive* (1974) and *It Lives Again* (1976), in which mutant babies create carnage. Perhaps, in part, this fear came from the rebellious nature of the children of the sixties and an underlying concern that the next generation might wreak even more cultural destruction. By the mid-1970s, Americans were, as Arlene Skolnick observes, "standing about in the ruins of structures that had, little more than a decade before, seemed stable and changeless—lifelong marriage, sexual morality, the 'traditional' family."[14]

Apocalypse Now

Fear of children was also fueled by more concrete concerns. In 1968, Paul Ehrlich published *The Population Bomb*, the first in a series of books concerned with overpopulation. Ehrlich predicted widespread famine in the 1970s and urged stronger regulations to limit population growth. His predictions became remarkably popular and he appeared on *The Tonight Show* some twenty-five times, spawning numerous followers and imitators.[15] These fears also found their way into American cinema in films such as *Soylent Green* (1973), in which humans are turned into food for the teeming populace, and *Logan's Run* (1976), in which a maximum age of 33 is established. During the early 1970s, overpopulation was joined by numerous other ecological concerns including a new ice age, planetary drying, and global warming as Americans became increasingly concerned about the fragility of life upon the planet.

Fears about the end of the world were also fueled by biblical interpretations of the growing troubles in the Middle East. Ecological concerns were fueled by an energy crisis sparked by the Arab oil embargo of 1973. The oil embargo and subsequent American energy crisis was the result of U.S. support for Israel in the Yom Kippur War of 1973, the largest of the Arab-Israeli conflicts. The military conflict between Israel and its Arab neighbors energized American fundamentalist religious leaders to predict the imminent end of the world. The final battle of Armageddon, between the forces of good and evil, was to take place in the Middle East, and the Arab-Israeli conflicts seemed, to many, to be the beginning of this ultimate ending. Hal Lindsey's book-length declaration that the Biblical end was nigh, *The Late Great Planet Earth*, sold approximately 10 million copies between 1970 and 1977.[16]

Apocalyptic Narratives

Tales of the end of the world, of course, date back as far as recorded history. Seemingly from the moment humans began to ponder the origin of their world they also began to speculate about the

traumatic moment of its demise. The sunrise at the birth of humanity, it seems, needed the counterpoint of a sunset at its end. These
speculations have been integral parts of religion, fiction, and culture, and they have long been part of the medium of film. As far back
as the beginning of the twentieth century, filmmakers have depicted
their own visions of the end of the world.[17]

Apocalyptic visions, as stated earlier, need not express a literal
end of the world but may entail a sense of the inevitable decay and
demise of broad social structures and order. Indeed, tales of the
apocalypse tend to arrive at moments when social upheaval and
chaos seem to be on the brink of overcoming the forces of stability
and order. While some tales of the apocalypse are presented as
prophecies of an inevitable—often religious—final moment, other
apocalyptic stories are presented more as critiques of the current
state of the world. In these narratives of the end, an apocalypse is
necessary because of the inherent failure of the world's moral character. As James Berger puts it, "the world is poised to end and is so
suffused with moral rottenness and technological, political, and
economic chaos and/or regimentation that it should end and must
end, and it must end because in some crucial sense it has ended."[18]

In contemporary, nonreligious depictions of the apocalypse, the
end often results from the decay and decadence of cultural and
moral order.[19] Civilization either withers away or is violently torn to
pieces as the broader structures of society begin to fail. In numerous
films in the 1960s and 1970s, the emphasis is on the literal end that
results from the social decay and chaos. Romero's *Living Dead* trilogy functions this way, as do such disparate films as *The Birds*
(1963), *Dr. Strangelove* (1964), *The Planet of the Apes* (1968), and
Mad Max (1979). In other films, the destruction of moral order is
subtler—the emphasis here is less on the end than what is revealed
in the unraveling of moral order. Any number of films suggest the
fragility of civilization and the gaping chasm of chaos that lies waiting at its edges, films such as *The Wild Bunch* (1968), *Deliverance*
(1972), and *Apocalypse Now* (1979).

Often, the apocalyptic tone is achieved through a spectacular display of violence and catastrophe. Apocalyptic visions have long
been rendered in terms of sexualized violence and debauchery—
consider Hieronymous Bosch's triptych of Hell—and in film these
tendencies became even more pronounced.[20] In spectacular displays of the apocalypse, screens were filled with images of buildings and bodies in decay and dismemberment. Disasters, violence,

and human suffering became commonplace in the American cinema of the 1970s, in part as a reflection of the apocalyptic tone in the broader culture.[21]

READING *THE EXORCIST* AND *THE TEXAS CHAINSAW MASSACRE*

Interestingly, both *The Exorcist* and *Texas Chainsaw* feature images of the sun in their opening moments. In Friedkin's film, the sun blazes over an archaeological site in northern Iraq. The sun gleams in a blazing white that fills the sky, but then quite suddenly, the color tone shifts and the bright sun strikes a strong contrast to a darker, reddish-brown sky. In Hooper's film, the grotesque images of a decomposing corpse being photographed are followed by the deep red and black swirls of solar flares on the surface of the sun.

These solar images suggest a broader apocalyptic tone in both films. The sun rises to bring life, but in its setting the light is removed and life comes to its inevitable end. Each of these openings visually emphasizes the contrast between the darkness and the light. In *The Exorcist*, this contrast is between the darkness of the sky and the brightness of the sun. In *Texas Chainsaw*, it is the darkness of the image that contrasts with our sense of the sun as bringing light and life. The sun rises in *Texas Chainsaw*, but it is not the glowing orb of life we might expect. In addition to emphasizing the distinction between light and dark, these opening solar images also focus our attention on the cosmic. The human dramas we will watch for the next hours are played out, in other words, within a broader cosmic framework. The struggle between good and evil is about something more than the individuals involved.

If these openings suggest a cosmic scale to the unfolding dramas, each film crafts this drama in distinctive ways. Fragments of radio news reports of horrific events accompany the dark, tumultuous sun in *Texas Chainsaw*: "Grave robbing in Texas is this hour's top news story." "Health officials in San Francisco fear they may have a cholera epidemic on their hands." "A sixteen-story building under construction in downtown Atlanta collapsed today killing at least twenty known persons. The engineering firm responsible for the design of the building could offer no explanation for the collapse." The credit sequence, however, has only limited connection to the subsequent narrative as the news reports of grave desecrations provide the impetus for the group to visit the grandparents' old home. More importantly, the opening provides a thematic tone for the film suggesting, as Sharrett puts it, "an evil age" of "a world dissolving into primordial chaos."[22] Within the film, this sense of a new age of evil and chaos is explicitly discussed by Pam, who reports the astrological signs: "When malefic planets are in retrograde, and Saturn's malefic, OK, their malefice is increased." There is, in other words, little hope for the future offered by the swirling dark sun.

The opening of *The Exorcist* suggests a much different approach to the impending apocalypse. The sun appears first in an equally bright sky, but the sky soon changes, becoming darker and more contrasted to the brightness of the sun. The state of the cosmos changes in these opening moments. Something dark has entered the world; a shadow has encompassed humanity. The dramatic shift is mirrored in the opening of the film where Father Merrin is alerted to an archaeological find—a fragment of an ancient demonic statue discovered along with a medallion of St. Joseph from a later era. The uncovering of these two artifacts, profane and sacred, furthers the film's general approach to its apocalyptic tone: forces beyond our comprehension are in conflict and, for this brief moment, that conflict will be played out before us. As with the astrological discussion in *Texas Chainsaw*, the sudden shift in the cosmos is noticed by one of the principles. As Father Merrin examines the demonic statue, a clock stops suddenly. Father Merrin's friend urges him to stay and continue working on the dig, but he explains, "There is something I must do." Returning to the dig, Father Merrin seems led to scramble up a small hill where he stands face to face with a larger statue of the demonic image. A strong wind blows in the space between the priest and his adversary, and dogs fight angrily in the distance. In this moment before the scene shifts to Georgetown and the beginning of Regan's possession, it is evident to the viewer: a fundamental struggle between good and evil has been joined.

In *The Texas Chainsaw Massacre*, the apocalyptic tone is one of the dawning of an inevitable age of degradation and destruction; *The Exorcist* maintains some hope that in the eternal struggle the forces of order and righteousness might still hold the line. The contrast between *The Exorcist*'s cautious optimism and *Texas Chainsaw*'s resigned pessimism casts each film's apocalyptic theme in very different tones. Beyond these more global differences, the dialectic tension between these two approaches can be mapped along a number of different points.

Transcendence/Degradation

One of the functions of apocalyptic narratives is to critique existing social structures. Interestingly, both *The Exorcist* and *Texas Chainsaw* engage some of the same social structures. For instance, both films point out the disparity between wealth and poverty. In *Texas Chainsaw*, the psychotic family is destitute after losing their jobs at the local slaughterhouse as a result of mechanization. They have fallen through the cracks in the broad network of social security systems and become a twisted version of the underlying logic of modern capitalism—the exploitation of others for profit. In the grotesque exaggeration of *Texas Chainsaw*, humans are literally turned into products to be sold and consumed.

The Exorcist also points out the disparity inherent in modern American capitalism. The scenes of Chris and Regan MacNeil enjoying the luxuries of their affluent life—discussing trips overseas, buying a pony, and so on—are juxtaposed through tight editing with Father Karras's struggle to find appropriate health care for his ailing and indigent mother. As he prepares to visit his mother in one of the city's deteriorating public hospitals, his uncle remarks, "You know, its funny. If you wasn't a priest you'd be a famous psychiatrist on Park Avenue. Your mother, she'd be in a penthouse instead of here." Ultimately, Father Karras's mother dies, and we are led to believe this was, in part, because of neglect. At the very least, Father Karras believes himself responsible for his mother's death, and this guilt becomes one of the principle weapons the demon uses against him. The loss of his mother, indeed, leads to Father Karras's loss of faith in the church and his place within it.

In both films, the economic consequences of modern capitalism are graphically displayed. However, in *The Exorcist*, the inequities of the American economic system are portrayed but unexplored. Father Karras's vow of poverty, the anguish of his mother, the frustration of his uncle, all these are laid aside in favor of the broader question of Father Karras's faith and his willingness to sacrifice himself for a higher calling. In the final moment of his sacrifice—as he brings the demon into himself and prepares to hurl himself out the window—a ghostly vision of his mother appears before him. While the moment is highly ambiguous, it is possible to interpret this final appearance as his mother's final blessing for his selfless sacrifice.

Each film, arguably, critiques the broader structures of modern society, but true to their unique apocalyptic tones, each does so in its distinct way. In Hooper's film, the degrading qualities of modern capitalism are taken to their logical conclusion: cannibalism. There is, in *Texas Chainsaw*, little hope for any other conclusion. While Sally escapes, there is no triumphant moment, no final victory of the forces of humanity. Sally avoids being cannibalized by the family. Yet, as she laughs and screams in the back of the escaping pickup truck, it is clear that she has been no less dehumanized. Sally's hysteria at the film's end is not surprising.

The tone of degradation is pervasive; the narrative structure of *Texas Chainsaw* itself disintegrates into an increasingly psychotic series of grizzly tableaus. During the "dinner party," Sally cries out "You're crazy," a sentiment likely shared by the audience. During this final sequence, the editing becomes increasingly nonlinear with repetitive tightly focused shots of Sally's eyeballs and her mouth, which interrupt the narrative development. As the insanity of the experience reaches its height, the scene suddenly shifts away to an ambiguous shot of an out-of-focus circle of light against a black backdrop. Accompanying this jarring out-of-focus shot is a mechanical whirring sound that might, for a moment, be mistaken for the sound of the film projector. In this ambiguous moment, our experience of this insane film is drawn into dramatic relief against this sudden jarring edit. However, if for a moment we imagine ourselves outside the madness of the Leatherface family's world, we are quickly disavowed of this notion. The focus pulls back to reveal the full moon in a dark sky, and the scene shifts back to a groggy Sally rousing herself. If there is any hope left that the madness has ended, it ends as Sally opens her eyes and screams. She is still in the house and the insanity continues. There is no escape.

In Friedkin's film, the brutality of poverty and inequity are merely manifestations of a broader, more transcendent struggle between good and evil. Father Karras's act of self-sacrifice embodies the broader Christian ethic of "loving they neighbor as thyself." The final triumph of *The Exorcist* calls its audience not to engage in critiquing the failures of existing social structures but to rise above them in pursuit of more transcendent truths.[23] Tellingly, the force of *The Exorcist*'s critique is aimed at scientific and medical technologies. Indeed, Regan's ordeal at the hands of medical equipment such as spinal taps and CAT scans seems almost as horrific as her experience with the demon. Ultimately, the film suggests, our arrogant attempts to understand our nature without reference to the transcendent spiritual world are as reprehensible as the forces of evil themselves. The truth lies not in our mortal material world but in a higher realm.

Spirit/Body

The tension between transcendence and degradation is most graphically evident in the way each film uses the human body. While *Texas Chainsaw* has the reputation for being one of the bloodiest and most violent films in history, it has virtually no onscreen gore. *The Exorcist* offers a vastly more graphic display of bodily fluids and disfigurement. The violence and bodily degradation in *Texas Chainsaw*, however, is in many ways far more disturbing. While both films use the body to emphasize the apocalyptic horror, their tones are markedly different.

Following its transcendent apocalyptic theme, *The Exorcist* frames the body as a site for a higher struggle. Wrapped within a broader religious affirmation of the spirit over the body, the increasingly grotesque and disfigured body of Regan becomes symbolic of the inner evil. As Paul West observes, "The religious framework ensures that we understand disgust in negative terms because religion assures us of the elevation of the spirit over the flesh."[24] Regan's contusions and contortions become, in the logic of the film, symbolic of the defilement of her spirit, a sense exemplified by the scene in which Regan's body becomes a literal page upon which her spirit writes the words "Help me."

Conceiving the defiled body as a text in need of interpretation lends credence to the film's implicit critique of scientific rationality. Medical physicians and psychologists are incapable of interpreting the signs of Regan's body, and even Father Karras misunderstands the biblical implications because of his scientific training. Only when Farther Karras abandons his psychiatric training and reclaims his religious faith is he able to resolve Regan's crisis and vanquish the demon. To ascertain the transcendent truth, the physical world of the body must be understood within a larger spiritual framework.

Texas Chainsaw, of course, has no such transcendent pretensions. In the degraded logic of the Leatherface family, the body is the totality of the human existence. Their home is decorated with the bones and skin of their victims, and they dine on barbecued human flesh. Their aging grandfather revives briefly after sucking on Sally's blood. In *Texas Chainsaw*, the world of the body is entirely devoid of spirit. It is animalistic savagery and sadism without an inkling of humanity. With the exception of Sally, all the killings are swift and unfeeling. Kirk is smashed in the head with a sledgehammer in an instant. Pam is unceremoniously hung on a meat hook and then ignored as Leatherface uses his chainsaw to carve Kirk's body. Jerry's death is equally quick and efficient. Early in the film the group of young adults discuss the banal slaughter of cattle in the nearby slaughterhouse, and the parallel between the killing of these animals and the murder of these young people is obvious.

The centrality of the corporeal body to *Texas Chainsaw* is also evident in the figure of Leatherface, who wears a series of different human flesh masks to display different personas: the "killing mask," "the old woman," and "the pretty woman." Wearing the "killing mask," Leatherface wields his chainsaw with savage efficiency. He snorts and screams while chasing down Pam and dragging her back into his slaughter room. However, later in the film when the Cook brings Sally back to the house, Leatherface wears the "old woman" mask and is seen fussing about the house and timidly preparing a family meal. As Kim Henckel, one of the film's scriptwriters observes, "Leatherface is one of those characters who is what he wears—his character changes according to the face he puts on."[25] The body, in other words, does not represent the inner workings of a spiritual soul; rather, there is only body.

Dangerous/Endangered Youth

Both *Texas Chainsaw* and *The Exorcist* focus on youth, and their attention to the plight of young people begs to be understood in terms of the wreckage of the youth rebellions of the late 1960s and early 1970s. The young people traveling through central Texas in their van are clearly remnants of the fragmented flower children. Their dress and speech are stereotypical of the late 1960s, as are their lengthy discussions of astrological signs and cosmic mysticism. Their seemingly aimless drifting across the Texas plains is reminiscent of the generation's determination to drop out. They travel without any sense of direction or responsibility. Parents are not mentioned, nor are schools, jobs or any other form of social support or expectation. For these young people, however, dropping out of society entails dropping into a primitive chaos for which they are utterly unprepared. If the youth movement sought to tear down the structures of society, the film suggests, they had best beware of what lies beneath.

Friedkin's film also gestures towards the tumultuous years of the youth rebellion. The "film within the film," that has brought Chris MacNeil and her daughter to Georgetown is titled *Crash Course*, and while we have no clue to the film's overall plot, we are witness to one of the film's scenes. In the midst of an enormous staged student protest, MacNeil, followed by cameramen and sound operators, fights her way to the front and begins a dramatic speech asking the students to relinquish the building they occupy. While there is no clear sense of the politics of this scene, it is telling that as our camera pulls back we witness the broader life of the campus surrounding the artificiality of the film set. Crowds of spectators, including Father Karras, gather to watch the spectacle of filming, but outside the set students stroll to class as the normal life of the university goes on.

As the politics of the youth rebellion are played for its spectacle and artificiality, the real fate of the youth is tied to the family structure. While Regan and Chris MacNeil are shown in a number of idyllic scenes of affluent happiness and camaraderie, the absence of Regan's father is palpable. In the scene immediately prior to Regan's first complaint about her "bed shaking," Chris rants at a telephone operator for being unable to connect to the hotel in Rome where the absent father is supposedly staying. "Jesus Christ! Can you believe this, he doesn't even call his daughter on her birthday for Christ's sake," Chris shouts. As the camera pulls back from this scene, Regan is seen eavesdropping on her mother's conversation. Despite her doting mother and loyal nanny, Regan, like the drifting youth of *Texas Chainsaw*, illustrates the negligent family structure.

Family is an important theme in both of films, and interestingly, both films explore the notion of family by juxtaposing two family structures—a kind of mirror image of the family. In *The Exorcist*, Regan's family is without a father and her salvation—here quite literally—is dependent on a Father who, tellingly, is without a mother. In *Texas Chainsaw*, the benevolent and freewheeling "family" of youths encounters the twisted and malevolent Leatherface family.

In each instance, the mirroring effect draws upon the broader theme of transcendence or degradation. Father Karras represents a "father figure," but his ability to fulfill this role is dependent not on his masculinity but on his divinity within the broader Catholic structure of the "family" of God. It is only in embracing his role as spiritual father that Father Karras is able to save Regan from

demonic possession. The failings of Regan's earthly father and subsequent disintegration of her earthly family cannot be reconciled
by any earthly intervention but, following the film's overall apocalyptic theme, must be transcended. As Barbara Creed observes,
"What better ground for the forces of evil to take root than the
household of a family in which the father is absent?"[26] Father Karras,
in his sacrificial act, thus fulfills the role of familial patriarch for
the MacNeil family. In the same way, Father Karras's guilt over ne-
glecting his earthly mother is forgiven in his act of transcendent
self-sacrifice. His mother's approving ghostly image acts as a sign
that in choosing the spiritual over the familial Father Karras has
chosen correctly.

Degradation, of course, is the key to the family-mirroring in *Texas
Chainsaw*. The Leatherface family exists in a macabre parody of
family life. The "father," the Cook, arrives home from work with the
family dinner, Sally, while the impudent son, Hitchhiker, complains
about his chores. Leatherface, now wearing his old woman mask,
prepares the family dinner and fusses about the house. The interaction of the family members is filled with violence, threats, and
curses. Where the MacNeil family lacks the protective authority of
a father, the Leatherface family lacks the nurturing support of a
mother. Leatherface, apparently, plays some distorted version of
that role, but it is telling that once Sally is brought into the family
home, she is treated as a kind of guest of honor and seated at the
head of the table. There is, of course, no sense that the family can
integrate Sally into its ranks or any serious possibility of sexuality
or affection. Still, during the "dinner party," Sally is placed at the
head of the table. Even in the midst of this depravity, Cook insists
on some level of courtesy and propriety: "Now, now, young lady,
you just take it easy there. We'll fix you some supper in a few
minutes."

Horror films since *Psycho* had continuously focused on the family as a cause of insanity and monstrousness. *Texas Chainsaw* marks
a turn in this tradition by focusing on the monstrous family, in
which all the members have collectively degraded into monsters.[27]
Lacking the moral stability provided by the traditional role of a
mother, the Leatherface family has devolved into the most animalistic and primitive version of patriarchal society: cannibals. While the
transcendent spirituality of Father Karras is capable of rescuing
Regan, Sally has no hope in lifting the Leatherface family out of
their depravity. Her only hope is to flee from the chaos she has

glimpsed, though the film's ending suggests she may never fully recover.

Both *The Exorcist* and *Texas Chainsaw* portray the moment of contact between functional and dysfunctional families. In *The Exorcist*, Father Karras's spiritually transcendent family is able to rectify the consequences of Chris MacNeil's failed marriage. Thus the functionally transcendent family of the church saves the dysfunctional family. The story in *Texas Chainsaw* is notably different. In *Texas Chainsaw*, it is the dysfunctional, degraded family that seeks to consume the generally functional family unit of the van, and only Sally's resilience saves her from being absorbed like her peers—literally—into the degraded cannibal family.

Across all four families, their problems stem, largely, from excessive permissiveness. The "van family" in *Texas Chainsaw* seems devoid of any real restrictions or responsibilities, and the Leatherface family exists in a pocket of chaos completely outside the strictures of society. The MacNeil family drifts in their own pocket of fatherless and overly permissive affluence, and Father Karras, perhaps most of all, has drifted away from his spiritual obligations and duties. "I'm unfit," he tells one of his superiors.

Lack of authoritative norms and boundaries, these films suggest, allowed for the invasion of chaotic evil into the world, and this invasion is focused on young people in both films. In *The Exorcist*, it is the young themselves, raised without clear guidance, who are dangerous—providing a portal for destructive apocalyptic forces of evil. In *Texas Chainsaw*, it is the youth, left adrift without guidance, who are endangered by the encroaching forces of primordial chaos.[28]

Violation

The tension evident in these two prominent horror films expresses the overall tension facing America in the 1970s. The overall sense that the American dream had not only failed but also fallen apart pervaded the country, and Americans were left with a basic choice. *The Exorcist* suggested one approach to the overarching failure of social structures: transcend the particulars of the world and embrace an overarching set of principles and values. *Texas Chainsaw* suggested a more pessimistic view of the aftermath of the dying American dream: prepare for the inevitable slide into chaotic, primitive violence. Whatever the difference in their approaches, it is clear that both films resonated with the broader apocalyptic tone pervading American culture. However, the dialectic tension between the ways the two films engage the apocalypse may help to explain how these two very different films became such instantly prominent parts of American culture.

Additionally, each film seeks to resolve this apocalypse in its own ways. *Texas Chainsaw* embraces the madness it unleashes; there is no clear resolution to the narrative. Sally has apparently gone mad, and the Leatherface family, sans Hitchhiker, can continue to practice their capitalistic cannibalism. In a world without hope, the film's final moments seem to suggest, one can only embrace the hysterical laughter. *The Exorcist*'s ending is far more ambivalent. According to the filmmakers, especially Blatty, the film ends on a positive note.[29] Along the lines discussed above, Father Karras's death at the bottom of those Georgetown stairs is a triumphant moment of spiritual self-sacrifice. Audiences, however, were less clear about the optimistic message. Many audience members reported believing that Father Karras's death is the result of the demon's wishes, and interestingly, this misreading of the film led Friedkin and Blatty to reinstate some scenes of dialogue for the film's 1999 re-release, *The Exorcist: The Version You've Never Seen.* Seemingly, the overarching cultural tone of pessimism was, on the surface, too great for Blatty's optimistic ending to overcome.

Whatever the resonance around the apocalyptic tone, both films violated their audiences' expectations. First, both films challenged preconceptions about the line between horror fantasy and reality. Both films were widely believed to be based on actual events, and each exploits this belief in different ways. *The Exorcist*, with its large budget, challenged the line between fiction and reality through an impressive array of often-gruesome visual effects. *Texas Chainsaw* drew the audience into the "reality" of its film through its use of unsteady, 16 mm handheld cameras and cinema verite style.

Additionally, and more importantly, these films broke ground in bringing these horrors into the realm of young people. While there were certainly other horror films that focused on young people, few had done so with as much brutality and violence, and none had done so as successfully.[30] The notion of the family as a space of security, first broken down in *Psycho*, was now fully dismantled and whatever illusions of safety had been fostered for the young were fully dispelled. Young people were both fully dangerous and eminently endangered.

THE LEGACIES OF *THE EXORCIST* AND *THE TEXAS CHAINSAW MASSACRE*

The focus on young people, so successful in these two films, would become an ironclad commonplace component in the late 1970s and 1980s. Horror would become almost exclusively the purview of young people. *The Exorcist* spawned numerous films that focused on dangerous young people, films such as *The Omen* (1976), *Carrie* (1976), *The Fury* (1978), *The Brood* (1979), *The Shining* (1980), and *Firestarter* (1984).[31] The legacy of endangered youth spawned by *Texas Chainsaw* is far more extensive. Every masked or disfigured slasher of the 1970s and 1980s, from Michael Meyers to Jason to Freddy to Chucky, follows in the footsteps of Leatherface and his family. While the formula for these endless stalk-and-slash films would be perfected in John Carpenter's *Halloween*, which is discussed in the next chapter, its genesis was in the macabre world of *Texas Chainsaw*.

Additionally, the combination of *The Exorcist* and *Texas Chainsaw* solidified the increasingly pessimistic and now openly apocalyptic tone of American horror films. The period from the 1970s into the 1980s is one characterized by paranoia. Endings were increasingly left open and often suggested that the forces of evil not only lived on but also triumphed.[32] These pessimistic tales were also told with an increasingly graphic and savage style in which the spectacle of special effects became a primary object of viewing enjoyment. Indeed, as the horror film developed into the latter part of the decade and into the eighties, the creativity and realism of the death sequences would become central to the genre's aesthetic.[33]

While the overall tone of pessimistic degradation, advanced in *Texas Chainsaw*, attained almost instant dominance within the genre, the other points of dialectic tension—spirit/body and dangerous/endangered youth—remained unresolved. Some films opted for invading spirits, such as those in *The Amityville Horror* (1979) or Hooper's later film *Poltergeist* (1986), while others focused on psychotic killer families, such as the ones in Wes Craven's *The Hills Have Eyes* (1978) or *Just Before Dawn* (1982). Some films depicted the dangers of supernatural children, while others used young people as prey for maniacs.

The synthesis of these points of dialectic tension would come in the form of a supernatural, psychotic young boy who returns home to prey on attractive young people, and it would occur on the most appropriate of days, *Halloween*.

6 *Halloween* (1978)

"You can't kill the bogeyman."

If imitation is the sincerest form of flattery, then John Carpenter's *Halloween* may be the most flattered film in the history of American cinema. While Carpenter's tale of baby-sitters stalked by a psychotic madman borrows heavily from all of the films discussed in the previous chapters—a point I'll take up in more detail later—its simple, stalk-and-slash formula would be repeated, almost verbatim, by innumerable imitators. These imitations, films such as *Friday the Thirteenth* (1980) and *Nightmare on Elm Street* (1984), would in turn spawn numerous sequels, as would *Halloween*. The age of the horror franchise had begun. As of this writing, *Halloween* has produced seven sequels, *Friday the Thirteenth* has reached number ten, *Nightmare on Elm Street* has seven, and if that weren't enough, Jason and Freddy, the respective killers in these two film series, have met in the appropriately titled *Jason vs. Freddy* (2003).

If the filmmakers are to be believed, the original *Halloween*, even with its ambiguous ending in which the supposedly slain killer vanishes, was not meant to begin a long cycle of sequels. The idea for the single film began with Irwin Yablans, a producer and distributor of small, independent films, who was looking for an angle on the low-budget, horror, exploitation film. Baby-sitters, Yablans realized, were an almost universal aspect of American culture. Almost every young person had either been a baby-sitter or been taken care of by one. In an effort to condense the plot and minimize the budget,

Yablans conceived of the story as occurring on a single night. After some research, he learned to his astonishment that the most horrific night of the year had never been the title of a film. Thus, the premise of *Halloween* was born.

Perhaps the most important element of this simple project was the choice of its director. Yablans contacted a young University of Southern California graduate with whom he had worked on a low-budget science fiction spoof titled *Dark Star* (1974) and an urban, action film titled *Assault on Precinct Thirteen* (1976), which received considerable acclaim in Europe. The young graduate, Carpenter, agreed to write and direct the film with one key stipulation: he would have complete autonomy over the production. Thus was forged the almost perfect combination of an intriguingly simple idea with a distinctively brilliant cinematic mind.

Interestingly, the basic components of Yablans's idea had been central to a small, Canadian horror film titled *Black Christmas* (1974). In *Black Christmas*, a killer stalks young girls in a boarding school during the Christmas holidays. The Canadian film, directed by Bob Clark and starring a young Margot Kidder, exploits the urban legend of the obscene phone caller who is actually calling from inside the house.

Whatever its similarity to this earlier Canadian film, there could be no comparison in terms of the later film's overall success. While the production of *Halloween* clearly follows in the footsteps of earlier low-budget, independent horror films such as *Night of the Living Dead* and *The Texas Chainsaw Massacre*, in terms of its immediate popularity it belonged more in the stratosphere of major studio films such as *Psycho* and *The Exorcist*. Made on a budget of $320,000, Carpenter's film set box-office records that would last for decades. Unable to interest a major studio for distribution, Yablans and executive producer Moustapha Akkad independently released the film regionally. Opening on October 1978 in Kansas City, *Halloween*'s box office grew rapidly based on word of mouth, and soon the film was an unqualified hit. In its initial theatrical release the film yielded world-wide box-office receipts of more than $55 million.

At first glance, the success of Carpenter's film can be attributed to his successful blending of the shocking elements of "exploitation" horror films—films such as *Night of the Living Dead* and *Texas Chainsaw*—with the appearance of big-budget production values. Tellingly, Carpenter spent much of his meager budget on a recognizable star for the brief but pivotal role of the psychiatrist, hiring

Donald Pleasance, who had previously appeared in such films as *The Greatest Story Ever Told* (1965) and the Bond film *You Only Live Twice* (1967). Perhaps more importantly, Carpenter insisted on shooting in 35 mm and using another major portion of his budget for Panvision's new Panaglide—their version of the Steadicam. While these decisions left very little for other cast members or crew and virtually nothing for special effects, they provided the film an over-all visual quality more akin to major studio releases.

The combination of quality production value with the shocks of an exploitation film, however, can hardly explain the film's over-whelming success. Indeed, in terms of the definition of cinematic success outlined earlier—the combination of popularity and lasting influence—Carpenter's *Halloween* is, arguably, the most successful horror film in American history. The formula for horror developed in the film was not only immediately successful but would dominate American horror films for the next decade. There was, then, some-thing about *Halloween* that captured not only a particular cultural moment but also captured a movement within American culture.

In this chapter, I argue that Carpenter's *Halloween* stands as a culmination of the various trends and tensions that had developed in the American horror film at least since its beginning in 1931. If 1974, with *The Exorcist* and *Texas Chainsaw*, was the pinnacle of the history of American horror films, then *Halloween* is the culmi-nation of that history. While I am not suggesting that the American horror film ended with *Halloween*, I am suggesting that the varied and contradictory elements of the modern horror film coalesced in Carpenter's carefully crafted tale.

Thus far, the story of the American horror film has been one of approaching chaos. A brief recap seems in order. In 1931, *Dracula* represented the sense of social upheaval and chaos that threatened Americans during the period between the two world wars. His was an invasive defilement but, at the same time, a seductive lure over the edge of civilized boundaries.

The danger of invasive chaos was brought closer, out of the Gothic past and into the conceivable world of the present. In *The Thing from Another World*, this all-too-real sense of encroaching cataclysm was masterfully contained within familiar bonds of human affec-tion and optimism by Howard Hawks.

In 1960, Alfred Hitchcock lured audiences into the theaters to view another advancement in the modern horror film as the horrific chaos lurking on the boundaries of American culture was brought next door in the sympathetic form of Norman Bates. However, where Hawks had contained the encroaching horror, Hitchcock delighted in tearing back the containing veil of human affection to reveal the inner sickness.

Amidst the turbulent late 1960s, a generation of Americans turned against the optimistic vision of American suburbia critiqued in *Psycho* and sought to reformulate American society through unity, peace, and harmony. Their failure became the backdrop for the next advancement of horror. In *Night of the Living Dead*, George Romero reflected the divisive failure of the counterculture dropouts and their inevitable reabsorption into the culture they had revolted against. The end of the counterculture revolution changed the overall tone of American culture as a general sense of apocalyptic pessimism engulfed the country. In 1974, Americans could consider two approaches to this apocalyptic moment—to seek the transcendent spirit of traditional values in *The Exorcist* or to be resigned to the degraded chaos of *The Texas Chainsaw Massacre*.

Halloween stands as a culmination of this apocalyptic movement in American horror films. Importantly, Carpenter's film not only draws on the elements of preceding horror films but also inverts the predominant sense of invading chaos. In *Halloween*, the monster no longer threatens to unleash chaos into an orderly world but, quite to the contrary, Michael Meyers functions as a punishing avenger who imposes order in an otherwise chaotic world.

SYNOPSIS

Carpenter's *Halloween* opens with an extended subjective shot in which our view is also that of some unknown figure lurking outside a typical suburban home. The figure with whom we share this point of view creeps around the house to spy on a young woman and her boyfriend embracing on a couch. As the couple head upstairs, apparently for a sexual encounter, the figure slips around the back of the house and into the kitchen where it retrieves a butcher knife. At the top of the stairs, the figure retrieves a Halloween clown mask and places it over its face, thereby partially obscuring our point of view. The figure approaches the young woman, now alone, who shrieks as the knife strikes her repeatedly. After the murder, the figure returns back down the stairs and out the front door where it is confronted with two adults, apparently the parents returning home. The mask is removed by the father, and at this point the camera reverses and

we now see the figure with whom we have shared this murderous point of view: a small, unexceptional, blonde-haired boy in a
Halloween clown suit.

After the opening credits, the story resumes fifteen years later. A
psychiatrist, Dr. Sam Loomis (Donald Pleasence), and a nurse are
seen driving to retrieve a patient from an asylum in order to fulfill a
court-ordered competency hearing. The inmate, Michael Meyers, is
the now-grown boy who had committed our opening crime. As the
duo drives towards the asylum they are delayed and, after Dr. Loomis
leaves the car, Michael terrorizes the nurse out of the car and then
drives it away.

The scene then shifts back to Haddonfield, the site of the original
crime, on Halloween, now in the present. Dr. Loomis is convinced
Michael will return there. In Haddonfield, Laurie Strode (Jamie Lee
Curtis) goes to the old Meyers house to drop off a key for her father,
a real estate agent. Tommy, the little boy whom Laurie will babysit,
warns her that the Meyers house is haunted, but Laurie ignores his
warning and drops off the key anyway. A dark figure appears in the
doorway as Laurie and Tommy walk away.

The two are soon followed by the mysterious figure we know to
be Michael. As Laurie returns home from school with her friends
Annie and Linda, she is followed by the dark figure, referred to in
the script as "the Shape." As darkness falls on Haddonfield, Laurie
and Annie begin their babysitting assignments in neighboring
houses. Annie soon drops her young charge off with Laurie and prepares to visit her boyfriend, but the Shape, who has been spying on
Annie, strangles her to death. Linda and her boyfriend, Danny, arrive
at the house where Annie was babysitting and, after sex, Danny goes
downstairs for beers. The Shape kills him with a butcher knife and
then heads upstairs. Entering the bedroom wearing a ghostly sheet,
Linda mistakes the Shape for her boyfriend until he strangles her
with a telephone cord.

Concerned about the lack of contact with her friends, Laurie
enters the neighboring house to find their dead bodies. She is then
chased back to Tommy's home, where she stabs the Shape in the
neck with a knitting needle. Believing the killer is slain, Laurie goes
upstairs to retrieve the two young children only to find that the
Shape has revived and is pursuing her again. As the Shape batters
through a door and into the closet where Laurie is hiding, she stabs
him in the eye with a coat hanger and then in the abdomen with the
butcher knife. Again believing the Shape to be dead, Laurie sends

the children off to get help. Dr. Loomis, who has been pursuing the Shape in Haddonfield, sees the children running and enters the house to find that the Shape has revived and is again attacking Laurie. Dr. Loomis shoots the Shape six times, and the killer falls over the balcony and into the back yard. However, when the psychiatrist looks over the balcony, the Shape has disappeared. The film ends with a series of still images of the places in the neighborhood where the Shape had been lurking.

Driven by a strong visual sense and a chilling soundtrack—also composed by Carpenter—*Halloween* is a horror tour de force. The plot is simple and straightforward and the pacing outstanding, a blend of long, teasing sequences of suspense and then sudden eruptions of violence. Additionally, Carpenter offers explicit nods to his predecessors. Not only does the film use Curtis, the daughter of Janet Leigh and Tony Curtis, but the psychiatrist is also named Sam Loomis, the name of Marion's boyfriend in *Psycho*. The television sets show a midnight-movie marathon featuring sequences from *The Thing from Another World* and Fred Wilcox's *Forbidden Planet* (1956).

More importantly, in *Halloween* Carpenter boiled the American horror film down to its most basic elements and created a formula that was both simple and appealing. The basic formula of the slasher film has received considerable critical attention. Carol Clover, in her influential *Men, Women and Chainsaws*, contends that the basic formula of the slasher films derives from *Psycho* via *Texas Chainsaw* but finds its most pure expression in Carpenter's film. The slasher formula, according to Clover, consists of the following:

1. A psychosexually confused killer
2. The use of primitive, usually phallic weapons such as a butcher knife or chainsaw instead of a pistol
3. A "terrible place" where the killer lives and chases or torments his victims
4. Sudden moments of shock—the natural legacy of *Psycho*'s shower scene
5. The victims—almost all sexually active young people and, while men and women are killed in about equal numbers, women suffer the more dramatic and lengthy murders
6. The final girl—usually a virginal tomboy who becomes the target of the killer's attention but, unlike her friends, survives his attacks

A similar configuration is offered by Vera Dika in *Games of Terror*, in which she demonstrates the similarity of the plot structures across numerous slasher films.[1] In her analysis, Dika finds the basic plot involves two basic acts: (1) some past traumatic event—Michael's murdering his sister as a child, and then, (2) a commemoration of the event in the present—the holiday, Halloween. Interestingly for both Clover and Dika, the success of this basic formula is attributable to underlying psychoanalytic tendencies. A similar tack is taken by Robin Wood, who explains the appeal of *Halloween* as the "revenge of the repressed," in which both Laurie and Michael are victims of repressed sexual desires that fuel both their identification and the carnage in the film.

The basic psychoanalytic explanation, with its focus on sexuality, repression, and punishment, seems appealing particularly as these films were largely popular among adolescents who were just beginning to struggle with their own sexuality and sexual identity.[2] However, the psychoanalytic explanation can do little to explain why this particular version of the horror formula became so prominent at the end of the 1970s. While the film does lend itself to an explanation in terms of sexuality and repression, a historical perspective suggests that these elements be placed into the broader cultural contexts with which they resonate and the ways in which this particular film articulates those elements in uniquely shocking ways.

CULTURAL CONTEXTS

Halloween appeared in American theaters just four years after *The Exorcist* and *Texas Chainsaw* had made their mark on the American psyche, and the film drew on many of the same cultural trends. However, if anything, the three major trends of the early 1970s—paranoid apocalyptic thinking, the general decline in the American family, and a growing hedonism—were reaching a turning point. These trends were prominent, but a backlash was beginning to develop. In the midst of disco and a growing sexual revolution, the seeds of a new, more conservative American culture were beginning to sprout.[3] It was in the midst of this cultural sea change that John Carpenter's *Halloween* struck such a sensitive nerve.

A Permissive Age

The general erosion of 1950s morality, with its strict limits on sexuality and promotion of the nuclear family, reached a zenith in the late 1970s. This erosion was, perhaps, nowhere more evident than in the explosive popularity of disco at the end of the 1970s. Disco entailed not only the catchy dance music that had long been prominent in the New York City club scene but also its broader lifestyle of drugs, free sex, gender bending, and sequined clothing.[4] Critics of both the music and the lifestyle promoted in the then widely popular American discotheques were quick to point out the superficiality and narcissism being promoted in such disco vehicles as the enormously popular film (and soundtrack) *Saturday Night Fever* (1977).

In addition to the suggestive lyrics and dance moves of disco, America's sense of sexual morality was also being challenged by the increasingly public popularity of sexually explicit books and movies. Films such as *Flesh Gordon* (1974) and *The Devil in Miss Jones* (1973) were gaining wider audiences, and books such as *The Happy Hooker* (1973) and *The Total Woman* (1976) were expanding American's conception of sexuality. The sexual liberation movement of the mid-1970s was particularly aimed at young women who were embracing the laxness of sexual morality as a manifestation of the expanding movement for women's rights.[5]

While the changes in sexual morality were often associated with the young, older adults were also embracing the sexual revolution of the 1970s. The "swinging" seventies were aptly named, as the suburban family home became a site of more permissive sexual activity. The practice of swinging, in which married couples would meet to have sexual relations with each other's partners or engage in more free-form orgies, extended the decade's shift away from traditional family values as both adults and their teenage children embraced a more experimental attitude towards sexual and familial relations.[6]

The overall texture of American sexual morality was also being changed by the open emergence of the gay and lesbian community into mainstream culture and politics. The gay rights movement gained momentum quickly in the 1970s after its most dramatic manifestation in the Stonewall riots of 1969 and demanded not only equal rights but also a place in American culture. Prominent television sitcoms began to acknowledge and even embrace homosexuality. Billy Crystal portrayed the first regular gay character in the sitcom *Soap* (1977–1981), and *Three's Company* (1977–1984) was based on the premise that one of its main characters pretended to be gay in order to live with female roommates. The late 1970s were radically transforming the traditional notions of not only family and sex but also gender and sexuality.

Certainly, many of the results of the sexual revolution of the 1970s were enormously positive. The changes in the cultural perception of women, gays, and lesbians helped promote greater tolerance and acceptance of sexual and gender diversity. On the other hand, much of the sexual permissiveness of the 1970s was wrapped in the hedonistic selfishness that manifested itself in the late 1960s. Whatever cultural revolutions may have been produced, they were largely founded on a deeply rooted cultural narcissism where the pleasure of the individual took precedence over communal values.[7] Seemingly, the failure of the sixties counterculture and the resulting sense of apocalyptic pessimism led to an increasingly introverted and self-serving American culture.

The Nostalgic Turn

The general tone of permissiveness and hedonism grew through the decade of the 1970s, but by the decade's end, a notable backlash was beginning to develop. The broader aesthetic tone of this backlash was a nostalgic return to the images and motifs of the 1950s. In television, *Happy Days* (1974–1984) and its spin-off *Laverne and Shirley* (1976–1983) portrayed the 1950s as a simpler, purer, and more wholesome time. These television sitcoms came out of a similar movement in film that included the progenitor of the 1950s revival, George Lucas's *American Graffiti* (1973). Nostalgia for the 1950s permeated the 1970s, promoting a kind of dialectic tension with the loose values of disco. Films such as the teen musical *Grease* (1978) and even the more raucous comedy *Animal House* (1978) relied on this sense of an earlier, simpler time. Seemingly, in the midst of destabilizing traditional values and institutions, Americans in the 1970s sought a definition of their culture from the seemingly simpler times of the past.[8]

For some cultural critics, this period of nostalgia also suggests a culture unable to progress into new cultural forms. The failure of cultural progress, in terms of new musical, filmic, or artistic developments, prefigured, for some critics, the rise of postmodernism. Literary critic Frederick Jameson has famously equated the nostalgic turn in 1970s cinema with a tendency towards cultural pastiche—the combination of old images and themes—that signaled the failure of the generation's inventiveness.[9] George Lipsitz insisted that the 1970s substituted "open plagiarism for originality."[10]

The Conservative Turn

The return to a 1950s aesthetic corresponded with a rise in conservative philosophy and politics. In California, former B-movie actor and past-president of the Screen Actors Guild, Ronald Reagan, was elected governor of California in 1967 and would make an unsuccessful bid for the Republican presidential nomination in 1976. While the failure of the Nixon administration significantly impeded the Republican Party in general and President Gerald Ford in particular, the trouble-plagued administration of President Jimmy Carter served as a kind of emblem of the chaotic unraveling of America in the 1970s. Crippled by the combination of economic inflation and stagnation and hampered by an ongoing oil crisis, the Carter administration was unable to fulfill the promises of the liberal Democratic Party. Economic difficulties, the significant rise in Middle Eastern terrorism, and a general sense that American morals were being eroded led to a growing sense of malaise that dominated the later years of the decade.

In these later years of the 1970s, the religious right became an increasingly prominent and vocal part of American culture and politics. This movement, an attempt to integrate fundamentalist religious principles with politics, can be traced back to Barry Goldwater's failed 1964 presidential bid, during which old McCarthy-era fears of communism were combined with concerns about "secular humanism." The movement gained momentum during the 1970s by exploiting fears about women's and gay rights. Phyllis Schlafly founded the Eagle's Forum in 1972 to oppose the Equal Rights Amendment, and Anita Bryant, a popular entertainer, led opposition to gay rights efforts in Florida and California during 1976 and 1977.[11] The emergent New Right promised, as Peter Carroll puts it, "to restore a world of simple virtues, an old America based on family, church and the work ethic."[12]

The Bogeyman

In a way, every tale of horror is a tale of the bogeyman. Folklorists trace the origin of this mythical figure of fear as far back as human history is recorded. The "bogey" or "boggle" was a generic term for some form of devil, ogre, or spirit that came to torment and, often, devour its victims. While the form of the bogeyman varies across cultures and historical periods, the essential quality of the bogeyman is his (or, at times, her) relationship to cultural boundaries. The bogeyman exists at the boundary point between cultural notions of right and wrong, and his position at the boundary entails a number of important cultural implications.[13]

Initially, the bogeyman's position at the boundaries of notions of cultural normalcy and propriety is a threatening one. As with many of the films previously considered in this book, the bogeyman embodies the chaos that exists on the other side of these cultural boundaries. The chaotic force of unleashed desire and wickedness waits at the edge of the systems of order and reminds us of the importance of these systems of restrictions. Following this line of cultural logic, figures such as Dracula or Norman Bates wait on the other side of the normal and sane. These kinds of monstrous figures have long served as warrants for the systems of morality—if you cross the boundaries of morality, these figures await you. The bogeyman's very body displays the transgression of boundaries. Mythic figures such as the Minotaur or the horrific Scylla, whose female torso is attached to serpent tails and hounds heads for a lower half, become monstrous by their physical violation of the laws of normalcy. In the same way, the living dead or the demonically deformed child become visual symbols for the threatening chaos, and their bodies represent the loss of order that might come from transgression.

In a similar way, the bogeyman becomes an example of what happens to those who transgress the boundaries. One of the earliest legends of the werewolf dates back to Ovid's *Metamophoses*, in which the cannibal King Lycano is transformed into a werewolf by Zeus. In American horror films, Dracula becomes one of the unholy undead because of his unnatural desires to cheat death, and Norman Bates becomes a demented killer through his Oedipal perversions. The cannibal clan in *Texas Chainsaw* is a twisted example of humanity deformed by its own depravity. In this way, the bogeyman standing at the edge of civilized boundaries serves not only as a boundary marker but also as a mirror, warning us what we might become if we stray to far. As Marina Warner notes in her extended study of the historical bogeyman, "Bogeys make present what we dread, and these fantasies include what we know we are capable of perpetrating ourselves."[14]

These two functions of the bogeyman, as threatening chaos and as an object lesson in morality, are common in the history of the American horror film. From *Dracula* through *Psycho* and into *The Texas Chainsaw Massacre*, the monsters in American horror films have mirrored back to our culture the threatening chaos that we might become. A third historic function of the bogeyman, however, has been largely absent or at least underplayed. The bogeyman, after all, has long inhabited the fairy tales told to children and, in this familiar format, his function has been as threatening punisher. The sandman, at least in his more threatening early incarnations, came to steal the eyes of children who stayed awake past bedtime, and the nineteenth-century tailor came to cut the thumbs off of children who continued to suck them.[15] Tales of the bogeyman have long served as a threat to unruly children who must conform to proper behavior or be menaced by these horrific figures. In this way, the punishing bogeyman stands in for the parents, providing a more severe disciplining threat to naughty children.

The bogeymen of American horror films embodied the chaos threatening the rigid structures of American cultural morality. By the 1970s, however, the fictional landscape had passed through the apocalypse, and now on the other side of this event, American society seemed to embrace the chaotic and degraded permissiveness that had long threatened.[16] By the end of the 1970s, Americans had become too permissive and hedonistic and it was time for a different kind of bogeyman.

READING *HALLOWEEN*

Halloween is essentially the story of a return. Michael returns to the scene of his initial crime, the killing of his sister. A crime from the past returns to threaten the present. The rhetoric of return is particularly evident in the film's tagline, "The Night HE Came Home!" The film represents not only a return but also a return home—to someplace familiar and traditional. While the return of Michael is hardly familiar or traditional, the return of past crimes to haunt the present is one of the earliest themes of American horror films.[17] In Carpenter's film, Michael's return to his home is only one aspect of the overall theme. In addition to the literal homecoming in the film's plot, *Halloween* presents two very different forms of return. On the one hand, the film is an aesthetic return, by which I mean to suggest the ways the film synthesizes the various themes of previous horror films. On the other hand, while *Halloween* embraces many of the familiar elements in the American horror tradition, Michael represents a very different aspect of the bogeyman. The masked Shape of *Halloween* comes not to bring cultural and moral chaos but to punish the wicked. In this sense, the punishing bogey-man of *Halloween* heralds a cultural return to a more conservative set of cultural values.

Aesthetic Returns

It is interesting that of all the horror films considered in this book, *Halloween* is the first directed by a film school graduate. At USC's film school, Carpenter participated in lectures with many of Hollywood's greatest directors, including John Ford, Orson Welles, Howard Hawks, and Alfred Hitchcock.[18] Carpenter's formal film education is evident throughout *Halloween,* and the film becomes a kind of homage to the horror films of the past. Indeed, as I've suggested earlier, *Halloween* can be seen as a kind of culmination of the preceding history of the horror film, at least in the sense that it is able to synthesize many of the elements that made these previous films successful.

Like *Dracula*, *Halloween* entails a kind of Gothic return of the past to haunt the present. As with Browning's film, Carpenter's film is driven by sexuality, in particular female sexuality, and while Michael's punishing look is vastly different from the seductive gaze of the count, both films gain momentum from the cultural boundaries around sexuality. If the overtones of Gothic sexuality permeate *Halloween*'s plot, the depiction of the murderous Michael is clearly derivative of Howard Hawks's *The Thing from Another World*. "The Shape," as Michael is called in the script, lurks and lumbers in the same kind of emotionless way as Hawks's alien invader. His blank mask renders his features in an alien, expressionless way, and as with Hawks's creature, the Shape is rarely seen in full view. He appears in the dark, often in the background of a scene, and while the characters in the foreground are unaware of his appearance, we are alerted by the sudden shift in the background music.

The most heavily drawn upon film, clearly, is Hitchcock's *Psycho*. Carpenter's film is filled with explicit references to its predecessor, and more importantly, the basics of the narrative structure are also derived from the tale of Norman Bates. Like Norman, Michael's motive for murder stems from issues of family sexuality—in his case, related to his sister. In both films the identity of the killer is obscured, in Hitchcock by misdirection and in Carpenter by the killer's mask and his seemingly supernatural nature. Additionally, as others have noted, the final girl of *Halloween*, Laurie, is a kind of amalgam of Marion and Lila Crane. She is clearly the target of the killer's attention. The killer follows her in his car and is seen peering at her in class, on her way home, and in her bedroom. However, unlike Marion, Laurie fights back and survives the killer's assault and, in this way, inherits the tough resilience of Lila.[19]

The most immediate contextual films for *Halloween*, of course, are *The Exorcist* and *Texas Chainsaw*. As discussed in the previous chapters, these two films addressed the same broad cultural theme of the apocalypse but did so in diametrically opposed ways. *The Exorcist* suggested that the apocalyptic moment of destruction and revelation recommends a transcendent turn towards the universal and spiritual. *Texas Chainsaw*, to the contrary, depicted a hysterical embrace of the degraded body as the only response to the apocalyptic moment. As I alluded at the end of the previous chapter, Carpenter's film offers a unique and appealing synthesis of these two responses. Michael is a psychotic killer and his methods are physical and brutal—two killings with a butcher knife and two strangulations—however, what Carpenter adds to the already familiar psychotic slasher formula is a transcendental vision of evil as a force of fate.

While Michael does not exhibit any explicit supernatural powers, he does seem to exert an unnatural influence over events. When Annie is sorting out her dirty shirt in the laundry room, the door slams mysteriously shut and locks itself. After Laurie escapes from Michael and locks herself into the Doyle residence, the side door is suddenly revealed to be open. The most dramatic display of these unstated powers occurs in the "room of horrors" sequence. After Laurie enters the Wallace residence in search of her friends, she finds Annie dead on the bed beneath the headstone of Michael's slain sister. As she recoils in horror, the closet door springs open revealing Linda's dead body. Then, as Laurie pulls away, the body of Linda's boyfriend swings out from another closet. Barring the construction of an elaborate mechanism of springs and pulleys in the few minutes between Linda's death and Laurie's entrance, the sudden opening of doors and dropping of bodies occurs through some supernatural means.

Of course, while no one in the film specifically attributes unnatural demonic powers to the masked killer, a great deal of discussion about Michael centers on a grand theory of evil. Dr. Loomis in particular invokes this language constantly. As Michael escapes, Dr. Loomis proclaims, "He's gone from here! The Evil has gone!"

When Dr. Loomis explains the danger to the Haddonfield sheriff he insists, "I realized what was living behind that boy's eyes was purely and simply evil." A more telling explanation of Michael occurs during Laurie's English class. As she stares out the window at the car we know Michael is driving, her teacher drones in the background, "You see, fate caught up with several lives here. No matter what course of action Collins took he was destined to his own fate, his own day of reckoning." Laurie is posed with the question of fate to which she responds, "Samuels felt that, well, fate was like a natural element like earth, air, fire, and water." In a strange non sequitur, the teacher responds, "That's right, Samuels definitely personified fate. In Samuels' writing fate was immovable, like a mountain, it stands where man passes away. Fate never changes." Interestingly, while Laurie explains fate as an elemental force, the teacher defines it is a personification. Given the framing of the shot, with the stolen asylum vehicle visible through the window, the conversation seems to offer a deeper understanding of the nature of Michael's evil. He is a force of nature, an embodiment of some transcendent fate. At the film's conclusion, in the brief moment before Dr. Loomis realizes that Michael's body has disappeared, Laurie sobs to him, "It was the bogeyman." Dr. Loomis replies, "As a matter of fact, it was."

Cultural Returns

One of the most notable and repeated aspects of *Halloween* is the choice of victims. Four people die on screen during the film. Michael's sister, Judith, is killed in the opening sequence immediately after what appears to be a sexual encounter with her boyfriend. Annie is killed by Michael after she drops off her young charge, Lindsey, with Laurie and prepares to go and retrieve her grounded boyfriend. Bob, Linda's boyfriend is killed immediately after a sexual encounter with Linda and as he rummages through the Wallace's kitchen in search of beer, and Linda is killed a few moments later. One other death occurs off screen, a tow-truck driver whose uniform Michael wears for the remainder of the film.

With the exception of the driver, whose death is entirely instrumental, each of the victims has engaged in some form of delinquent sexual behavior.[20] Linda and Danny are killed in the postcoital moment. Annie's case is, in a way, more interesting. Annie is killed before she has engaged in an onscreen sexual act, but she is preparing to engage in illicit sexual behavior. When her boyfriend accuses her of only thinking about sex, she responds, "I think about lots of things. Now why don't we not stand here talking about them and get down to doing them." During this conversation, Michael is seen lurking outside the window. Apparently, in the punitive logic of the film, not only does sex lead to death, but sexual intent also leads to death.

All the delinquent behavior—let alone the murders that follow it—is facilitated by the noticeable absence of parents. Michael's parents appear only after the murder of his sister. Laurie's father is viewed only briefly early in the film as he asks his daughter to drop off the keys at the Meyers's house. In this regard, the role of both sets of parents is to facilitate the subsequent crimes. Michael's negligent parents set the stage for all the murderous acts in the film. Laurie's father is not only absent but also sends Laurie to the terrible place of the Meyers's house where, apparently, the killer fixates on the young baby-sitter.

The one parental figure who does play a significant role in the film is Annie's father, the sheriff. Still, even in his dual authoritative role as parent and law enforcement officer, his presence does nothing to deter either the delinquent behavior or the murderous consequences. As Laurie and Annie drive to their babysitting assignments, they smoke a marijuana cigarette and discuss their romantic feelings. Blue Oyster Cult's *Don't Fear the Reaper* wafts tellingly in the background. During this scene, they see Annie's father, who is investigating a break-in we are led to believe Michael has committed, but the father says nothing about the marijuana smoke that must still be lingering in the vehicle. Despite Laurie's insistence that "I think he knew. I'm sure he could smell it," the sheriff/father seems largely unconcerned about his daughter's behavior. In this way, the sheriff's permissiveness stands as an explanation for the negligent behavior of the film's entire parental community.

In this reading, Michael functions as the punitive bogeyman that stands in for the disciplining parental figure. Meyers watches the teenagers of Haddonfield more closely than their largely absent parents, he judges their naughty behavior more severely, and he punishes with extreme prejudice. The appearance of Michael Meyers, however, can be read as corresponding not only to the teenagers' wicked behavior but also to the absence of their parents. It is, in a way, the absence of the disciplining parents that calls forth the monstrous bogeyman.

Michael Meyers is the bogeyman, and it is interesting that the younger children, Tommy and Lindsey, are the first to recognize this. As Tommy leaves school, he's surrounded by taunting bullies who chant that the bogeyman is going to get him. The bogeyman, Michael, follows the young boy and then returns to stalking his baby-sitter, Laurie. Only Laurie and the children, first Tommy and later Lindsey, see Michael for what he is, a punishing bogey who represents danger to those who transgress cultural boundaries. In this regard, it is notable that the only ones to survive Michael's onslaught are the two young children and Laurie.

Why is it that Laurie survives the killer's attacks when the other teenagers do not? Michael attacks Laurie four times, and each attack is more ferocious than the last. In the first attempt, he stabs her but catches only the edge of her arm, cutting her sleeve but doing little real damage. In the second, he stabs at her but misses entirely, embedding the knife into the couch instead. In the third attempt, Michael batters his way into the closet where Laurie is hiding but is fended off with a coat hanger and then is himself stabbed with the offending butcher knife. Finally, as Michael Meyers again rises from an apparent death, he attempts to strangle Laurie but is interrupted when Laurie pulls off his mask and then further thwarted by the appearance of Dr. Loomis and his revolver.

Laurie does not succumb to these numerous attacks because she, unlike her compatriots, did not engage in sexual activities. While she entertains romantic notions over one of her classmates, confessing to Annie that she has feelings for Ben Tramer, even these feelings are squelched in the film as she later calls Linda and begs her friend to call off the proposed date with the young boy. Laurie is, as other critics have noted, sexually prudish. While she is clearly attractive, she is awkward around boys. "Guys think I'm too smart," she confides to her friend. She is too capable and too dedicated to her studies—she complains that she has forgotten her chemistry book at school. She is, in other words, a kind of model teenager: studious, prudish, loyal, and obedient to her parent's wishes. After all, she obeys her father's order to go to the Meyers's house despite Tommy's warning about the bogeyman.

Beyond her overall goodness, Laurie is, perhaps more importantly, the "good mother" in the film. She takes care of not only her charge, Tommy, but also of Lindsey, who is Annie's responsibility. As she takes charge of the two children, Laurie says to herself, "The old girl scout comes through again." We see Laurie with Tommy on a number of occasions in which she assuages his fears, chastises him for naughtiness, and even tries to elevate his reading material (criticizing his choice of comic books over King Arthur). In each of these instances, Laurie displays not only her inherent goodness but also her inherent maternal quality. Even during Michael's pursuit of her, Laurie's first and foremost concern seems to be for the children. She locks Tommy and Lindsey into a secure bedroom closet and hides herself behind a more flimsy door. When she imagines that she has killed Michael after this assault, she sends the children out to a neighbor's house to call the police.

Perhaps it is this good mother quality that explains Michael's fascination with Laurie. She represents, in a way, the kind of loving and limiting parental figure that he missed in his early childhood. Indeed, one can surmise that had Michael been attended to by some strict parental figure instead of his overly amorous sister, the events of the film would not have taken place. Thus, Michael's fascination with Tommy might be considered the real point of identification for the killer—he sees in Tommy a vision of himself as he might have been. The key distinguishing factor in their difference is the presence of the loving, maternal figure embodied by Laurie. Only this nurturing figure can ward off the harsh hand of the bogeyman's punishment.

Violation

In an age of permissiveness and declining family values, *Halloween* depicted a bogeyman not dissimilar to the many fairytale figures from folklore that came out of the darkness to punish naughty children. That such a tale of punishment and traditional values would be popular among a horror audience made up primarily of adolescents is a bit odd. On one level, perhaps the film resonated with some desire for authority and restrictions, the disciplining, parental love that adolescents growing up in the permissive 1970s might have lacked. Perhaps, in the midst of their own delinquent behaviors, the young people lining up in droves to watch Carpenter's film were purging themselves, at least symbolically, of their own guilt.

Carpenter's film clearly resonated with the typical American youth. This resonance may have come from guilt, but it was surely compounded by the familiarity of the film's setting. Haddonfield is meant to be a generic American suburban town. Horror had, since *Dracula*, been slowly creeping its way closer to the real-life experiences of its audiences, but even films such as *Night of the Living*

Dead and *Texas Chainsaw* placed their horrific scenarios outside of the suburban and urban streets familiar to their audiences. In *Halloween*, horror is not out there, somewhere to be stumbled upon by the unwary; rather, *Halloween* was the night that horror came home—to the suburban homes of its audience members. Carpenter's film introduces a kind of "suburban Gothic," in which the horror of a Gothic bogeyman comes to haunt the remarkably familiar streets of the American youth.[21] As the sheriff explains to Dr. Loomis, "Doctor, do you know what Haddonfield is? Families, children all lined up in rows up and down these streets. You're telling me they're lined up for a slaughterhouse."

In addition to synthesizing the Gothic and the suburban, *Halloween* also more intimately synthesizes killer and victim (or target). Carpenter's film masterfully switches us back and forth from the perspective of the killer to the perspective of the victim (or in Laurie's case, the target). Such a formulation takes the ambiguously sympathetic relationship of Norman Bates and Marion Crane to another level. Where in *Psycho* we moved from one perspective to another—the two separated by the shock of the shower murder—in *Halloween* we are made to juggle these two positions almost from the beginning. To illustrate the point, consider the scene in which Annie spills butter on her shirt. We begin inside the kitchen with Annie as she removes her soiled clothing. We shift outside to stand with Michael as he moves in for a closer look through the window and, in so doing, knocks over a hanging plant. We shift back inside with Annie, who hears the noise, then back outside to Michael. This shifting back and forth continues.

The shifting point of view allows the audience to inhabit both wicked behavior and its punishment almost simultaneously. The murderous moment is, thus, a culmination of both the urge to punish (embodied by Michael) and the urge to be punished for inappropriate behavior (embodied by the victims). Fortunately, we are freed from this potentially sadomasochistic cycle of punishing and being punished by the figure of Laurie who, through her goodness and maternal instincts, breaks the cycle of punishment and survives.

In a similar fashion, *Halloween*'s most notable blurring of established boundaries is between audience and film. Again following Hitchcock's lead, *Halloween* forces its audience members to implicate themselves in the acts of killing and being killed. The powerful opening sequence, shot so explicitly from the killer's point of view, suggests not only the powerful implications of the voyeuristic gaze but also draws the audience even more directly into the cycle of sin and punishment that drives the murderous acts of this modern bogeyman.[22]

In the film's final moment, the monster vanishes, and the film withdraws from its narrative in a series of still shots of the various, mundane suburban locations in which Michael terrorized his victims. The message seems clear. The punishing bogeyman of Michael has not been vanquished but merely dispelled for the moment by Laurie's virtue.

Potentially, this cycle of punishment, and its eventual disruption through Laurie, resonated so powerfully with its young audience because they sought discipline or to purge their guilt. Perhaps by becoming so deeply involved in this story of guilt and punishment, the audience fashioned for themselves a way to prepare for the inevitable discipline to come. Discussing the fearsome bogeyman, Warner notes the way children like to play at being the monster, almost as "a defensive response that is frequently adopted in real experience: internalizing the aggressor in order to stave off the terror he brings." The permissive age of the 1970s could not last forever; a new age of order and authority was on the horizon. Perhaps as much as anything else, Carpenter's film somehow resonated with the shifting political and cultural winds and foresaw the end of the permissive, liberal 1970s and the back-to-basics rise of the conservative 1980s.

HALLOWEEN'S LEGACY

The election of Reagan to the presidency in 1980 brought the permissive, aimless era of the 1970s to both a literal and a symbolic end. During Reagan's two terms in office, his simplistic, conservative politics permeated the culture. Reagan's conservative agenda incorporated many familiar Republican themes: bigger defense budgets, lowered taxes, and fewer social welfare programs. Yet, Reagan's politically conservative agenda would also entail a culturally conservative position. The 1980s saw a dramatic rise in the religious Right as a new breed of politically savvy and vocal religious fundamentalist would come to dominate American culture. Driven by a literal interpretation of the Bible and a commitment to the idea that the America of the 1950s was a better, simpler, and more holy time, this "moral majority" would fight to roll back the cultural permissiveness and experimentation of the previous two decades.

While in no way a conservative film, *Halloween* resonated with this rise in conservative sentiments. True to this form, the horror films of the 1980s overwhelmingly would be dominated by the repetition of Carpenter's tale of a punishing bogeyman pursuing naughty teenagers through suburbs, campgrounds, and their own unconscious minds. In a way, Carpenter's simple, condensed version of the familiar American horror genre fit with the simplistic condensed version of cultural politics promoted in the 1980s.

The growing conservative trend in American culture was, indeed, well reflected in Carpenter's own career. *Halloween* was followed by another, more Gothic, horror film, *The Fog* (1979), in which ghosts from the past return to seek revenge on the town that betrayed them, and then a science fiction film in which the Reagan-era fears of the debauched American city became a hyperbolic caricature, *Escape from New York* (1981). Both films were well received and successful. By the early 1980s, Carpenter was widely regarded as one of America's rising stars. Then, in 1982, as Carpenter prepared to release his most accomplished film to date—a remake of Howard Hawks's *The Thing*—the filmmaker became concerned. As Carpenter explains, "I was sitting in my office at Universal a few weeks before the movie came out, and I got to read a little study, a demographic study—it was the first time I ever saw one of these things—and they discovered that the market for horror movies had shrunk by 70 percent over like six months."[23] Steven Spielberg's *E.T.* (1982) had been released to unexpected success only a few months earlier, and it was clear that the country's mood had changed. Carpenter's apocalyptic, pessimistic, and graphic tale of paranoia and alien invasion was met with lukewarm box-office receipts and an almost overwhelming critical condemnation. Spielberg's film of a charming, benevolent, father-figure alien had captured the spirit of the times. Carpenter's shape-shifting, blood-letting alien appeared in the wrong place and at the wrong time. The Reagan era was a time for Frank Capra-esque fantasies, not doom-laden Hawksian tales of invasive threats, and Carpenter's career would never fully recover from this misstep. While Carpenter would go on to direct a number of interesting and provocative films, he would never reclaim the cultural prominence that promised to be his.

7 *The Silence of the Lambs* (1991)

"Don't you feel eyes moving over your body, Clarice,
and don't your eyes seek out the things you want."

Horror in the 1980s was dominated by the supernatural killer who stalked and slaughtered countless young males and females for their sexual transgressions. By the end of the 1980s, however, the story had become far too familiar. Seemingly endless sequels of these stalk-and-slash films relied on either graphic and increasingly ridiculous death scenes or the development of preposterous background stories. By the late 1980s, for instance, Freddy Krueger, of the *Nightmare on Elm Street* franchise, had become a ubiquitous and largely comical figure—appearing in a short-lived television series as well as the increasingly campy films—and new slasher films either debuted on video or were quickly relegated there. The remarkably successful formula developed in *Psycho* and *The Texas Chainsaw Massacre* and perfected in Carpenter's *Halloween* had largely lost its power to shock and horrify. By the beginning of the 1990s, the horror genre had grown predictable and, therefore, moribund.

One irony in the increasingly banal nature of the onscreen slasher was the dramatic rise in prominence of the real-life serial killer in the 1980s. During this decade the serial killer became an almost mythic figure. As Richard Tithecott observes, "Contemporary monstrosity assumes its most compelling form for us as the serial killer."[1] In addition to the growing media coverage—at times bordering on hysteria—of real-life serial killers such as David Berkowitz, Ted

Bundy, and John Wayne Gacy, the pursuit of serial killers became a remarkably popular narrative in literary fiction. Perhaps the most prominent producer of serial killer fiction was Thomas Harris. Harris's first novel, *Black Sunday* (1975), was a successful political thriller about a terrorist attack on the Super Bowl, but it was Harris's second novel that would solidify his fame and establish him as one of America's most successful novelists. In *Red Dragon* (1981), Harris details the forensic and psychological procedures used by the FBI in their pursuit of a serial killer. The compelling narrative balances these procedural details with a fast-paced plot and a convincing portrait of a haunted FBI profiler who is brought out of retirement for one more assignment. The novel also introduced the figure who would become the most prominent monster of the coming decade, Dr. Hannibal "the Cannibal" Lecter.

Harris's *Red Dragon* was an enormously successful novel, and despite the largely unsuccessful film adaptation by Michael Mann, *Manhunter* (1986), Harris's next novel would be a sequel titled *The Silence of the Lambs* (1988).[2] Like its predecessor, the novel of *Silence* was a bestseller and was soon optioned by Hollywood.[3] Gene Hackman initially planned to make the tale of a female FBI trainee's search for a serial killer his directorial debut, but the venerable actor eventually passed on the project, feeling it was too dark and violent. Orion Pictures, which had optioned the film for Hackman, passed the film on to an up-and-coming young director named Jonathan Demme, who assembled a strong, though not star-studded, cast including Academy Award winner Jodie Foster and the distinguished Welsh actor, Anthony Hopkins.[4]

Filmed on a modest budget of $22 million, *The Silence of the Lambs* opened the day before Valentine's Day 1991 on the heels of a limited though visually strong promotional campaign. Despite being released by a smaller studio during the usually weak post-Christmas period, *Silence* achieved an unprecedented level of popular and critical success. By the end of its initial release, the film had earned more than $130 million in North American, and its worldwide box office of $250 million equaled that of Tim Burton's mega-hyped *Batman* (1989).[5]

Beyond the remarkable box office, *Silence* would achieve the highest critical praise of any horror film in American history, becoming only the third film of any genre to sweep the "big" Academy Awards. The Academy members honored *Silence* with the awards for Best Picture, Best Director, Best Actress in a Leading Role, Best

Actor in a Leading Role, and Best Adapted Screenplay. Only *It Happened One Night* (1934) and *One Flew over the Cuckoo's Nest* (1975) also were able to take all of the major awards. The Academy's sentiments were generally shared by the critics. While there were some vocal opponents to the film—some objected to the violence, others to the homophobic overtones in the film's depiction of Buffalo Bill—most popular and academic critics embraced the film as not only a successful film but also an important one. Feminist critics such as Amy Taubin and B. Ruby Rich thought Demme's film transformed the typical gender politics of the horror film, and Judith Halberstam observed that the film undermines the murderous gaze of patriarchy.[6]

Clearly, *Silence* took horror in a new direction. *Halloween* represented a culmination of the long trajectory of American horror films, and in the post-*Halloween* era, horror had become essentially tied to the synthetic formula of supernatural killers and punished transgressions. By the end of the 1980s, these films had become so formulaic as to be of interest only to the youngest of audiences; older audiences could find little to identify with in the increasingly graphic and ridiculous plots of 1980s horror films. Horror had become remarkably artificial and removed from the cultural reality of audiences, especially the older audiences who had once shuddered at Michael and Jason and Freddy.

In the long history of horror films, the monster had been creeping closer and closer to the audience's lived experience. In a way, then, *Silence* takes the next step. *Silence* brought its monster and the resultant horror into the real world—a world filled not only with horrors but also with issues, politics, and complexities.

SYNOPSIS

Demme's *The Silence of the Lambs* begins in a dark and foggy wood where a woman is seen running. Within seconds, it is obvious that the woman, Clarice Starling, is running an obstacle course, and within a few minutes, her run is interrupted by a course instructor who sends her to see Jack Crawford. As she enters the FBI Academy building in Quanitco, Virginia, Starling encounters Crawford, director of the Behavioral Science Unit, and learns of his latest prey—the serial killer "Buffalo Bill." Bill, we learn from newspaper clippings, abducts and kills women, removing portions of their skin in the process. Crawford, however, has summoned Starling, an FBI trainee, to ask her help not with Buffalo Bill but in interviewing incarcerated serial killers. Starling is to interview the cannibalistic psychiatrist, Dr. Hannibal Lecter.

Starling visits Lecter, who toys with her and then prepares to send her away insulted. A lewd assault on Starling by an inmate changes Lecter's disposition, and he offers her a vague clue about one of his former patients. Starling pursues the clue and finds a severed head in a jar. After further investigation, Starling finds that this head has a moth inserted into its throat—the same kind of moth found inserted in the throat of a victim of Buffalo Bill. To find out what Lecter knows, Starling agrees to trade personal information about herself for clues to the identity of Buffalo Bill.

The film also follows Buffalo Bill, whose real name is Jame Gumb, as he abducts a young woman, Catherine Martin, from her apartment building's parking lot. He asks for help while wearing a fake arm cast, a trick employed by real-life killer Bundy. The remarkably resourceful young woman is later seen captive in Bill's basement, where she uses a chicken bone and a bucket to capture his poodle in an effort to escape. We learn that this young woman is the daughter of a junior senator from Tennessee. Desperate to gain some information, Starling and Crawford make a fake offer to Lecter of a transfer to a V.A. hospital and a yearly vacation in exchange for information. The deal falls through, thanks to the nefarious efforts of Lecter's warder, Dr. Frederick Chilton, and Lecter is moved to Tennessee, where a real deal for cooperation is offered.

As time is running out, Starling visits Lecter again and is urged to think more about what Buffalo Bill covets. As Starling pursues this lead, Lecter escapes. Following his tip, Starling visits the hometown of the first victim, Belvedere, Ohio, under the assumption that the killer knew this victim. At the same time, the FBI believes they have traced the killer to Chicago. The Chicago address turns out to be a fake, and soon Starling comes face to face with the killer. Starling learns that Bill has been sewing together a "woman suit" made out of the skin of his victims, in what Lecter describes as a desperate attempt to create a new identity. In the tense climax, Starling chases Buffalo Bill—a.k.a. Jame Gumb—into his labyrinthine basement, where she shoots the serial killer to death and rescues the senator's daughter. The film concludes with Starling's graduation ceremony from the FBI Academy, during which her supervisor, Jack Crawford, and the now-at-large serial killer, Lecter, both congratulate her.

CULTURAL CONTEXTS

The conservative movement that had begun in the late 1970s, dominated the 1980s and early 1990s. The Reagan revolution represented a major reconfiguration of American politics, economics, and culture. Not only were the utopian, leftist dreams of the counterculture dead and buried, but former flower children were working as cutthroat venture capitalists. The era of peace and love had been largely replaced by a decade of power and greed. For movie-going audiences in the early 1990s, the repercussions of this dramatic decade of change were still being felt, and Americans once again were seeking direction in this, the last decade of the twentieth century.

Rise of the Yuppies

Reagan's two terms as president dominated the majority of the 1980s—from 1980 to 1988—and he was succeeded by his vice president, George H. W. Bush. For twelve years, the Republican Party held sway over American politics and pushed a unique vision of America. The epitome of the Reagan-era American was the "yuppie"—an acronym for young urban professional. A yuppie combined the egocentric behavior of the 1970s with newly conservative politics and a vastly more ruthless attitude towards career and success. As Leonard Quart and Albert Auster define the term, "The archetypal yuppie jogged, ate health food, was obsessed with brand names and what was fashionable and was a workaholic. Work was a means to greater status and a more affluent life-style, and happiness only could be realized by relentlessly pursuing one's own needs. And little sense of larger social, moral, and communal concerns were allowed to intrude on this hunger for personal mobility."[7]

The Reagan doctrine pushed three interrelated political goals: increased spending on defense, lowered taxes (especially for the wealthy), and reduced federal involvement in regulating the economy and providing basic social security services.[8] "Trickle-down" economics was founded on the notion that the more affluent drive the overall economy and, thus, that tax cuts for the wealthy will trickle down to the rest of the citizenry. The underlying principle for the Reagan-era economic citizen, therefore, was greed. Oliver Stone's corporate caricature Gordon Gecko, the venture capitalist antagonist in *Wall Street* (1987), captured the decade's spirit, "Greed is good." Traditional American values of modesty, altruism, and community were being replaced by an overwhelming desire for personal gain. Joseph Stiglitz notes that by the early 1990s, Americans were being told "not only should they feel no guilt in greed; they should feel pride."[9]

The cultural effect of the unrestrained pursuit of personal wealth was the further erosion of concepts of community and the bonds of affection that hold people together. The yuppie was a self-motivated and self-interested creature for which notions of ethics were meaningful only to the extent they promised personal gain. The national focus on military power and individual responsibility was mirrored in the ways individuals saw themselves in relation to their overall community. The Reagan-era policies, as Quart and Auster note, provided a "distorted moral vision [which] gave sanction to an age of narcissism."[10]

The Backlash against Feminism

The virtually unrestrained individualism of the Reagan/Bush era was, however, not distributed equally. Not only were the disadvantaged and lower classes left out of the process, so were women. The rise of the New Right, a mix of religious fundamentalism and the Republican Party, was motivated, in part, by the sense of moral decay prevalent in the 1970s. The rise in antifeminist rhetoric and organizations in the late 1970s began to have a broader political impact in the 1980s. The New Right targeted the reproductive rights guaranteed by *Roe v. Wade* and the programs of affirmative action, which had been designed as a remedy for the historical disadvantages endured by women and minorities. Additionally, the Reagan-era conservatives targeted feminism and feminists specifically.[11] These were among the first major salvos of what James Hunter would call the "culture wars," a clash between progressives and conservatives over issues of cultural values and practices.[12]

Susan Faludi, in a book published the year *Silence* was released, defined the entire decade of the Reagan/Bush presidencies as "the backlash decade" and charged that it "produced one long, painful, and unremitting campaign to thwart women's progress."[13] The ascendance of the New Right's traditional, patriarchal values and rhetoric was paralleled by an equally dramatic decline in the feminist movement itself. During this period, as Sheila Tobias notes, "Feminism began to lose its luster and its freshness, its popularity and its power to convert. By the end of the Reagan/Bush era, the feminist 'revolution' was in retreat."[14]

The backlash against the feminist revolution was evident not only in politics but also in popular culture. Marsha McCreadie, for instance, describes a growing trend of films in the mid-1980s as "backlash films," films in which women were portrayed as deviant and dangerous and were subsequently punished.[15] This trend was perhaps best captured in Adrian Lyne's *Fatal Attraction* (1987), which depicted both the doting and subservient wife (Anne Archer) and the dangerously deranged, independent, and sexualized other woman (Glenn Close). The only solution to the "woman problem," this film and others suggested, was to either keep women in line or destroy them; for women, survival increasingly was equated with subservience.

By the beginning of the 1990s, American women were caught in a new version of the double bind. Where once women were meant to be simultaneously chaste and sexually ravenous, in the age of the yuppie women were to be both professionally successful and relationally subservient. The new myth of the "superwoman" as an aggressive professional and a nurturing wife and mother did not represent a new egalitarian reality as much as a new mode of subjugation. Women were to embody both the traditional male and female roles and to feel guilty for failing at either. Perhaps it is this cultural tension that made 1991 an oddly positive moment in the depiction of women in film. This year saw the appearance of Linda Hamilton's remarkably aggressive, protective mother in James Cameron's *Terminator 2* as well as the feminist retelling of *Butch Cassidy and the Sundance Kid* in Ridley Scott's *Thelma and Louise*. Of course, 1991 also saw the appearance of FBI trainee Clarice Starling.

Serial Killing

As novelist Brett Easton Ellis grasped so readily, the figure who most epitomized the cultural contradictions and excesses of the eighties was the serial killer. Ellis's scathing critique of the Reagan era's narcissism, misogyny, and greed, *American Psycho*, was published in 1991 to great controversy and condemnation. The yuppie killer whose psychotic musings fill its pages slaughters coworkers and women with no remorse or fear of discovery. These killings—whether real or imagined—typify the combination of ruthless capitalism and antifeminist misogyny that were undercurrents in the rise of the New Right.

While Ellis's novel courted controversy with its grotesquely detailed graphic descriptions, the novelist captured not only the dark underside of the Reagan/Bush era but also the perfect eighties monster. The serial killer, of course, had been part of America's cultural imagination since Jack the Ripper's East London murders achieved infamous notoriety. The mythic figure of the anonymous, repetitive killer achieved even greater prominence during the 1980s. In part, this prominence came from a number of high-profile cases of serial killers—especially Bundy, who courted the media throughout the decade in a failed attempt to avoid the Florida death penalty. Whatever the sources of the serial killer narratives that pervaded the decade, it is clear that the serial killer replaced other monsters as the principal bogeyman of the 1980s.[16] As a lone killer satisfying his inner desires with no concern for the lives of others, the serial killer embodied many of the cultural patterns of the 1980s. The serial killer was, as Mark Selzer observes, not only horrifically abnormal but also "abnormally normal."[17] In Selzer's reading of the serial killer as cultural icon, these murderers achieve a version of the American vision of success, albeit a distorted version. The killer achieves both notoriety and anonymity. He (almost always a "he") is both chameleon-like in his ability to appear in different forms and spectacularly distinct in leaving his signature upon the frightened culture. The killer is, therefore, both powerless in the sense of being outside the authorized realms of power and amazingly powerful in his ability to hold entire cities, even the nation as a whole, in his grip of fear. The cultural potency and ambiguity of this new monster is suggested by Philip Simpson who argues, "The 'serial killer' ... is a fantastic confabulation of Gothic/romantic villain, literary vampire and werewolf, detective and 'pulp' fiction conceits, film noir outsider, frontier outlaw, folkloric threatening figure, and nineteenth-century pseudo-sociological conception of criminal types given contemporary plausibility."[18]

READING *THE SILENCE OF THE LAMBS*

As the Bush administration reached the final years of its first and, as it would turn out, last term in office, 1991 marked an odd transition period for American culture. The narcissism that had driven the economic and cultural trends in the 1980s became the target of increased criticism and derision. The yuppie became a foolish icon of a past decade just like *Miami Vice* jackets, day-glo socks, and Duran Duran. It became increasingly clear that the New Right's promise of economic prosperity had trumped its promise of a return to traditional values, and the country seemed to be fragmenting into a culture of self-promoting narcissists. Even the Bush administration recognized the excessive individualism in the country as the president promoted a largely unfunded initiative to develop community-based, voluntary social services. While Bush's "thousand points of light" failed to achieve the promise of sparking a new age of community and civic responsibility, the sense that Americans had sacrificed unity in their pursuit of economic success became palpable. The gap between rich and poor was wide and growing wider, and most Americans spent their time at work to the neglect of family and the abandonment of community.[19]

In the midst of these various cultural anxieties, Demme's *The Silence of the Lambs* struck a powerfully resonant note with Americans. The film became not only successful but also "important." Like *The Exorcist*, the film demonstrated that horror could be mature and of high quality, but in a way unlike that film, *Silence* suggested that horror films could directly inform the cultural debates of their day. With *Silence*, the horrors that had moved from Transylvania to the Gothic suburbs of *Halloween* emerged into the complicated and politically tense world of reality. The monster was drawn, indeed quite closely, from the real monsters who terrorized citizens and occupied maximum security cells, and the pursuit of the villain was wrapped up in the kinds of daily troubles and obstacles that mark the real life of average Americans.

My reading of the film focuses on the notion of community and the difficulty involved in becoming part of, but not being consumed by, communal relations. In this reading Starling and Buffalo Bill represent contrasting versions of the same struggle to develop a clear sense of identity. For both these characters, identification with others holds the key to developing a mature identity, but community also holds the dangers of being consumed by rigidly defined roles. Ultimately, Buffalo Bill veers too far away from community, failing to achieve identification and, instead, falls into objectification. Starling, on the other hand, achieves partial success, though the end of the film suggests her struggle to maintain balance between individualism and community continues.

Starling and Buffalo Bill: A Search for Identity

In a fashion familiar in American horror films, Demme drives his plots through the interactions of opposed pairs, or "doubles." For many critics, both academic and popular, the opposed pair of *Silence* is Starling and Lecter. However, the pairing of Starling and Buffalo Bill seems most pressing. The plot is driven by Starling's and Bill's activities—Bill's effort to finish his identity suit and Starling's effort to track the killer. Additionally, the audience spends considerable time with both of these characters. Starling is our primary point of identification within the film as we follow her activities and empathize with her experiences, but we also share the point of view with Buffalo Bill, including two chilling scenes in which we view the world through Bill's green night-vision goggles. Finally, and perhaps most importantly, Starling and Bill both are portrayed, at least at times, as victims of a brutal, insensitive society, and it is this abusive society that places them on their collision course.

Considerable critical attention has been paid to Starling and her struggle to overcome the leering intrusion of men. This struggle is given its most sympathetic voice through Crawford but is shown as well in her mesmerizing relationship with Lecter. Starling's nature is revealed to us through four interactions, with four different men, early in the film. Her first substantive conversation is with Crawford, and the dialogue is almost a caricature of institutional bureaucracy. Crawford refers to her as "Starling, Clarice M." while he reviews her resume and recalls a previous encounter with her in a seminar he taught at the University of Virginia. The discussion serves to give the audience a glimpse of Starling's background, credentials, and talents, but it also provides us an insight into her motives. Reviewing her official paperwork, Crawford notes, "Says here when you graduate you want to come work for me in Behavioral Sciences," to which she replies, "Yes, very much sir, very much." Institutional success and ambition define Starling.

This professional definition of Starling is repositioned during her encounter with Dr. Chilton. During their walk through the asylum en route to Lecter, Starling parries Dr. Chilton's offensively obvious advances saying, "I graduated from UVA, Doctor. It is not a charm school." In this scene we find that Starling's accomplishments and ambitions are a defense against objectification. Thus, in addition to her institutionally defined success and her ambition, a third element of her identity becomes clear: her use of those aspects to resist objectification.

Where Dr. Chilton fails to unsettle Starling with his overt sexual advances, Lecter is far more successful, striking at the core of her identity: ambition. Lecter begins by observing that her credentials are temporary, that she is not "real FBI," and then moves to invert the construction of institutional success and identity. Mocking her accent, Lecter hisses, "You're so ambitious, aren't you. You know what you look like to me with your good bag and your cheap shoes? A rube, a well-scrubbed hustling rube with a little taste." The appearance of authority and advancement are, for Lecter, merely illusions to be dispelled—hiding insecurities for Lecter to uncover and consume.

Lecter's interrogation is clearly devastating for Starling, and while the unpleasant incident with Multiple Miggs[20] establishes a more productive relationship with Lecter, she leaves the asylum rattled. As she walks to her car we have our fourth revelatory encounter in a flashback to her childhood. As a young Clarice sneaks up on her father, a town marshall, we glimpse the reason for her ambition. While many critics have focused on the relationship to her father, often as a figure of patriarchal authority, we might also observe the context of this encounter. The setting is a simple street on a sunny day. Leaving his car, Marshall Starling waves to a neighbor walking by. "Hey Bill," he says. As father and daughter go into their house, the camera lingers on Bill, who waves to a passing truck as a dog in the back barks. The light soundtrack and the birds singing in the background suggest a kind of idyllic setting, a neighborhood where people walk down the street and wave to passersby. This, then, is community for Starling, and her marshall father becomes the core of her understanding of community. To become part of community is to achieve a place of authority and success; her ambition is not to live up to her father but to take his place in a broader, supportive community.

Buffalo Bill gets considerably less screen time than Starling but is also explicitly defined in terms of his struggles to attain an identity. We see Bill as a cunning predator in his stalking of Martin and as a sadist, tormenting his captive. The film, unlike the novel, gives no glimpse into Bill's background, and we never see Bill interacting with people save for his victim and his pursuer. Bill, thus, is visually defined in terms of the absence of community, alone in his basement with his poodle and moths. Interestingly, it is this sense of community that Bill uses to lure Martin into his van. Wearing an arm cast and struggling to put a couch into the back of the van, Bill's appearance of need draws her to offer him assistance.

While Bill is portrayed as separated from community, establishing an identity is also his quest. Bill's route to identity, however, is not through interaction with others but through a solipsistic construction of a self, a self pieced together from the skin of his victims. When we see Bill at work in his basement, he is alone at his sewing machine, asking his image in the mirror if he is desirable, or dancing in front of a video camcorder to create an illusion of femininity. Bill, according to the all-seeing Lecter, "hates his own identity" and learns to "covet" the identities of those around him. To him, murder becomes a means for transformation. Systematically abused as a child, Bill, in contrast to Starling, seeks an identity in the absence of community. The multiplicity of identities that Bill has attempted is, indeed, momentarily visible during the various scenes in his basement. The rotting walls are covered with Nazi paraphernalia, snapshots of himself with female strippers, and tellingly, an American flag that is framed into the shot of Bill's death.

Thus, the main players of the film are established. Placed at odds both by the plot and by their position in terms of identity—Starling seeking one through communal relations and Bill seeking one in isolation from community—Starling and Bill become contestants in a struggle for identity. Ultimately, Bill and Starling are diametrically opposed. If Bill achieves his identity, Starling fails and vice versa.

The Obstacle Course Metaphor

The sense that the film involves a kind of contest is developed in the opening sequence of the film. Here we see, initially, a shot of a wooded area soon identified as "near Quantico, VA," but as the credits appear on the screen, this generic commonplace, the dark and scary woods, is disturbed by the appearance of a woman, Starling, in sweats and climbing up a rope. At this point it becomes clear that we are not watching some "damsel in distress" but a competent and powerful woman running an obstacle course.

Her run on the obstacle course appears interrupted when a male instructor directs her to see Crawford. Still, the visual sense of the film maintains the feel of an obstacle course as Starling enters the building, climbs stairs, passes through various training sessions, and in one of the more stark visuals of the film, enters an elevator surrounded by larger men all wearing bright red shirts. Out of the elevator, the camera follows Starling as she walks the labyrinthine halls, finally ending up in Crawford's office.

Once in the office she is confronted not with Crawford but with evidence of the man who will be her competitor in this contest, Buffalo Bill. The evidence of Bill's brutality is harsh: photographs of mutilated bodies and crime scenes stuck to a bulletin board. As Starling looks at photographic evidence of her opponent, we assume her point of view, gazing at the aftermath of violence. Interestingly, the setup of this scene involves a "shot-reverse shot" in which the audience first shares Starling's point of view and then the camera reverses, effectively taking the point of view of the bulletin board filled with the photographic remnants of Bill's carnage. The editing of this scene suggests, at least in part, a kind of dialogue beginning between Starling and Bill.

Transfixed by the photos, Starling does not see Crawford enter the scene, and for a few seconds, his blurry figure is visible to us as he stands observing Starling. It is interesting that when Crawford first suggests a need for Starling, her first assumption is that it is to help in the pursuit of Buffalo Bill. In this initial conversation, however, Crawford offers Starling the "interesting errand" of interviewing Lecter, the incarcerated serial killer.

Before returning to these two men who serve as the extreme poles in the film's struggle for balance, a few other instances of the obstacle course theme deserve attention. Indeed, the next major sequence of the film involves Starling's dealing with Dr. Chilton, the lecherous administrator of the asylum where Lecter is incarcerated. Here the obstacle course is both physical, traversing serpentine hallways and numerous metal gates, and psychic, as Starling endures the advances, hostility, and "petty torments" of Chilton.

The physical sense of an obstacle course continues a few scenes later as Starling pursues a clue offered by Lecter into a dark and menacing storage unit. Indeed, this theme appears over and over as Starling negotiates the obstacles of patriarchy, savagery, and memory during the autopsy of one of Bill's victims, again as she slips past guards to see Lecter in Memphis, and again as she stumbles blindly through the darkened basement of the serial killer Buffalo Bill. These various obstacles all stem either from the oppressive norms of patriarchal community (to which Starling ostensibly aspires) or from the savage appetites of a rogue individual (i.e., Lecter or Bill).

Two Extremes: Crawford and Lecter

As suggested, however, the danger is not merely physical nor is the goal only survival. Both Starling and Bill are seeking fulfillment of their ultimate goal, a sense of identity, and the greatest danger they face is succumbing to one of two extremes presented in the film: Crawford and Lecter. In different ways, both Starling and Bill are pursued by Lecter and Crawford. Beyond the protagonist/ antagonist relationship, the two men represent extreme points in the struggle between individualism and community. In one sense, Lecter and Crawford parallel the mythic Narcissus and Echo—one solely focused on self-gratification, the other a caricature of communal power relations.

Lecter, the ultimate expression of self-obsession, is an all-consuming force utterly unbound by the conventions of society, and like some wild beast, we first meet the cannibal behind a glass cage. Throughout the film Starling is warned that Lecter is "toying" with her and only satisfying his own desires. Lecter expresses his philosophy of life when Starling chastises him for giving false leads to the Justice Department officials. "You've got to learn to get more fun out of life," Lecter replies. Beneath Lecter's civilized veneer lies a sadistic and savage hunger that thrives on consuming both the flesh and psyches of those around him. The contrast between the genteel psychiatrist and the horrific animal is revealed most graphically in his escape scene. The scene is the only onscreen graphic violence in the film and is a kind of sudden and visual assault on the audience's expectations. Lecter murders the two prison guards with both savage efficiency and a clear sense of ravenous joy. In the aftermath, covered in blood, Lecter stands, transfixed by the soft strains of classical music, interrupted only by the struggles of one of the dying guards. The contrast is clear, but Lecter seems untroubled by the deep contradiction between his actions and tastes. He is an entity of pure consuming desire, a ravenous id, unleashed from the bonds of morality or obligation.

Where Lecter is narcissistic hunger unbounded, Crawford functions as his exact opposite, the embodiment of communal order. There is no sense of Crawford's life outside his profession. The first interaction between Starling and Crawford invokes the power relations of the bureaucratic institution, and their relationship stays on a professional plane.[21] In this first interaction, he recalls his position as Starling's instructor during a course at the University of Virginia, and his role as mentor/instructor always is wrapped up in the official hierarchical structures. As others have observed, Crawford functions as a stand-in for Starling's deceased father, and in this way Crawford's position within the broader official structure reinforces the assumptions of patriarchy. After Starling shoots Bill, it is Crawford who escorts her out of the house and fends off the encroaching cameramen, his arm encircling her in a protective manner. Indeed, in the film's final moments, Crawford makes his connection to Starling's law enforcement officer explicit. "Your father would've been proud today," he tells Starling as they share a professional though intimate handshake. Demme's Crawford is the epitome of an FBI agent, professional and traditional to the point of being explicitly misogynistic. When Starling rebukes Crawford for the use of a sexist stereotype, he is a representative for the whole community: "It matters Mr. Crawford. Cops look to you to see how to act. It matters."

As suggested earlier, the obstacles Starling faces throughout the film are manifestations of one or the other of these extremes. Starling continually resists the efforts by members of her chosen community, the law enforcement community, to put her in her gendered place. When Starling comes to assist with a murder investigation in West Virginia, the local—and decidedly male—officers surround her with inquisitive if not quite intimidating stares. Throughout the film, Starling is leered at and approached sexually—by Chilton and even, in a humorous come-on, by an entomologist. Male law enforcement officials continually disrupt her investigation.[22] On the other hand, Starling is also endangered by those individuals who have utterly rejected the norms of community—people such as Multiple Miggs, Buffalo Bill, and Lecter himself. This tension becomes most evident at the end of the film where the Lecter/Crawford pair, who instigated the events of the film, appear again.

Resolution

If the film can be read as a desperate attempt to resolve the conflict between the restrictive relations of community and the dangerous desires of individualism, then the key question is how the film resolves this tension. There are two interrelated resolutions offered in the film. The first is the plot resolution that occurs in Buffalo Bill's darkened basement where Starling shoots the killer to death. The second resolution, a kind of antiresolution, occurs at the very end of the film where, as Starling receives her "real FBI" credentials, she interacts with the two polar opposites, Lecter and Crawford. Crawford gives her a firm handshake and congratulates her, saying her hard work will not be forgotten. Lecter, via a phone call, assures her that she has nothing to fear from him. These two resolutions give us two different senses of community that emphasize rather than resolve the overarching tension of the film.

The first resolution can be read as reinforcing a conservative "rhetoric of hate" wherein the outsider is enemy. While Bill's crimes are horrific, we are told early in the film that Bill is a victim himself of systematic child abuse. Why then, do we cheer for the killing of this horrific albeit horribly misguided victim? Because killing Buffalo Bill reinforces the existence of the community. As Roderick Hart contends, "For each community in existence ... there is also an 'uncommunity,' an assembly of the befouled and besotted who have heard the Word [of community] and rejected it."[23] In the film's logic, Bill failed to keep his balance, falling too far into an objectified narcissism (a la Lecter). His inability to find a communal identity makes him not an object of pity but of hate.

This is not to suggest that the film takes an entirely conservative tone—that the dangerous other must be destroyed and the traditional community reestablished—rather the film offers a more ambivalent view of the tension between individual desires and communal restraints. The second antiresolution, in which both Crawford and Lecter continue to loom large in Starling's future, suggests that the balance between the consuming relations of community and the consuming desires of individualism cannot be taken for granted. Starling's success is achieved not only by the death of Buffalo Bill but also by the balance she maintains between her desires and the attempts by others to turn her into an object of desire. Starling is, thus, able to achieve communal respect while maintaining her separate identity. This balance, however, once achieved must be maintained.[24]

In Demme's *Silence* there is no conclusion, no final victory, only a precarious balance—a quest for equitable human relationships that comes at a cost and can never be abandoned. Starling's identity could not be established, however precariously, without the death of her opposite. The cost of community is Buffalo Bill's final gasp, and like Starling, we are left in a world where the temptations of community and the lure of individual desires offer all too easy solutions to the complex question of a humane community.

THE SILENCE OF THE LAMBS'S LEGACY

In a way, the conflict between community and individual desires was reenacted in some of the more incendiary reactions to the film. *Silence* became an object of controversy particularly among gay and feminist critics. In some of the more heated exchanges, it becomes clear that many gay and lesbian critics focused on the elements of the rhetoric of hate embodied in the film's depiction of Buffalo Bill and the way in which his deviance is brutally resolved in the film. For many feminist critics, the key was Starling's achievement of a balance between her aspirations and the maintenance of her personal integrity. As the controversy raged among critics, it became clear that both sides felt betrayed by the other and that these two communities, typically allied in the struggles over sexual politics, were divided in their understanding of this film.[25]

Of course, much of *Silence*'s notoriety was based on its explicit sexual politics. By infusing the horror genre with explicit cultural politics, Demme infused the fading slasher genre with new life. Indeed, Demme's film almost single-handedly created the "serial killer profiler" genre that would become a prominent aspect of American popular culture in the 1990s. *Silence* spawned numerous imitators—films focused not only on serial killers but also engaged with mature questions of cultural politics, films such as Dominic Sena's *Kalifornia* (1993), Oliver Stone's *Natural Born Killers* (1994), Jon Amiel's *Copycat* (1995), David Fincher's *Se7en* (1995), and Gary Felder's *Kiss the Girls* (1997). *Silence* also paved the way for such television shows as *The X-Files* (1993–2002), *Millenium* (1996–1999), and *Profiler* (1996–2000).

Demme's film also sparked interest in the "Hannibal Lecter" franchise, and within months of the film's successful run, Dino DeLaurentis, the producer of *Manhunter* and owner of the rights to Harris's characters, announced plans to film the next Lecter novel. Ten years later, Harris released the odd tale of Hannibal Lecter's return from exile and the increasingly romantic relationship between the cannibal and the FBI agent. *Hannibal* (2001), while considered unfilmable in many ways, became a highly profitable film. While Demme and Foster passed on the film, suggesting it was too violent and too dark, Ridley Scott and Julianne Moore stepped into these vacancies, and the film broke box-office records for opening weekend of an R-rated film. Scott's *Hannibal* began the process of turning the psychiatrist into a kind of monstrous figure of fun and was followed in this vein by another successful Lecter film, Brett Ratner's *Red Dragon* (2002), which was a remake of *Manhunter*.[26] By the end of the 1990s, Hannibal Lecter had become the same kind of ubiquitous cultural monster that Freddy Krueger had been at the end of the 1980s. The films, while successful, had begun to lose their horrific edge.

8 *Scream* (1996)

"It's all a movie, all a great big movie, only you can't pick your genre."

On June 17, 1994, all three major networks interrupted their broadcasts, including the NBA Finals, a news show, and a popular crime drama, for a live broadcast from Los Angeles, California. A white Ford Bronco, traveling at approximately 35 miles per hour, was leading a fleet of LAPD patrol cars and helicopters on one of the most bizarre police chases in American history. Inside the Bronco was O. J. Simpson, the former football star, who was wanted on the suspicion that he had murdered his wife, Nicole Brown Simpson, and her friend, Ronald Goldman. For most of that evening, the major networks maintained coverage of the slow-speed chase until finally, late in the evening, Simpson surrendered himself.

Thus began the long and complicated saga of the O. J. Simpson trial, an event that would touch on many of the major issues facing Americans in the mid-1990s: racism, sexism, class, and of course, the impact of the overwhelming presence of the news media on the stories they reported. Three years before the Simpson event, the videotaped beating of Rodney King and subsequent acquittal of the offending police officers had set off massive riots in the city of Los Angeles, and these riots themselves had become media spectacles. So, as the Simpson trial proceeded, an enormous number of Americans watched the daily, almost continuous, television broadcasts. The unfolding drama of the trial raised many important topics for public discussion, including racial injustice, spousal abuse, and celebrity justice. However, the general gravity of these issues and the specific seriousness of a murder trial were almost overshadowed by the intense level of media scrutiny of every aspect of the trial, its participants, and eventually, the media itself. The Simpson trial was certainly not the only or even the first carnival-esque media spectacle in American history, but it had the distinction of being televised to millions of homes across the country on a daily basis.

Among the many cultural trends accentuated by the trial were the pervasiveness of the media and the blurring of the lines between television spectacle and reality. In theory, a trial ought to be one of the more rational and dispassionate procedures in our culture, but the Simpson trial was as much about public relations, photo opportunities, and "spin" as it was about evidence or argumentation.[1] As Paul Thaler contends, "In the final analysis, the media did not just report the Simpson case but were instrumental in creating it. They transformed a murder trial into a cultural event the likes of which we had never seen before.... Simpson was a cultural happening, a Woodstock of the courtroom, with its own pulsating beat and adulating audience calling for more."[2] Ultimately, the question of Simpson's guilt or innocence became irrelevant as the media attention to the event and the event itself merged. It was no longer a state of "style over substance" but a point where style was everything and substance was largely irrelevant. America had embraced the postmodern era.

In the previous chapter, I argued that one of the innovations in Demme's *The Silence of the Lambs* was the way it brought the familiar slasher bogeyman into the complicated and political realm of reality. However, the blurring of the line between reality and fiction goes both ways. The Simpson trial and many other examples suggested that, by the 1990s, reality seemed to be slipping into the realm of mediated fiction. Reality, in other words, just wasn't what it used to be, and so, the American horror film was reconfigured to address the broader anxieties of a culture that found it increasingly difficult to differentiate realistic cinema from cinematic reality.

It is fitting, in a way, that the director who captured the tension underlying this blurred sense of cultural reality was Wes Craven. Craven's career in horror films began with the intensely controversial exploitation film *The Last House on the Left* (1972) and continued with a number of shocking and intelligent films such as *The Hills Have Eyes* (1977), but Craven's lasting fame came from a badly scarred and dead former janitor named Freddy Krueger. In many ways, *A Nightmare on Elm Street* (1984) followed the highly familiar slasher bogeyman formula established by Carpenter. However, in Craven's remarkably popular version of the familiar tale, the bogeyman came from the dreams of his victims, and this general theme of the blurring of the line between fantasies and deadly realities is a major theme in almost all Craven's films. In *The Serpent and the Rainbow* (1988), which was based on "true events," a medical researcher tries to distinguish hallucinations from real voodoo magic; in *Shocker* (1989), the serial killer is a being of electricity who can come out of the television set; and in *Wes Craven's New Nightmare* (1994), the monstrous Krueger emerges out of the fictional world of the film to terrorize the actors and creators, including Robert Englund, who played Krueger, Heather Langenkamp, and even Craven himself. Of all the major horror auteurs, Craven was clearly prepared to explore the horror lurking in the space between reality and fiction.

Of course, Craven's habitual worrying of the line between reality and fiction had not been especially successful in the 1990s. Craven's three films in the early 1990s, *The People under the Stairs* (1991), *Wes Craven's New Nightmare* (1994), and the Eddie Murphy vehicle *A Vampire in Brooklyn* (1995), were all critically and commercially unsuccessful. So, in 1996 when Miramax contracted Craven to direct a hip, self-referential horror script by Kevin Williamson, expectations were not especially high. The presence of Drew Barrymore, even in a minor role, helped to create some buzz around the project, but it was always a modest movie with a budget of approximately $15 million. Another horror film filled with young actors, many from minor television programs, held little hope for reviving the stagnant horror genre.

An examination of *Scream*'s weekly domestic box office offers a clear picture of the impact word of mouth can have on a film. Released on December 22, 1996, with limited fanfare, *Scream* grossed a little more than $6 million in its opening weekend. By the end of its first week it had grossed more than $21 million. The next week added $18 million, its third week saw another $11 million, and the fourth an additional $14 million. By the mid-1990s, most films opened big and faded each week. *Scream* displayed the opposite trend. The film stayed in American movie theaters into July 1997, and by the end of its initial domestic run it had grossed more than $100 million, and its worldwide box office was more than $160 million.[3]

Somehow a director from an earlier era took an overly familiar version of the horror genre, the teen slasher film, and made it relevant to the young, media-savvy moviegoers of the last few years of the twentieth century. The success of the film was due in some part to tight pacing and direction as well as to the delicate balance between humor and horrific shocks. However, *Scream* also violated the traditional formulaic rules of the slasher film by acknowledging and even referencing them. The killers, victims, and survivors in *Scream* knew the rules of a slasher film and even, to a lesser extent, knew that they were in a slasher film. With *Scream*, the boundary between fiction and reality was, once again, blurred as the rules of the genre leaked into the narrative itself. The postmodern horror film emerged from this confusing blend of horror and humor with self-reference and slaughter.

SYNOPSIS

In many ways, both implicitly and explicitly, Craven's *Scream* is a reworking of Carpenter's *Halloween*. Both films begin with a short and tightly paced introductory murder. In *Scream*, the first victim is Casey (Drew Barrymore), who receives a series of annoying phone calls from a deep-voiced man who refuses to give his name. The conversation turns to scary movies, and Casey confesses she is about to watch a video. The conversation soon turns nasty, and the caller reveals that he has abducted Casey's boyfriend, Steve, and will kill him if she fails to answer questions about scary movies correctly. When she misses one of the questions, the killer disembowels the captive Steve, whom Casey can see strapped to a chair on her back patio, and then begins stalking the young girl through the house. When the killer is finally seen, he is wearing a long black robe and a Halloween mask resembling Edvard Munch's painting *The Scream*. Eventually the killer catches up to Casey, killing her and hanging her body in the front yard. Her parents find her mere moments after she is killed.

The film then shifts to the bedroom of its protagonist, Sidney "Sid" Prescott (Neve Campbell), as she is visited by her boyfriend, Billy Loomis (Skeet Ulrich). Billy climbs in through her window and leaves after a brief discussion of their limited physical relationship. Sidney's father, who reminds his daughter that he is leaving town for the week on business, briefly interrupts the visit. When Sidney arrives at school the next morning, the building is surrounded by television news crews, and the students are abuzz with rumors about the murders of Casey and Steve. In the midst of these developments, we learn that Sidney's mother had been raped and murdered a year ago and that the killer, Cotton Weary, was convicted based on Sidney's eyewitness testimony.

The killer stalks Sidney, and soon all attention is on her. A prominent tabloid-television news reporter, Gale Weathers (Courtney Cox), has written a book about the year-old rape-murder and is convinced that Sidney identified the wrong person. Weathers, too, begins tracking the girl's movements. The night after the murders of Casey and Steve, the killer attacks Sidney in her home, but she escapes. As she waits for the police to arrive, Billy again appears at her bedroom window. When his cell phone drops from his pocket, Sidney and the police are convinced that he is the killer.

Billy is soon cleared after his cell phone records are searched. The search for the killer intensifies as the high school is closed and a citywide curfew is imposed. Sidney's friends convince her to attend a "quiet" get-together, which soon turns into a large, drunken party. The party is watched over by Deputy Dewey (David Arquette) and his new friend, Weathers. Sidney's friend Tatum (Rose McGowan) is murdered during the party, but the death goes unnoticed. When news arrives that the high school principal has also been murdered, most of the guests leave to view the scene of the murder. Sidney and Billy have sexual relations, and moments later, the killer appears and slashes Billy across the abdomen. Sidney and the killer engage in a protracted game of cat and mouse. In the course of this pursuit, the killer seriously wounds the deputy, the news reporter, and Randy, a horror movie fanatic who is one of Sidney's friends. He also kills a television cameraman.

The film climaxes with the revelation that Billy was not actually wounded but faked the attack and that he and his friend Stu (Matthew Lillard) have been working together as the masked killer. They disclose their plan to frame Sidney's father, who is found bound and gagged in the house. Billy admits that the pair had killed Sidney's mother a year before. Billy blames Sidney's mother for breaking up his parent's marriage, and Stu follows along with his friend's murderous plans.

While the two boys prepare to stage their elaborate ruse, which involves stabbing each other before they kill Sidney and her father to give the appearance of a multiple murder/suicide, Sidney slips away and turns the tables. As the two wounded murderers track her through the house, she kills Stu by pushing a television onto his head. Weathers, who was wounded, shoots and kills Billy while struggling with him. Moments later, as the survivors stare down at the body, Randy notes that at this point in a horror movie, the killer rises for one last scare. When Billy does lurch forward, Sidney shoots him in the head and says, "Not in my movie." The film ends with Weathers broadcasting her exclusive report on the night's events.

The plot of *Scream*, despite its intriguing twists and turns, offers very little innovation to the traditional slasher films derived from *Halloween*. The major addition to the traditional formula is the degree to which the film references other horror films. Jancovich contends that the film seeks to present itself as a "clever, knowing and ironic reworking of the slasher movie."[4] This self-referential style—the way that the film constantly works to remind audiences about the "rules" of a slasher film—is a crucial aspect of the film's overall aesthetic and of its popularity. However, the heavy reliance on the well-known conventions of earlier horror films has led some critics to dismiss *Scream* and its progeny. Wells, for instance, contends that *Scream*'s obsession with the rules of the genre affords the film only a limited cultural importance, and Humphries dismisses the film as "highly derivative."[5] These dismissals of the film—that it has little cultural relevance and that it is overly derivative—seem off target given the broader developments in American culture. By the mid-1990s, America had a uniquely postmodern cultural attitude, one that was simultaneously highly derivative and deeply aware of its own derivative status.

CULTURAL CONTEXTS

The term "postmodern" had bounced around academic circles since the 1970s, but by the mid-1990s it had begun to permeate the culture. Most Americans had only a limited grasp of what postmodern meant, but the term seemed to capture some sense that the world had changed. The spin of images that marked the media age seemed to be picking up velocity, and whatever firm foundation had once anchored the culture to sure principles or ideals seemed to have eroded, if not completely vanished. The yuppies' narcissistic, inward gaze had, it seemed, finally achieved its ultimate expression in the next American generation—a complete cultural implosion, out of which emerged a whirlwind of cultural texts. A new generation of Americans was emerging in the 1990s, a generation of young people who had grown up amid the narcissism and cynicism of the 1970s and who appeared to feel more comfortable with a computer than a newspaper. With the emergence of this so-called Generation X, a new form of horror was needed.

Postmodern America

The aesthetic styles of MTV, *The Simpsons*, and films such as *Blade Runner* (1982) are all described as postmodern as, at times, is the broader culture itself. Despite the ease with which this term has entered into our regular parlance, it continues to be a difficult concept to define. The notion of the postmodern and postmodernity is the topic of wide-ranging academic conversations and debates. For some, the ascendance of the postmodern—a cultural trend emerging in the aftermath of the Second World War and maturing in the 1980s—is a natural development in the trajectory of modern Western civilization, and for others it is a regrettable aberration.

The extent and intricacies of these discussions make it impossible for me to offer a concise summary, and for present purposes, such a comprehensive survey is unnecessary. To consider the ways that Craven's reconfiguring of the slasher film resonated with a new generation of American young people, it is important only to get a general sense of the contours of the culture that many would come to describe as postmodern. Towards this end, the general concept of "postmodern" can be conceived in three interrelated ways: as a cultural moment, as an aesthetic movement, and as a critical project.

To define the postmodern, it is important to begin with the modern. Modernity generally is conceived of as a historical period encompassing the first half of the twentieth century. More important than its temporal placement, modernity entailed an attitude towards the world. The modern perspective was based on a belief in the linear progress of society. Society was, in the modernist perspective, getting better. Technology was improving, people were learning more about our world, and economic and democratic structures were becoming more just and effective. In particular, modernity placed a great deal of faith in the notions of scientific progress—the accumulation of more and better knowledge—and in political emancipation—the freeing of the human potential. *The Thing from Another World* encompasses some of this modernist faith. While the folly of Dr. Carrington almost destroyed the group, it was, ultimately, one of the scientists who devises the plan to kill the marauding alien with electricity. Also, while the group might have fallen to pieces in the face of the great threat to humanity from the unemotional invading creature, the group maintained faith in itself and survived.

The French philosopher who helped to introduce the cultural concept of postmodernity, Jean-François Lyotard, defined postmodernity as "an incredulity" towards these broad notions of progress and emancipation.[6] Across the western world, in other words, people became increasingly skeptical of the progress of science and the emancipation promised by governments and politicians. Western civilization began to lose faith. This is not to say that science or politics were openly rejected but to say that the cultural tendency was moving towards a skeptical lack of faith. This general drift away from modernist faith has been evident in the history of horror films traced in this book thus far. Since Hitchcock, the tendency of horror films has been more to explicitly engage the cynical, at times paranoid, condition of a culture that felt bereft of foundations or certainty. In a way, each of these post-*Psycho* films has attempted to grapple with the difficulties of living in a world without such cultural faith or, in other words, to grapple with the growing postmodern cultural tendency in American life.

A second aspect of the broader cultural drift towards postmodernity was its unique aesthetic style. The aesthetics of postmodernity are best depicted in examples from television such as MTV or *The Simpsons*. While MTV began as an outlet for popular music videos, it has become a cultural entity all its own, and one of the facts of MTV that has drawn the most attention is its style of fast-paced editing. The MTV-style video is filled with a rapid succession of loosely related images, often in different visual styles and using varied film stocks. The artistic term for this is pastiche, a style that draws bits and pieces from other styles to form a kind of artistic collage of disparate chunks. The MTV style thrives on pastiche and adds to this artistic style a frenzied pacing that makes the aesthetic experience of the rapid succession of disjointed images more important than any sense of narrative coherence.

The Simpsons (1989–) embodies another important aspect of the postmodern aesthetic, intertextuality. The venerable cartoon sitcom fills each episode with a plethora of allusions to other cultural texts. These allusions to other cultural texts—hence the phrase "intertextual"—offer a sustained cultural parody. As Brian Ott and Cameron Walter note, "In each 30-minute episode, *The Simpsons* regularly incorporates fifteen to twenty parodic allusions, ranging from *Citizen Kane* (1941) and Michael Dukakis' 1988 presidential campaign to *Married with Children* (1987–1998) and the O. J. Simpson Bronco Chase."[7] Part of the fun in watching a show like *The Simpsons* is in attempting to keep up with the fast-paced allusions to other cultural texts. The show is, in a way, a kind of cultural trivia game in which the audience tries to connect the dots. The rapid pace and amazing variety of these intertextual references mean that even when an audience member is puzzled by one reference, another, perhaps more familiar, allusion is on its way. Watching becomes a kind of game, and this is an important aspect of postmodern aesthetics. The often-rapid mix of cultural images and ideas adds playfulness to the overarching skepticism of the postmodern attitude. Rationality, coherence, and progress may have broken down, but their failure also opens up a potential space for creative play with the irrational and incoherent.

The optimistic aesthetic of postmodernity plays into the final aspect of this cultural tendency, its critical edge. For many, particularly academic critics, the postmodern era is an important step away from the rigid optimism of the modern age. The 1950s, as many are quick to point out, is only an idyllic age in television reruns. For many of those living in that decade, America was rife with racism and sexism as well as the hysterical oppression of the Cold War. Postmodern critics contend that the apparent unity of the "golden American age" was built on the silencing of those who did not fit into its white, male, middle class image. In a melting pot, these critics point out, objects lose all their individuality and are melted into an amalgam. Postmodern critics pushed for the opening up of notions of "America" and "American history," and pushed the notions of multiculturalism as a way to embrace the fragmented nature of American culture and history. While many of these critical exchanges took place in the densely theoretical terminology of academics, this critical project reached out beyond the realms of education to impact on cultural, political, and economic realms.

Generation X

In 1991, Douglas Coupland's *Generation X: Tales for an Accelerated Culture* helped to coin the term that would stand in for the first post-baby boomer generation of Americans.[8] The generation born between 1965 and 1981 were not participants in the tumultuous sixties or the debauched seventies. Beginning to attain a mature identity at the end of the 1980s, Gen-Xers seemed an enigma to their political and culturally rebellious parents. *Time* magazine defined Generation X as having "few heroes, no anthems, no style to call their own. They crave entertainment but their attention span is one zap of a TV dial."[9]

Despite their seemingly enigmatic aimlessness, Generation X developed some generally accepted traits. Perhaps the most prominent of these traits was their antipathy towards the baby boom generation.[10] Gen-Xers perceived their parents' generation to be hypocritical in their nostalgia for a cultural revolution they, effectively, sold out for the profits of the Reagan era. The older generation had a similar distaste for the cultural tendencies of Generation X, which became "a Boomer metaphor for America's loss of purpose, disappointment with institutions, despair over the culture, and fear for the future."[11]

Unlike its politically incendiary predecessors, Generation X was largely perceived as uninterested in the world of politics and revolutions. Stephen Bennett and Eric Rademacher examined the political attitudes of Generation X and concluded, "Its members are, on balance, indifferent to public affairs, unlikely to vote or take part in other kinds of political activities, disinclined to follow media accounts of public affairs and generally uninformed about government and politics. In fact, a variety of evidence seems to indicate that apathy and disengagement are even more pronounced among Xers than among young people in years past."[12]

Generation X's political apathy seemed to come, in part, from its overwhelming cynicism. Members of this generation were characterized as adrift in a social anomie and filled with an abiding mistrust of others, especially those in power. William Strauss and Neil Howard observed in their book *Generations* that cynicism was no longer a function of age and experience but that skepticism had replaced idealism as the attitude of the young.[13] In a way, it is not surprising that Generation X evidenced a deep distrust of politics and government, having been raised during the increasingly contentious political era of the 1970s and 1980s. Generation Xers grew up in an era filled with unprecedented failures: Vietnam, Watergate, the OPEC oil embargo, the Iran hostage crisis, and "stagflation."[14] The cynical edge that was evident in the horror films of the late 1960s and 1970s had become the cultural norm, and Generation Xers began with the assumption that nothing was sacred and no one could be trusted. In this way, Generation X was perfectly adapted to the cultural terrain of postmodern America.[15]

Media Spectacles

In the early 1970s, Marshall McLuhan had become a popular public intellectual based on his innovative theories about the impact of media technology on culture.[16] According to McLuhan, "the medium is the message," meaning that the dominant form of media is more important for understanding culture than the content of cultural messages.[17] While McLuhan's theories and celebrity had faded by the mid-1990s, the expansion and impact of mass media, especially television, during the decade would offer his theories a great deal of support.

As suggested at the beginning of this chapter, media spectacles dominated the 1990s. In fairness, of course, the blurring of the line between reality and media spectacle had been occurring for years. The presidential election of Ronald Reagan, a former B-movie actor and president of the Screen Actor's Guild, added substantially to this blurring. The Reagan presidency was filled with cinematic images, from his Star Wars defense plan to "evil empires," and furthered the sense that the entire society was a media creation. The 1990s continued this trend. The Gulf War, for instance, was widely regarded as a made-for-TV war. Night-vision videos of bombing runs played continuously on cable television networks, and the overall image of the war was a masterful coup by the Pentagon public relations department. The war itself hardly seemed like a war—the sanitized images of smart bombs resembled video games.[18]

At the same time that the real world of politics and war seemed more like the special effects in a film, the growth of cable television and video-rental outlets was making films more readily available. During the 1980s, the dramatic expansion of VCR technology and the concomitant emergence of the videotape retail industry meant that films were increasingly available to a wider audience.[19] At the same time, the emergence of cable television meant that most American households could access a growing number of specialized movie and entertainment channels. Generation X was the first generation to have a wide array of media entertainment products at its immediate disposal.

During the 1980s and early 1990s, American culture was inundated with mediated entertainment, and simultaneously, cultural events began to resemble media events. The age of the media spectacle had begun, and Generation Xers were the first to live in an age so pervaded by mass-mediated images. In the postmodern pastiche of mediated images and motifs, a new generation embraced an age of fragmentation, incoherence, and cynicism.

READING *SCREAM*

The Silence of the Lambs resonated deeply with the maturing baby boomers who had thrilled to the punishing bogeymen of the slasher films. In *Silence*, those terrifying fantasies had been updated and placed within the same complicated world of sexual and professional politics in which the boomers found themselves. While *Silence* was, undoubtedly, popular among members of the younger generation, its deeper messages were not meant for them. Generation X was far too familiar with the odd mix of 1980s slasher films and cable-televised trials of real serial killers. The cynical, media-savvy Generation Xer faced a world where nothing was real and everything was a fast-paced spectacle. They were too jaded to be frightened by the same old knife-wielding psychopath and the same sexually repressive rules. Or so they thought.

Boomers versus Generation X

While *Scream* is heavily dependent on the boomer-era slasher film in its plot and tone, the film takes pains to accentuate the division between the two generations. Many of the adult characters give voice to the pervasive criticism of Generation X. First, Generation X is portrayed as enigmatic to the older generation. When asked whether he believes young Billy Loomis capable of the murders, the sheriff exclaims, "Twenty years ago I would've said not a chance. But these kids today, hmm, damned if I know." Twenty years before the events of the film would have placed it squarely in the mid-1970s, precisely the period in which the boomer slasher film emerged. While Michael Meyers and many of his brethren were in fact young people, they were monstrous aberrations. The sheriff's condemnation, echoing the thoughts of many older Americans, encompasses the entire younger generation.

If the sheriff expresses uncertainty about Generation X, the high school principal, played by former *Happy Days* star Henry Winkler, gives strong voice to the most negative stereotypes about the youth. Chastising students for wearing the "ghost face" masks to school for a prank, the principal shouts, "You make me so sick. Your entire havoc-inducing, thieving, whoring generation disgusts me." This portrayal of a chaotic and immoral generation might describe many generations, so the principal offers a clear explanation of the real problem with this younger generation. They are, the principal explains, "heartless, desensitized little shits." If the first description points to the generation's destructive lack of direction, the second notes the reason they are so dangerous. Desensitized by endless hours of mediated violence, Generation X has lost any perspective on limits or decorum.

Many of these criticisms seem accurate given the actions of many of the young people in the film. Of course, Billy and Stu embody the sense of a dangerous, desensitized generation. Yet, even beyond these two, the young people of *Scream* are portrayed as insensitive and callous. In a telling scene that occurs immediately after the principal's condemnation, two girls enter a bathroom where the traumatized Sidney, having just survived the first attack by the killer, is hiding. The two begin criticizing Sidney, conjecturing that either she made up the attack story for attention or that Sidney herself is the killer, driven by anger over her mother's death and jealousy for Casey's boyfriend. One of the catty girls asks the other, "Where do you get this shit?" The other explains, "Ricki Lake."[20] Interestingly, virtually none of the young people express even the slightest mourning over the death of Casey and Steve or genuine concern for Sidney.

While the younger generation is portrayed as desensitized and callous, the older boomer generation does not fare better. Typically, the police are largely ineffective, and the only officer who plays any real role in the developing plot is the twenty-five-year-old Deputy Dewey. Weathers, the news reporter, does help stop the killers, but it is clear throughout the film that her real motive is the fame and fortune that might come from an exclusive story.

Unlike the earlier generation of slasher films, parents do play a role in *Scream*, albeit an ambivalent one. Some parents are portrayed in a sympathetic light. The shock and grief of Casey's parents in the opening moments of the film seems genuine and moving, but parents also play key roles in the horror of the film. Billy's father, for instance, seems largely unconcerned about the possibility that his son has committed murder and more interested in the inconvenience of the police interrogation. More importantly, Sidney's parents become an intimate part of the film's plot. While her father is ultimately revealed as a victim of the murderous pair, through much of the film he is used as a believable red herring. The film exploits the willingness of its young audience to imagine the murderous rage of a psychotic, grieving father.

A more important role is played by Sidney's mother, Maureen Prescott. Ultimately, Maureen's sexual promiscuity is the cause of the film's events. Her affair with Billy's father led to the divorce that so traumatized the young killer, and her seduction of Cotton Weary leads to his unfair imprisonment. Even though she dies a year before the events of the film, Maureen's presence haunts the proceedings. In a telling scene, Sidney confesses her fears about the role models provided by the older generation to Billy, "I'm really scared that I'm going to turn out just like her." The promiscuous mother stands in for the hypocrisy of the baby boomers who engaged in wildly rebellious behavior as youths but now look on with condemnation at the recklessness of their children.

Media/Reality

Perhaps the most noticeable aspect of *Scream* is the blurred line between media spectacle and reality. Media and media technology is pervasive, and the characters within the film are acutely aware of the mediated nature of their situation. Like most Gen-Xers, the young characters are surrounded by technologies of communication. Telephones and the relatively recent innovation, cellular telephones, play a prominent role in the film, as do televisions, VCRs, and even the computer, which Sidney uses to call 911 and escape the killer. As the film progresses, however, the line between spectacle and reality becomes increasingly blurred.

The first blurring occurs at the level of the mutual influence between the young people and the media. Clearly, the killers are heavily influenced by the mass-mediated depictions of slashers and use their knowledge of scary movies as models for their crimes and as a mode of torture for the victims who are forced into the deadly trivia game. As Stu explains their method of murder late in the film, "watch a few movies, take a few notes."[21] On the other hand, it is clear that the young killers also have an enormous influence on the media. The morning after the initial killings, television reporters clamoring for a story swarm the high school. The media reporters and the killers are, in a way, symbiotic. The killers seek out the media attention, staging their murders in spectacular, almost artistic ways so as to draw attention, and in turn, the news reporters seem to hope for more carnage. When the deputy explains that the killer is not yet a serial killer because there haven't been enough deaths, Weathers says, "Well, we can hope can't we."

A deeper relationship between the media and the killings becomes clear as the film progresses. Most of the characters begin to display a kind of self-conscious realization that they are, indeed, in a formulaic slasher film. Randy, the video store clerk and movie fanatic, is the epitome of this self-consciousness. Randy insists that the plot itself is obvious, "There's a formula to it! A very simple formula!" It also is Randy who explains the rules of the horror film: (1) sex equals death, (2) drugs and alcohol lead to death, and (3) never say "I'll be right back." For the most part, these simple rules play out within the film. Soon almost all the participants, including killers, victims, and pursuers, are aware that they are following along with the well-worn generic rules of a slasher film. However, in spite of their hip self-consciousness and media awareness, most of these characters succumb, in one way or the other, to the rules of the genre.

By the film's climax, the thin line between media and reality is not merely permeable but has imploded, and the two realms have become indistinguishable. This intermeshing of mediated violence and reality are evident in two telling scenes near the end of the film. As Deputy Dewey enters the house seeking the killer, a video of *Halloween* plays in the background. As the deputy moves through the house, the soundtrack of Carpenter's film becomes the soundtrack for Dewey's movements. The line between the videotape and the real crime scene become indistinguishable.

This blurring is even more complicated in an earlier scene, which deserves some careful delineation. As Randy, now alone, watches the final moments of *Halloween*, we notice the killer lurking behind him. Randy cries out to the television screen, "Jamie, behind you!" The levels of blurring in this moment are remarkable. Randy calls out a warning to the television image of Jamie Lee Curtis that echoes what the audience wants to shout to him. To add to this complication, the actor portraying Randy is the well-known Jamie Kennedy, so the character Randy is calling out to "Jamie" to turn around and avoid the killer. Adding another layer to this, we re-view the scene through a hidden camera, surreptitiously placed in the house earlier by Weathers. The camera, however, has a thirty-second delay, so we watch the scene again but this time through the monitor in the television news van along with the cameraman and Sidney. As these characters shout for Randy to look behind him—just as he shouts to

"Jamie" to look behind her—the end of the scene is finally revealed to us, the audience. The killer does not attack Randy but instead leaves the house to pursue Sidney. Only at this moment does the cameraman recall the thirty-second delay. Immediately, his throat is slashed, and the killer continues his pursuit of Sidney. In a way, this scene is the epitome of the film. Wrapped up in the mediated spectacle of the near-attack on Randy, the cameraman and Sidney imperil themselves. Ultimately, there is a great irony in that it is the cameraman, the ostensible purveyor of these spectacular images, who dies because he confuses the mediated image of violence with the real thing.

Sidney

Most of the characters in the film fall victim to the same confusion that kills the cameraman. Their self-conscious awareness that they are operating within the parameters of the slasher genre does little to spare most of them from death or, at least, severe wounding. The one person who doesn't succumb to the attacks of the killer is Sidney, and tellingly, she is also the one character in the film who blatantly refuses to be enmeshed within the formulaic rules. Only Sidney rejects the idea that her life has become confused with a film, insisting to Billy that "this is life, it isn't a movie." Of all the young people in the film, Sidney is the only one who takes the carnage seriously, mourning the deaths of Casey and Steve and refusing to take part in the callous joking about the crimes. While she is continuously victimized, often in small ways, her insistence on taking the events surrounding her seriously and refusing the ironic attitude of others saves her.

Sidney is, in many ways, the ultimate final girl.[22] She is the target of the killer and must survive a horrific gauntlet of torments to survive. However, unlike her predecessors Sally (from *Texas Chainsaw*) and Laurie (from *Halloween*), Sidney does more than run. She is a final girl who has learned the lessons of Clarice Starling and uses her strength and competence to fight back and refuse her positioning within the genre. Sidney, for instance, breaks the rules by having sex with her boyfriend but, in an important move, refuses the consequences. In the end she outsmarts the killers, who foolishly allow her to live while they celebrate their own cleverness, and turns the tables on them. She steals their cell phone and mask and begins stalking them. Sidney calls the police and then torments the two killers as they bleed from their self-inflicted wounds.

In the final struggle she kills both, and the means of their death is instructive. Stu dies when Sidney pushes a television set on his head, a moment of poetic justice for the killer who admitted to having no real underlying motive. In the end, Stu's confusion of televised violence and reality becomes literal. As Stu's death is the symbolic epitome of the media-confused youth of Generation X, Billy's death represents the defining moment of Sidney's refusal of this confusion. As the young killer lies, apparently dead, Randy articulates the rules of the final moment when the killer returns for one last scare. When Billy jolts back to life, Sidney calmly shoots him between the eyes. As she explains "Not in my movie," it is clear that Sidney has not only refused to be entangled in the violent confusion that has claimed the lives of her friends, but also that she has claimed ownership over her own story.

Sidney represents the real hope for Generation X. She refuses to fall into the battle against the older generation. In the end she unties her father, embraces her elders, and rejects the media driven world around her. Importantly, she also refuses to follow the lead of the older generation, rejecting her mother's pained efforts towards self-esteem.[23] In her refusal, Sidney becomes a powerful symbol of the final girl, a woman who rejects the murderous relations broadcast to her and refuses to be desensitized to the needs of those around her. In the end Sidney is saved not through knowledge of the genre— indeed, she professes distaste for slasher films—but by her own inner strength of character.

SCREAM'S LEGACY

In addition to reviving Wes Craven's career as a master of horror, *Scream* launched a short but intense revival of the slasher horror film. A sequel, filled with witty and self-conscious discussions of the cultural phenomena of repetitions and sequels, followed in 1997, appropriately titled *Scream 2*. In 2000, *Scream 3* appeared to round out the trilogy. Along with Craven's takes on the slick postmodern slasher film, a number of similarly themed and identically fashioned films followed close on their heels. Kevin Williamson, the screenwriter for the *Scream* films, branched out to write another slasher film populated by attractive young people, again played by former television stars, in *I Know What You Did Last Summer* (1997), which was followed by *I Still Know What You Did Last Summer* in 1998. Others followed: *Urban Legends* (1988), *Urban Legends: Final Cut* (2000), and *Valentine* (2001), to name a few.

Still, the rapidity of the postmodern horror film could not be sustained, and this version of the horror genre soon imploded under its own cynical, satiric façade. In 2000, the talented Wayans brothers played "Abbott and Costello" to the self-conscious slasher films in the highly successful *Scary Movie*, directed by Keenen Ivory Wayans. The postmodern parody would gross more than $150 million and launch two sequels, *Scary Movie 2* (2001) and *Scary Movie 3* (2003). The fine line between postmodern horror and postmodern humor had become completely blurred.

9 *The Sixth Sense* (1999)

"I don't want to be scared anymore."

Within a few years, the postmodern turn in horror films had played itself out. Tales of hip young characters outsmarting, or failing to outsmart, a masked killer had only a limited number of variations, and by the end of the 1990s, the horror genre was again considered moribund. However, 1999 was more than just the end of a decade or century; it was the end of the millennium. For many Americans 1999 represented more than just a change in the calendar. It represented a final moment, an end of what had been known, and the beginning of an unknown era. The twenty-first century had long stood as a mysterious age of the "future," and as America prepared to enter it, anxieties were high.

Considered in relation to the new millennium, the return of the horror film in 1999 should not be surprising, and neither should the form it took. A very traditional form of Gothic horror emerged into American theaters at the end of the twentieth century, in part as a reaction to the tongue-in-cheek, postmodern version of the genre, and in part as a reflection of the millennial anxiety that permeated American culture. The end of the millennium was haunted, haunted by ghosts from the past who demanded and received remarkable amounts of attention.

Two films, released within days of each other, marked this trend, and they shared several things in common. Both depicted fairly traditional ghost stories, both were from relatively new directors, and both were staggeringly successful. M. Night Shyamalan's third film, *The Sixth Sense*, grossed more than $290 million in its initial domestic release, and Daniel Myrick and Eduardo Sanchez's *The Blair Witch Project*, released in the same month as *The Sixth Sense*, grossed more than $140 million.

In many ways, *Blair Witch* is a fascinating case study of a culturally significant horror film. Much in the vein of Romeo, Hooper, and Carpenter, Myrick and Sanchez put together a skeleton crew and a group of earnest young actors and pieced together a largely improvised and realistic film about lost college students apparently pursued by ghostly spirits. The film opened in limited release but soon exploded into the popular culture. However, as much as there is to recommend *The Blair Witch Project* in this final chapter of the book, I will focus on only Shyamalan's *The Sixth Sense*. I make this choice for a few reasons. First, *Blair Witch* has already received a remarkable amount of attention.[1] Second, it is difficult to separate the film from the innovative and impressive marketing strategy, which made millions of people believe that the film was actual "found footage" of real events. The marketing strategy included an impressive Web site, recreated court and press documents, and a promotional television program aired on MTV. A third reason to attend to *The Sixth Sense* is that its version of Gothic fiction had a greater impact on subsequent films in this vein; *Blair Witch*'s driving gimmick, the presentation of the film as real, could not be easily repeated.

Additionally, of course, *The Sixth Sense* clearly meets the threshold of a cultural phenomenon. Filmed on a $55 million budget, the film featured Bruce Willis, cast against type as a frustrated child psychologist, and introduced Haley Joel Osment as his young patient. The film opened in August 1999 with a healthy though not staggering $26 million box office in its first week. However, in a manner similar to *Scream*, rather than seeing a considerable drop off for the next week, *The Sixth Sense*'s box office dropped only slightly. Word of mouth spread quickly, and the film's twist ending became a powerful lure to millions of Americans. Shyamalan's film maintained huge audiences for weeks and, beyond its financial success, soon permeated the culture. The film's popular catchphrase, "I see dead people," was commonly used as a punch line in late-night television talk shows and prime time sitcoms. Osment became a major Hollywood star, and Bruce Willis further cemented his reputation as more than just an action star. The film also launched the career of one of the few distinctive directorial voices of the twenty-first century. To date, M. Night Shyamalan has continued to direct interesting and well-received fantasies with twist-endings, including *Unbreakable* (2000), *Signs* (2002), and *The Village* (2004).

SYNOPSIS

The Sixth Sense opens with a light bulb illuminating a dark, cold cellar. A woman, the wife (Olivia Williams) of Dr. Malcolm Crowe, descends to retrieve a bottle of wine. Returning to her husband, the couple celebrates Dr. Crowe's (Bruce Willis) recent citation for outstanding work in child psychology. As they retire to their bedroom, they discover a break-in and find the intruder, a man stripped to his underwear, standing in their bathroom. The disturbed young man reveals that he is a former patient and that despite the doctor's promises, he was not helped. After a tense conversation, the young man shoots Dr. Crowe in the stomach and then kills himself.

The story shifts forward to fall as Dr. Crowe waits for his new patient, Cole Seer (Haley Joel Osment). Cole is an introverted young boy with few friends and strange habits. Despite a loving and devoted mother (Toni Collette), Cole is filled with fears and anxieties. The film proceeds with a series of conversations between Cole and Dr. Crowe in which Cole reveals more and more of his inner fear. These conversations are punctuated by scenes focusing on Cole's growing anxiety and alienation and scenes of Dr. Crowe's increasingly estranged relationship with his wife.

In a pivotal sequence, Cole is hospitalized after having a fit while locked in a closet at a friend's birthday party, and Dr. Crowe visits him in the hospital. In this conversation, Dr. Crowe tells the story of the young man who shot him and how he feels responsible for the tragedy. Cole also reveals his secret: that he "sees dead people," that he sees them all the time, and that they walk around like regular people, seeing only what they want to see. Initially, Dr. Crowe interprets this revelation as schizophrenia and believes Cole may need hospitalization. However, as Crowe's relationship with his wife deteriorates, he decides to transfer Cole to another doctor. Cole reacts badly to this news and is even more disturbed to find that Dr. Crowe does not believe him. In the midst of his guilt over failing another young patient, Dr. Crowe notes the similarity in the two cases, and returning to the earlier case file, finds evidence that both young men were actually visited by undead spirits.

At this point, the audience begins to see the world through Cole's point of view and observe the undead spirits who haunt the boy throughout his daily life. Eventually, Dr. Crowe suggests that these spirits may want something and that the best way to get them to leave is to find out what these needs are. Cole is visited by another spirit, a young sick girl, and fights back his fear to find out what the girl needs. Cole and Dr. Crowe then attend the girl's wake. While there, Cole slips into the dead girl's bedroom where the spirit gives him a box containing a videotape. Cole gives the tape to the young girl's father, who watches it and discovers that the mother was poisoning the young girl with cleaning fluids to keep her sick.

The revelation of the ghost's purpose frees Cole from his anxieties, and we later see him as the star in the school play, where his makeup job is attended to by another dead spirit. Cole and Crowe bid each other farewell, and Cole goes on to reveal his secret to his mother, passing on a poignant message of love and reconciliation to his mother from his grandmother. Dr. Crowe returns to his wife, and talking with her while she is asleep, apologizes for his absence. In this conversation, he realizes that his relationship has not been estranged but that he himself is a ghost, having died in the shooting incident at the film's beginning. After reconciling with his wife, Dr. Crowe says his goodbye and the film fades to white. An image of the couple's wedding appears briefly and the film ends.

CULTURAL CONTEXTS

Writing less then five years after the release of Shyamalan's popular ghost story, it is impossible discern the complex web of events and issues that were, and probably still are, affecting American culture. Therefore, in this section I will attend to only one broad and pervasive cultural movement that would help set the stage for the overwhelmingly positive reception of *The Sixth Sense*: the millennium. In 1999, the end of the twentieth century was imminent, and in this context the country was forced to consider its position in relation to its past and its future.

Millennial America

Even in modern, technological American society, religious conceptions of the end of the world continued to be prominent, and the eschatological beliefs of many Christians involved a relationship between the end of the world and the millennium.[2] In various readings of the Biblical book of *The Revelation of Saint John the Divine*, the final return of Christ is related to the notion of a millennium. For some this millennium occurs before the return of Christ, and for others the millennium is a period in which Christ reigns on earth before the final conflict that signals the end of the world. The coming end of the millennium, thus, added a direct impetus to these millennial beliefs about the apocalypse. The inevitable countdown to January 1, 2000, gave the religious convictions and concerns a greater rhetorical emphasis.[3]

Adding to the change in the calendar was a growing fear concerning America's considerable technological infrastructure. In 1992, a Canadian computer scientist named Peter de Jager observed a potentially devastating problem in the lines of code used in millions of computers.[4] To save time and effort, computers had been programmed to use only the last two digits to indicate the year. Logically, it was possible that these computers would then record accounts opened in 2001 as having been opened in 1901. This programming glitch was soon dubbed the "Y2K Bug," and predictions of its potential effects ranged from disabled financial institutions and failures of essential infrastructure services to the utter collapse of modern society. As Michael Barkun noted, "Y2K has functioned as a lightning rod with which free-floating millennial anxiety are discharged."[5]

By 1999 "millennial madness" was reaching a peak, and millions of Americans were purchasing generators, bottled water, firearms, and other survival implements. Some took the predictions of technological failure and spiritual rapture even more seriously, and various apocalyptic communities withdrew from society and into secluded encampments.[6] Predictions of an end appeared everywhere.[7] Just as in the 1970s, America was again wrapped up in narratives of the end.

All apocalyptic narratives, however, are not the same nor are the societies that are drawn to them.[8] Apocalyptic themes and anxieties appear in relation to specific cultural realities, and the narratives produced to express these themes and anxieties are crafted so as to fit these particular cultural realities. In this way, as Stephen O'Leary observes, the messages of "apocalyptic rhetoric" were fashioned in such a way as to address specific concerns and anxieties.[9] The typical sense of apocalyptic narratives, and certainly the way these themes emerged in the mid-1970s, is that they address cultural feelings of disorientation and dissatisfaction. Apocalyptic narratives, in this typical sense, appear in relation to moments of social upheaval and disconnection.[10] Thus, the apocalyptic rhetoric in films such as *Night of the Living Dead*, *The Exorcist*, and *The Texas Chainsaw Massacre* were shaped by the deeply troubled times in which they were produced.

Apocalyptic Reconciliation

However, the 1990s were not the 1970s. The economy, generally speaking, was strong and there were no major, pressing global conflicts. The end of the Cold War at the beginning of the decade had been a momentous moment in American history. The fall of the Berlin Wall on November 9, 1989, precipitated the inevitable unraveling of Soviet hegemony, and by 1991 the Warsaw pact was dissolved. 1991 also saw the end of another oppressive system as South Africa dismantled apartheid, its legal system of racial segregation and repression. Around the globe, parties involved in long-standing conflicts were turning away from violence and seeking productive methods of engagement. For example, a treaty and power-sharing agreement was signed in Northern Ireland in 1998, and near the end of the decade the Israelis and Palestinians seemed on the edge of an unprecedented peace agreement. As much as there were horrific things that occurred in the 1990s, civil strife in Africa for instance, the general tone of the decade had been one of growth and peace. For many good reasons, Americans were largely optimistic.

The unique contours of American culture in 1999 required a different type of narrative response. The coming millennium sparked traditional concerns about the apocalypse, but as noted, the nation was not wracked by domestic or international strife. The earlier narratives of apocalypse as decay, degradation, and destruction did not fit with the broader cultural tone. The different sense of apocalypse that seemed to emerge at the end of the twentieth century was characterized by, as Mark Kingwell put it, "the unspectacular but essential virtue of hope."[11] Even the Biblical depiction of the end suggests that the final act of the apocalyptic drama is one of joyous optimism and a new beginning of an everlasting life. Interestingly, this climactic moment is symbolized through the union of marriage, the final reconciliation of humans and their creator.

Reconciliation was a vitally important cultural trend in the late 1990s. The efforts of South Africans to reconcile their long history of racial injustice through the Truth and Reconciliation Commission seemed to be a model for the world. Similar efforts were underway throughout Eastern Europe and in Northern Ireland. The essential question of reconciliation was, as Erik Doxtader put it, "how to recollect the past in the name of making the future," and in this way, the prominence of reconciliation at the end of the millenium made sense.[12] Faced with a momentous punctuation point in the long stretch of human history, people around the world began to contemplate the ways they might reconcile with their past and others in the name of crafting a more promising future. Reconciliation promised the potential to overcome the problems of the past, to transform the character of human relationships, and to build new forms of life. As O'Leary observed, "every End is an opportunity for a new beginning."[13]

READING *THE SIXTH SENSE*

Two narratives of millennial apocalypse emerged in the final year of the twentieth century and both used a traditional, almost classical, sense of the Gothic.[14] As discussed in chapter 1, Gothic fiction depicts the ways that the past returns to haunt the present. This confrontation involves the intermingling of two distinct worlds: the world of "day," the rational, natural world, and the world of "night," the realm of the irrational and supernatural. In Gothic literature, we are haunted by those things we have left behind. The past returns to us through the world of night and slowly invades the world of day. In staging this confrontation between the rational and irrational— between day and night—Gothic art serves as a way for its audience to reconcile itself to change and instability. As Charlene Bunnell argues, Gothic art requires its audience to reconsider their own attitudes about what is considered normal, natural, or rational. This educational function is furthered by the reader's participation in the fiction.[15] The readers of Gothic fiction or the viewer of such film is drawn into the mystery and must struggle to find their own explanation for the inexplicable events. It is, in other words, not merely a matter of identifying with the characters as they encounter mysterious Gothic events but also an active effort on the part of audience members to discern the Gothic secret.

Blair Witch, of course, is deeply Gothic in tone and presentation. The film clearly uses a Gothic format in which a mysterious spirit of the past haunts the present. The film was marketed as "true events" recorded on film and videotape and subsequently found, a trick used in Gothic literature as far back as *The Castle Otranto* (1765). This "found" quality of the film worked as more than just an illusion of truth but also required the audience members to participate in "filling in the gaps" in the fragmented film. We are shown very little in *Blair Witch*, and there is no narrative framework that explains the events of the film. With *Blair Witch*, what you see is what you get, and the viewers are required to bring their intellectual, cultural, and emotional senses to the experience of the film. In *The Blair Witch Project*, of course, the three young filmmakers succumb to the violent spirits of the past and are lost forever in the labyrinthine woods. In Meyer and Sancez's narrative, the protagonists are unable to reconcile themselves to the legends of the past or to each other and are, thereby, doomed. This version of apocalyptic narrative is strikingly similar, at least in tone, to the line of apocalyptic horror emanating out of *Night of the Living Dead*.

Shyamalan's *The Sixth Sense* is also an overtly Gothic film. The spirits of the past return to haunt the present, and while the film does not present itself as real in the way *Blair Witch* did, the film is presented in a straightforward and serious tone. In this way, the Gothic films of the end of the 1990s had a markedly different tone than the tongue-in-cheek, self-conscious slasher films of the mid-1990s. Yet, while *The Sixth Sense* and *Blair Witch* share a number of Gothic elements, they differ substantially in their attitude towards the Gothic. Where *Blair Witch* perpetuates the chaotic, destructive sense of apocalypse that permeated the horror films of the 1990s, *The Sixth Sense* provides a more optimistic sense of the end— a vision of apocalyptic reconciliation.

Known and Unknown

At the most obvious level, all Gothic fiction is about the tension between the known and the unknown. Shayamalan's film offers a clear visual sense of the encounter between known and unknown in its opening moments. After the credits have rolled, the dark screen is slowly illuminated by the glowing filament of a light bulb. As the camera pulls back from the glowing bulb, we see a woman descending into a basement where she selects a bottle of wine. The sequence is archetypal Gothic tension. The image of a beautiful woman descending into a dark, cobweb-filled basement helps to establish a fairly clear Gothic tone for the subsequent film. The slow and unsteady light of the bulb foreshadows the subsequent plot. Additionally, the glowing bulb helps to clarify the depth of the darkness that surrounds it. As the woman descends into the basement, it is the light of the bulb that casts lingering shadows in such stark contrast. As the woman retrieves the bottle, she looks over her shoulder and pulls her shawl more tightly around her shoulders. Her attitude is clearly one of foreboding

The play of shadow and light continues as a motif throughout the film. A prominent example occurs a few minutes into the film in the pivotal scene in which Dr. Crowe is shot by his former patient, Vincent. As Dr. Crowe and his wife enter their bedroom, their mood is celebratory and frisky. The mood changes dramatically as they discover a shattered window and overturned nightstand, and their fears are confirmed as a shadow passes across the room. In this moment, the direction of the film is established. The shadow of the past—which we later learn is Vincent—has returned to haunt Dr. Crowe. In the conversation with Vincent, the encounter of known and unknown is even more explicit. The clearly disturbed young man accuses Dr. Crowe, "You don't know so very much." As Dr. Crowe struggles to remember who the young man is, Vincent repeats his accusation that Dr. Crowe's promise to help, contingent upon the doctor's knowledge, had failed.

In a familiar theme, *The Sixth Sense* suggests the limits of human knowledge. Just as with *Dracula* and *The Exorcist*, scientific knowledge is confronted with the unknown and is found wanting. Dr. Crowe failed Vincent because he was unable or unwilling to embrace the unknown. Armed with only his psychiatric knowledge, Dr. Crowe could not overcome the mysterious of the nocturnal world. As Dr. Crowe encounters Cole, he is still wrapped within his psychiatric knowledge and unable to reach the young boy. His struggle to understand the boy parallels the audience's efforts to understand the film. Interestingly, while we see Cole's reaction to his haunting experiences, it is only after he has confessed his secret to Dr. Crowe that we first see the ghosts through Cole's eyes. At the moment Cole utters his famous phrase, "I see dead people," our eyes are opened to the unknown, and so, as Cole returns to his home, we begin to see the dead people who haunt the young boy.

Dr. Crowe, however, continues to be wrapped up in his psychiatric knowledge and initially diagnoses Cole's confession as a sign of childhood schizophrenia. As Cole's encounter with the unknown pulls him further away from Dr. Crowe's "knowledge," the two become alienated from each other, and the doctor decides to abandon the troubled boy. At this point, our protagonists are divided by the chasm between the world of the known and the unknown, and the resolution of the plot requires an effort at reconciliation between these two worlds. As Dr. Crowe laments the alienation between Cole and himself, he returns to his past and revisits the case of Vincent Grey, the boy who shot him. It is in turning to the past that Dr. Crowe finally reconciles himself to the unknown, and it is this reconciliation that allows him and Cole to resolve the plot.

The film's eventual twist ending is also driven by this encounter between the known and unknown. Only after Dr. Crowe has reconciled the known and unknown for Cole is he able to embrace his own death. Ultimately, Dr. Crowe is another spirit coming to Cole for help. In his dramatic confession, Cole establishes the rules: the dead are everywhere, they don't see each other, and they don't know that they are dead. At its core, the problem of both the living and the dead is their inability to reconcile the known and the unknown, and this problem is only resolved as Cole and Dr. Crowe learn to embrace the unknown and thereby find peace.

Past and Present

The very notion of a haunting suggests a conflict between the past and present. The underlying premise of *The Sixth Sense* is driven by this sense of conflict as we learn that Cole is haunted by spirits who seek his help in accomplishing some unfinished business. So, just as Vincent returns from Crowe's past to trouble him, so too Cole is troubled by the past. Only by reconciling the past and present can either character achieve some level of peace in his life.

The film is driven by an underlying confusion about time.[16] Dr. Crowe explains his lateness to his wife, "I just can't seem to keep track of time." The temporal confusion, the blurring of past and present, is more pervasive than he realizes at that moment, and it is this inability to reconcile past, present, and future that drives the film. The intrusion of the past into the present lies at the heart of this confusion. The spirits of *The Sixth Sense* intrude into Cole's life in the same way that unbidden memories intrude upon our lives. Memories of the past carry with them not only that strange juxtaposition of present and past but also bring an inherent sense of loss. Whether memories of joyous events or grievous moments, the act of remembering is always an experience of the distance between

where we are now and where we were then.[17] We are always separated from the things, events, or people we remember, and it is this
sense of separation that lies at the heart of the film's temporal confusion. Cole's separation from the phantoms creates his fear and alienation, and Dr. Crowe's separation from his wife is created from his
own ghostly existence. Only in reconciling themselves to this separation, in bridging the gap of memory through an act of faith and
selfless love, can Cole and Crowe attain peace.

In this way, it is telling that the central relationship in the film is
between the older Dr. Crowe and the young boy, Cole. This relationship lies in stark contrast to the antagonist relationship between
generations that was a central part of recent horror films such as
Scream. Discussing his citation from the city early in the film, Dr.
Crowe's wife describes his work as teaching "children to be strong,"
and in this way there is a reconciliation of generations at work in
the film. Dr. Crowe, who has no children himself, takes on a parental role for his clients, teaching the younger generation to be strong,
but his relationship to Cole is mutually instructive. In helping Cole
reconcile himself to the spirits who haunt him, Dr. Crowe is reconciled to his own loss.

Individual and Community

Dr. Crowe and Cole are connected not only in their fear of the
unknown and intertwined fates but also in their mutual feelings of
alienation. Other than in the opening sequence, Dr. Crowe never
interacts with any character except for Cole. In a number of scenes—
as he sits with Cole's mother, with the emergency room doctor, at
both school plays, in the young girl's funeral, and in various scenes
with his wife—Dr. Crowe is seen with other people but has no connection to them. While this disconnect is explained in the end by
Dr. Crowe's spectral nature, through the course of the film it reinforces a sense of his abiding alienation.

This sense of isolation and alienation is even more poignant with
Cole. He is an outcast among his classmates, who make only a pretense at bonding with the young boy. His "friend" Tommy walks
him to school but only to appease his mother, and when Cole does
attend a birthday party he is tormented by two young boys who lock
him into a closet that, unbeknownst to them, contains one of the
haunting spirits. He is described by others as a "freak," a description he uses for himself. Cole's sense of his own alienation is

expressed in his continual insistence that people "not look at him in that way." His friends see him as an outcast, as do most of the adults in his life. When Cole recounts the horrific executions that occurred in the schoolhouse during an earlier era—the gruesome remnants of which we later see along with Cole—his teacher stares at him in a judgmental way. As the teacher stares, Cole shouts at him, "I don't like people looking at me like that!" The ugly encounter ends with the teacher stammering at his young pupil, "Shut up, you freak!"

Cole's alienation from others makes his relationship with his mother all the more important. Indeed, it is the importance of this relationship that leads the young boy to keep his ghostly visitations a secret from her. As he explains to Dr. Crowe, "I don't tell her things ... because she doesn't look at me like everybody else and I don't want her to." Throughout the film Cole questions his mother's perception of him asking, "What are you thinking, mama?" And in each instance his mother maintains her love and support for him. The secret, however, begins to strain their relationship. In one of the film's more touching moments, the mother explains to Cole, "If we can't talk to each other we aren't going to make it." Cole's most intimate and important relationship can only be maintained and strengthened if he is able to resolve his conflict and become more open and honest with his mother, and in this way, the film's theory of reconciliation is made explicit. To avoid a breach in his relationship with his mother, Cole must reconcile the known with the unknown and the past with the present.

The importance of this theory is reinforced by the parallel story of Dr. Crowe. His relationship with his wife is in deep trouble in the aftermath of his shooting. In the several scenes shared by Dr. Crowe and his wife they never speak, and it is clear that this breach deeply troubles the psychiatrist. In the tense moments before Dr. Crowe finally is convinced to believe Cole's amazing claims, he is sure that the only way to save his marriage is to abandon the troubled young boy. "I haven't paid enough attention to my family. Bad things happen when you do that," he explains to Cole. Still, just as with Cole, Dr. Crowe cannot reconcile himself to his wife without bridging the chasm between his own past and his present. On one level, Dr. Crowe is so racked with guilt over his failure to help Vincent that he cannot reestablish an intimate relationship with his wife. Of course, by the end of the film we are able to add another level of complexity to this theory of reconciliation. In the final moments, he learns of his own death and must reconcile himself not only to his past failure with Vincent but also to the unknown realm that lies beyond death. Only in reconciling the known and unknown can Dr. Crowe find peace for himself and, ultimately, for his wife as well.

Where some Gothic films emphasize the deterioration of relationships as the central focus, Shyamalan's film is interesting in that it focuses on the promise of reconciliation. The film's parallel endings reinforce this message. Having accomplished his ghostly mission and passed the dead girl's message on to her father, Cole finally achieves a genuine connection to others. Cast in the lead of the school play by the teacher who shouted at him earlier, Cole is finally embraced by his classmates and achieves acceptance.

More importantly, Cole finally gains the courage to reveal his secret to his mother, as they are stuck in a traffic jam after an accident. In revealing his secret, Cole tests his mother's willingness to embrace precisely the elements with which he has struggled. As he explains that he sees ghosts and that he can see the dead victim of the accident walking past, his mother must choose whether to accept the reconciled worlds of the known and unknown. Cole asks his mother, "Do you think I'm a freak?" She responds as she has to previous such queries, "I would never think that about you, ever!" Having chosen to accept the reconciled worlds of the known and unknown, Cole's mother is able to take the next step, reconciling the past and present. Cole describes the visits from his dead grandmother and passes on an important message from the estranged relative. Speaking from beyond the grave, the grandmother is finally able to express her love and admiration for her daughter. In the final moment of Cole's story, the various fragmented and alienated aspects of his life are reconciled.

The conclusion of Dr. Crowe's story provides a similar message. While the most dramatic element of this conclusion is the revelation that he is also a ghost, the more poignant aspect is his final reconciliation with his wife. As he speaks with his sleeping wife, he apologizes for his absence and can finally make peace with what we now understand to be his grieving widow. A videotape of their wedding plays in the background, and it is clear that both Dr. Crowe and his wife must reconcile themselves to their past, and their loss, in order to move forward. Crowe tells his wife, "I think I can go now. I just needed to do a couple of things, I needed to help someone, I think I did. ... I love you. You sleep now, everything will be different in the morning." Then as the screen fades to white, a final image of the newlywed couple embracing appears momentarily. At the film's end, the past with all its pain, loss, grief, and crimes has been reconciled to the present and from this reconciliation a new future can begin.

THE SIX SENSE'S LEGACY

In addition to sparking the career of M. Night Shyamalan, whose capacity for telling tales of the unknown has made him the next Rod Serling, *The Sixth Sense* spawned a number of similarly toned films. Among those films that launched the new millennium's return to Gothic horror were: *A Stir of Echoes* (1999), *What Lies Beneath* (2000), *The Others* (2001), and *The Ring* (2002). As America entered into the new millennium, a very traditional version of Gothic horror seemed to resonate most clearly with the strange experience of entering a new era.

The resurgence of Gothic horror at the turn of the millennium should not be surprising. American horror has always been about what lies lurking just beyond the boundaries of vision and normalcy. When American horror emerged in 1931, the creature lying at the edge of civilization was the seductive embodiment of chaos, Dracula. As horror moved closer and closer to the everyday lives of Americans, that chaotic horror evolved and transformed to match the anxieties of its day, but as Americans stood poised at the end of one age, another was dawning. The Gothic reconciliation offered in Shyamalan's film and picked up by a number of imitators offered not only a way to resolve the problems of the past but also a way to enter boldly into the future.

Conclusion

As I write these final pages, the American horror film has fallen back into one of its periods of slumber. A number of horror films have been released in the twenty-first century ranging in quality from excellent to dismal, but none have captured the attention of the wider culture. Horror is, once again, a moribund and all too predictable genre. Perhaps adding to this sense, or coming from it, has been the latest trend in horror films, the remake. In 1999 Joel Silver and Robert Zemeckis formed Dark Castle Entertainment, inspired by the works of William Castle, the master of gimmicky filmmaking in the 1950s and 1960s, and began producing remakes of his horror films. Their remake of *House on Haunted Hill* appeared in 1999 and *Thirteen Ghosts* in 2001. 1999 also saw a remake of the 1963 film *The Haunting*. While these films were at the most adequate, their relatively low budgets made them profitable, and a bandwagon effect was created. In 2003, an utterly wretched remake of *The Texas Chainsaw Massacre* limped into theaters with much hype and nothing of the style or shock value of Hooper's original. A remake of Romero's *Dawn of the Dead* was released in 2004. While this film added a few new wrinkles—the zombies, for instance, ran instead of their usual slow lumbering—it gave up any sense of the political commentary in Romero's 1978 classic.

If any film showed the promise of creative remakes—or "reimagining" to use the contemporary buzz term—it was the 2002 British film *28 Days Later* directed by Danny Boyle. While not technically a remake, the film essentially boiled down the plots of all three films in

Romero's *Living Dead Trilogy* into one film. Boyle managed to add a number of new innovative twists—for instance, his zombies are victims of a designer virus called rage that drives its victims into a frenzied and highly contagious homicidal state—but also kept the political attitude of Romero's earlier films. Indeed, when I first saw *28 Days Later*, I believed that it might attain the same cultural status as the films discussed in the preceding chapters. Of course, as with most predictions about the future, I was wrong. The film was remarkably well made, chilling, relevant, and largely ignored by audiences.

Reflecting on this recent trend of unremarkable and ineffective remakes, it does not seem entirely surprising. The beginning of the twenty-first century seems a bit like a remake. Another George Bush is in the White House, America is again at war with Iraq, and a general sense of hysteria, fear, and paranoia have gripped the country, perhaps justified, perhaps not. In the "post–September 11" world, as we are prone to call it, horror films may have been muzzled for a time. Romero, for instance, reports that he was in negotiations to begin a fourth chapter of the *Living Dead Trilogy* in the days immediately preceding the terrorist attacks in New York, D.C., and Pennsylvania but that in the aftermath of these events the negotiations were ended.[1] In a climate racked with fears, some justified and some not, and where "terror" has become a point of great political energy, manipulation, and contention, perhaps allegorical terrors cannot suffice. The fears at large in the real world have been so magnified and intensified that for the time being Americans prefer their projected fears to be more tame and predictable.

If the history of the American horror film suggests anything, it is that around the time we imagine the fictional world of horror to be desolate, a new form of monster and a new variation on the familiar story will emerge. This next important horror film may come from a big studio or from a group of first-time, independent filmmakers; it may explode into theaters with a flurry of hype or creep across the country driven by word of mouth. In any event, if the trajectory holds true, another film will emerge to shock the nation. It will capture the spirit of the times, resonating with the underlying cultural conflicts and anxieties and making audiences writhe in their seats as their expectations are systematically violated.

The American horror film was, after all, born in the midst of social turmoil. As Americans stared into the encroaching abyss of economic, political, and global turmoil, they found projected there the seductive visage of embodied chaos, Count Dracula. In the intervening seventy-four years, the monstrous image came from many different places—the stars, the psyche, the devil—and in many different forms—the boy next door, a child, legions of the undead. In each appearance, American horrors spoke to the culture in ways uniquely relevant to that moment in time and in ways that could not have been predicted. These monsters, the ones that captured our collective imagination, came to confront us with our own fears, and in so doing, provided a useful space in which to reflect on these fears and our relationships to them.

No matter how dire the current state of horror films may seem, the genre has shown a remarkable capacity to transform itself and reconnect, no matter how irrelevant it may seem, to the cultural currents of the day. It is this adaptability, the ways that each film connects with its unique moment, that makes it impossible to make blanket statements about the politics or cultural implications of the genre. Taken as a whole, the horror genre is clearly about our general fears and anxieties, but each rendering of these elements has a distinct message and a unique potential to reflect our concerns back to us. From this perspective, each film must be understood individually in terms of the cultural moment with which it resonates and the expectations it violates.

The ten films examined in the preceding chapters certainly achieved this delicate balance of familiarity and shock, resonance and violation, and in so doing they each changed the direction of the entire genre. Perhaps the case could be made for other films to be included in this list. Over the course of this project a number of such additions have been recommended to me: *King Kong* (1933), Brian De Palma's *Carrie* (1976), Ridley Scott's *Alien* (1979), Stanley Kubrick's *The Shining* (1980), among others. These and many other films may, arguably, belong among the list of films that have captured America's collective imagination. My argument has not been so much for an exclusive list of great American horror films as for a list of films that was indisputable. Other films may belong among these ten, but it would be difficult to argue that any of these films do not merit their place on this list.

The history of the horror film, at least as I've tried to understand it, is as much about American culture as it is about film. These films emerge at particular points in time, and in my reading, it is their relationships to the cultural moments that has energized their reception. In this way, the successful, groundbreaking horror film tells us a great deal about the culture that reacts to it, about its fears and dreams, its anxieties and aspirations. Read in this way, the horror film is an important barometer for the national mood and an important cultural space into which citizens may retreat to engage and examine the tendencies in their culture and to make choices about how to interpret and react to them. In the final analysis, the lesson of the history of the American horror film is clear: the things that we fear, and the ways that we express this fear, tell a great deal about us.

Notes

Introduction

1. Robin Wood, "Gods and Monsters," *Film Comment* 12 (1978): 19.

2. Elizabeth Cowie, "The Lived Nightmare: Trauma, Anxiety, and the Ethical Aesthetics of Horror," in *Dark Thoughts: Philosophical Reflections on Cinematic Horror*, eds. Stephen Jay Schneider and Daniel Shaw (Lanham, MD: Scarecrow Press, 2003), 26.

3. James Naremore, "American Film Noir: The History of an Idea," *Film Quarterly* 49 (1995–1996): 14.

4. Andrew Tudor, "Genre," in *The Film Reader*, ed. Barry Grant (Austin: University of Texas Press, 1986), 7.

5. S. S. Prawer, *Caligari's Children: The Film as Tale of Terror* (New York: Oxford University Press, 1981), 69.

6. Edward J. Ingebretsen, "Monster-Making: A Politics of Persuasion," *Journal of American Culture* 21 (1998): 25.

7. Tzvetan Todorov, *The Fantastic: A Structural Approach to a Literary Genre* (Ithaca, NY: Cornell University Press, 1975), 64.

8. For more on Greenblatt's theory of "resonance" and "wonder," see his "Introduction," *Genre* 13 (1982): 3–6; *Learning to Curse: Essays in Early Modern Culture* (London: Routledge, 1990); and "Intensifying the Surprise as well as the School: Interview with Noel King," *Textual Practice* 8 (1994): 114–127. For a good review of this approach to reading films, see Noel King's "Hermeneutics, Reception Aesthetics, and Film Interpretation," in *Film Studies: Critical Approaches*, eds. J. Hill and P. C. Gibson (New York: Oxford University Press, 2000), 210–221.

9. James Ursini, "Introduction," in *Horror Film Reader*, eds. Alain Silver and James Ursini (New York: Limelight Editions, 2000), 5.

10. Prawer, *Caligari's Children*, 60.

11. See Morris Dickstein, "The Aesthetics of Fright," in *Planks of Reason: Essays on the Horror Film*, eds. Barry Keith Grant (Metuchen, NJ: Scarecrow Press, 1984), 65–78.

12. Paul Wells, *The Horror Genre: From Beelzebub to Blair Witch* (London: Wallflower, 2000), 3.

13. Cowie, "Lived Nightmare," 30.

14. Rhetorical theorist Kenneth Burke described literature as "equipment for living," suggesting the ways that fiction supplies us with symbolic resources for living in an ever-changing world. This argument has been skillfully applied to films, particularly horror films, by Barry Brummett. See his "Burke's Representative Anecdote as a Method in Media Criticism," *Critical Studies in Mass Communication* 1 (1984): 161–176; and "Electric Literature as Equipment for Living: Haunted House Films," *Critical Studies in Mass Communication* 2 (1985): 247–261.

15. My approach is best defined as rhetorical criticism, an approach to film best outlined by Thomas Benson and Carolyn Anderson in their *Reality Fictions: The Films of Frederick Wiseman* (Carbondale: Southern Illinois University Press, 1989), see esp. 26.

16. David Bordwell makes the point in his important *Making Meaning: Inference and Rhetoric in the Interpretation of Cinema* (Cambridge, MA: Harvard University Press, 1989). In this book, Bordwell urges film critics to curb their flights of interpretive fancy and attend more closely to the historical context, to have an "awareness of historically existent options" that an audience would use for interpretation as it enters the theater (p. 268).

Chapter 1: *Dracula* (1931)

1. Rosemary Jackson, *Fantasy: The Literature of Subversion* (London: Methuen, 1981), 118.

2. Reported in Mark Vieira, *Hollywood Horror: From Gothic to Cosmic* (New York: Abrams, 2003), 31.

3. Reported in David Skal, *The Monster Show: A Cultural History of Horror*, rev. ed. (New York: Faber and Faber, 2001), 116.

4. Vieira, *Hollywood Horror*, 29.

5. Skal, *Monster*, 116–117.

6. Reported in David J. Skal, *Hollywood Gothic: The Tangled Web of Dracula from Novel to Stage to Screen* (New York: W. W. Norton and Company, 1990), 144.

7. Vieira, *Hollywood Horror*, 35.

8. Joseph Maddrey, *Nightmares in Red, White and Blue: The Evolution of the American Horror Film* (Jefferson, NC: McFarland, 2004), 12.

9. Vieira, *Hollywood Horror*, 29.

10. Ibid., 30.

11. Alain Silver and James Ursini, *The Vampire Film: From Nosferatu to Bram Stoker's Dracula*, 2nd ed. (New York: Limelight Editions, 1994), 67.

12. For example, Roy Kinnard, *Horror in Silent Films: A Filmography, 1896–1929* (Jefferson, NC: McFarland, 1995), 1–2.

13. Bill Ong Hing, *Defining America through Immigration Policy* (Philadelphia: Temple University Press, 2004), 34.

14. These immigration laws drastically reduced immigration by establishing a quota system that was particularly stringent on Eastern European countries.

15. Michael LeMay, *From Open Door to Dutch Door: An Analysis of US Immigration Policy since 1820* (Westport, CT: Praeger Publishers, 1987), 71.

16. Donald S. Strong, *Organized Anti-Semitism in America: The Rise in Group Prejudice during the Decade 1930–1940* (Westport, CT: Greenwood Press, 1941), 14.

17. Naomi W. Cohen, *Jews in Christian America: The Pursuit of Religious Equality* (New York: Oxford University Press, 1992), 93.

18. Skal, *Monster*, 114.

19. John Flynn, *Cinematic Vampires: The Living Dead on Film and Television* (Jefferson, NC: McFarland, 1992), 30.

20. Wells, *Horror Genre*, 47.

21. George Mowrey, *The Twenties: Fords, Flappers, and Fanatics* (Englewood Cliffs, NJ: Prentice-Hall, 1963), 173.

22. Angela J. Latham, *Posing a Threat: Flappers, Chorus Girls, and Other Brazen Performers of the American 1920s* (Wesleyan University Press, 2000), 18–19.

23. Skal, *Monster*, 114.

24. Kinnard, *Horror in Silent Films*, 2.

25. For a vivid account see Skal, *Monster*, 44–47.

26. Jackson, *Fantasy*, 118.

27. Stephen D. Arata, "The Occidental Tourist: *Dracula* and the Anxiety of Reverse Colonization" in *The Horror Reader*, ed. Ken Gelder (New York: Routledge, 2000), 165.

28. Richard Wasson, "The Politics of *Dracula*," *English Literature in Transition (1880–1920)* 9 (1966): 24–27.

29. Arata, "Occidental Tourist," 171.

30. Judith Halberstam, *Skin Shows: Gothic Horror and the Technology of Monsters* (Durham, NC: Duke University Press, 1995), 92.

31. Roger Ebert, *Dracula* (2004), available at http://rogerebert.suntimes.com/apps/pbcs.dll/article?AID=/19990919/REVIEWS08/909190301/1023&template=printart.

32. Reported in Skal, *Monster*, 126.

33. Daryl Jones, *Horror: A Thematic History in Fiction and Film* (London: Arnold, 2002), 85.

34. Flynn, *Cinematic Vampires*, 39.

Chapter 2: *The Thing from Another World* (1951)

1. Richard A. Schwartz, *The 1950s: An Eyewitness History* (New York: Facts on File, 2003), 104.

2. Bill Warren, *Keep Watching the Skies: Volume I* (Jefferson, NC: McFarland, 1982), 151.

3. *Invasion of the Body Snatchers* (1954), *Robot Monster* (1953), *Forbidden Planet* (1956), and *The Blob* (1958).

4. Peter Bogdanovich, "Interview with Howard Hawks," in *Howard Hawks: American Artist*, eds. Jim Hillier and Peter Wollen (London: British Film Institute, 1996), 62.

5. Vieira, *Hollywood Horror*, 163.

6. Ibid.

7. Warren, *Keep Watching*, 54.

8. Patrick Lucanio, *Them or Us: Archetypal Interpretations of Fifties Alien Invasion Films* (Bloomington: Indiana University Press, 1987), 1.

9. Warren, *Keep Watching*, 2.

10. Stanley Sandler, *The Korean War: No Victors, No Vanquished* (Lexington: University Press of Kentucky, 1999), 227.

11. Sandler, *Korean War*, 230.

12. Ibid., 227.

13. Russel Earl Shane, *An Analysis of Motion Pictures about War Released by the American Film Industry, 1930–1970* (New York: Arno Press, 1976), 31.

14. Per Schelde, *Androids, Humanoids, and other Science Fiction Monsters: Science and Soul in Science Fiction Films* (New York: NYU Press, 1993), 94.

15. Peter Biskind, *Seeing is Believing: How Hollywood Taught us to Stop Worrying and Love the Fifties* (London: Pluto, 1983), 103.

16. Andrew Tudor, *Monsters and Mad Scientists: A Cultural History of the Horror Movie* (Oxford: Blackwell, 1987), 220.

17. James Darsey, *The Prophetic Tradition and Radical Rhetoric in America* (New York: NYU Press, 1997), 150.

18. Joseph Maddrey, *Nightmares in Red, White and Blue: The Evolution of the American Horror Film* (Jefferson, NC: McFarland, 2004), 30.

19. Hannah Arendt, *On Violence* (San Francisco: Harvest/HBJ Book, 1970), 18.

20. Mark Jancovich, *Rational Fears: American Horror in the 1950s* (Manchester: Manchester University Press, 1996), 19.

21. Richard Weaver, *The Ethics of Rhetoric* (South Bend, IN: Regnery/Gateway, 1953), 213.

22. Alan Nadel, *Containment Culture: American Narratives, Postmodernism, and the Atomic Age* (Durham, NC: Duke University Press, 1995), 14.

23. Nancy A. Nichols, "What Happened to Rosie the Riveter?" in *Reach for the Top: Women and the Changing Facts of Working Life*, ed. Nancy A. Nichols (Cambridge, MA: Harvard Business Review Books, 1994), 3.

24. Nancy Baker Wise and Christy Wise, *Women at Work in World War II* (San Francisco: Josey Bass, 1994), 168.

25. Mary P. Ryan, *Womanhood in America: From Colonial Times to the Present* (New York: Harper & Row, 1975), 83.

26. Brandon French, *On the Verge of Revolt: Women in American Films of the Fifties* (New York: Frederick Ungar, 1978), xxi.

27. W. T. Lhaman Jr. *Deliberate Speed: The Origins of a Cultural Style in the American 1950s* (Cambridge, MA: Harvard University Press, 1998), 7.

28. Lucanio, *Them or Us*, 12.

29. Vieira, *Hollywood Horror*, 163.

30. Robert Ray, "Classic Hollywood's Holding Pattern: The Combat Films of World War II," in *Howard Hawks: American Artist*, eds. Jim Hillier and Peter Wollen (London: British Film Institute), 190–191.

31. For more on this element see Lawrence H. Suid, *Guts & Glory: The Making of the American Military Image in Film* (rev. and exp.) (Lexington: University Press of Kentucky, 2002), 67.

32. Robin Wood, *Howard Hawks* (London: British Film Institute, 1981), 109.

33. Jacques Rivette, "The Genius of Howard Hawks," in *Howard Hawks: American Artist*, 27.

34. Wood, *Howard Hawks*, 186.

35. Naomi Wise, "The Hawksian Woman," in *Howard Hawks: American Artist*, 113–114.

36. Warren, *Keep Watching*, 51.

Chapter 3: *Psycho* (1960)

1. Raymond Durgnat, *A Long Hard Look at* Psycho (London: British Film Institute, 2002), 3.

2. Reported in Stephen Rebello's fascinating and comprehensive history of the film's production, *Alfred Hitchcock and the Making of* Psycho (London: Mandarin, 1990), 23. Much of the production history in this section is derived from Rebello's excellent book.

3. Ibid., 22.

4. Reported in Janet Leigh (with Christopher Nickens), Psycho: *Behind the Scenes of the Classic Thriller* (New York: Harmony Books, 1995), 99–100.

5. Robert Hatch, "Films," *The Nation,* July 2, 1960, 18.

6. Rebello, *Alfred Hitchcock*, 163.

7. Amanda Sheahan Wells, Psycho: *Directed by Alfred Hitchcock* (London: York Press, 2001), 8.

8. Robin Wood, *Hollywood from Vietnam to Reagan … and Beyond* (New York: Columbia University Press, 2003), 87.

9. Gary A. Tobin notes, "The period between 1950 and 1960 was the decade of greatest suburban expansion in American history." See Gary A. Tobin, "Suburbanization and the Development of Motor Transportation: Transportation Technology and the Suburbanization Process," in *The Changing Face of the Suburbs*, ed. Barry Schwartz (Chicago: University of Chicago Press, 1976), 106. For more on this movement see Dolores Hayden, *Building Suburbia* (New York: Pantheon, 2003).

10. In relation to these reasons for fleeing the city see Ernest Mower, "The Family in Suburbia," in *The Suburban Community*, ed. William Dobiner (New York: G. P. Putnam and Sons, 1958), 152; and David Reisman, "The Suburban Sadness," in Dobiner, *Suburban Community*, 397

11. Reisman, "Suburban Sadness," 375.

12. Roger Silverstone, "Introduction," in *Visions of Suburbia*, ed. Roger Silverstone (London: Routledge, 1997), 8.

13. Gary Cross, "The Suburban Weekend: Perspectives on a Vanishing Twentieth-Century Dream," in Silverstone, *Visions of Suburbia*, 109.

14. Ernest Mower observes that "much more of the time of both husband and wife tend to be spent in the home." Mower, "Family in Suburbia," 157.

15. Reisman, "Suburban Sadness," 387.

16. Cross, "Suburban Weekend," 111.

17. For more on this gender fluctuation see Reisman, "Suburban Sadness," 387; and Mower, "Family in Suburbia," 156.

18. Lynn Spigel, "From Theatre to Space Ship: Metaphors of Suburban Domesticity in Postwar America," in Silverstone, *Visions of Suburbia*, 221.

19. See Cross, "Suburban Weekend," 111 (for "rootless"); and Reisman, "Suburban Sadness," 377 (for "aimless").

20. Lynn Spigel makes this argument in relation to the growth of science fiction and interest in rocketry. See Spigel, "From Theater," 221.

21. Avi Friedman, *Planning the New Suburbia: Flexibility by Design* (Vancouver: UBC Press, 2002), 28–32.

22. Cynthia Golomb Dettelbach, *In the Driver's Seat: The Automobile in American Literature and Popular Culture* (Westport, CT: Greenwood Publishing, 1977), 119.

23. Spigel, "From Theater," 225.

24. See on this matter, Jancovich, *Rational Fears*, 220.

25. In particular, I would recommend Raymond Durgnaut's detailed reading of *Psycho*, *A Long Hard Look at* Psycho (London: British Film Institute, 2002); Tania Modleski's feminist analysis, *The Women Who Knew Too Much: Hitchcock and Feminist Theory* (New York: Routledge, 1988); William Rothman's highly detailed *Hitchcock: The Murderous Gaze* (Cambridge, MA: Harvard University Press, 1982); or Robin Wood's *Hitchcock's Films Revisited* (London: Faber and Faber, 1991). Additionally, readers interested in pursuing Hitchcock's vision of film would benefit from some of the following excellent autobiographies and interviews: François Truffaut's *Hitchcock* (New York: Simon and Schuster, 1967); Donald Spoto's *The Dark Side of Genius: The Life of Alfred Hitchcock* (New York: Ballantine, 1984); and Peter Bogdanovich's *The Cinema of Alfred Hitchcock* (New York: Museum of Modern Art, 1963).

26. Reported in Sheahan Wells, *Psycho*, 10.

27. Ibid.

28. Interestingly, this sequence was the first time a toilet was flushed on screen in American cinema.

29. James Naremore, *Filmguide to* Psycho (Bloomington: Indiana University Press, 1973), 20.

30. The voyeuristic aspects were commented on as early as 1968 in Leo Braudy's influential essay, "Hitchcock, Truffaut, and the Irresponsible Audience," *Film Quarterly* 21 (1968): 21–27.

31. This topic is taken up dramatically in Laura Mulvey's influential article, "Visual Pleasure and Narrative Cinema," *Screen* 16 (1975): 6–18.

32. J. P. Tellotte, "Faith and Idolatry in the Horror Film," in *Planks of Reason: Essays on the Horror Film*, ed. Barry Keith Grant (Metuchen, NJ: Scarecrow Press, 1984), 29.

33. Explicit terms referring to birds include "Phoenix" and "Crane." In addition, Norman says to Marion, "You sure eat like a bird," the conversation between Norman and Marion in the parlor is overseen by menacing stuffed birds, when Norman comes to clean up the murder scene he knocks a picture of a bird to the floor, and so on. Of course, it is also interesting that Hitchcock's next film was *The Birds* (1963).

34. On the connection between the editing of the shower murder and the means of murder, see Kaja Silverman, *The Subject of Semiotics* (New York: Oxford University Press, 1983).

35. I am not, of course, equating the audience's voyeuristic gaze with an actual murder but suggesting that the experience of Marion's fictional death is a symbolic assault on the audience in ways that other on-screen deaths are not.

36. Wells, *Horror Genre*, 75.

Chapter 4: *Night of the Living Dead* (1968)

1. Todd Gitlin, *The Sixties: Years of Hope, Days of Rage* (New York: Bantam Books, 1987), 407.

2. Quoted in Paul R. Gagne, *The Zombies that Ate Pittsburgh* (New York: Dodd, Mead and Company, 1987), 36.

3. Kevin Heffernan, *Ghouls, Gimmicks, and Gold: Horror Films and the American Movie Business, 1953–1968* (Durham, NC: Duke University Press, 2004), 219.

4. Interestingly, Romero worked as a production assistant on Hitchcock's *North by Northwest*. For this and many other fascinating facts about Romero and his films, consult Gagne, *Zombies*.

5. Roger Ebert, "Just Another Scary Movie?" *Reader's Digest* (June 1969): 127–128.

6. At the time of writing, industry news indicates that Romero has received funding for a fourth *Living Dead* film.

7. Reynold Humphries, *The American Horror Film: An Introduction* (Edinburgh: Edinburgh University Press, 2002), 113.

8. See Gagne, *Zombies*, esp. 21–40.

9. Interestingly, 1968 saw the end of the restrictive Production Code and the beginning of the MPAA rating system—to which *Night of the Living Dead*'s distributor, Walter Reade Organization, did not submit the film for rating.

10. Tom Shachtman, *Decade of Shocks: Dallas to Watergate, 1963–1974* (New York: Poseidon, 1983), 124.

11. Todd Gitlin reports that "more babies were born in 1948–54 than in the previous thirty years." Gitlin, *Sixties*, 13.

12. Reported in Shachtman, *Decade of Shocks*, 127–128.

13. Gitlin, *Sixties*, 213.

14. Irwin Unger and Debi Unger, *Turning Point: 1968* (New York: Charles Scribner's Sons, 1988), 6.

15. On this point, see Howard Brick, *Age of Contradiction: American Thought and Culture in the 1960s* (New York: Twayne Publishing, 1998), esp. chap. 7.

16. Gitlin, *Sixties*, 287.

17. Brick, *Age of Contradiction*, 163.

18. Stephanie A. Slocum-Schaffer, *America in the Seventies* (Syracuse: Syracuse University Press, 2003), 14.

19. Unger and Unger, *Turning Point*, 3.

20. David Rossinow, "'The Revolution Is about Our Lives:' The New Left's Counterculture," in *Imagine Nation: The American Counterculture of the 1960s and 70s*, eds. Peter Braunstein and Michael William Doyle (New York: Routledge, 2002), 99.

21. See Marilyn Young, "Foreword," in *Imagine Nation*, 3.

22. Excellent histories of the studio system are available in, *The American Film Industry*, ed. Tino Ballio (Madison: University of Wisconsin Press, 1985); and Thomas Schatz, *The Genius of the System: Hollywood Filmmaking in the Studio Era* (New York: Pantheon Books, 1988).

23. These various strategies are detailed in Heffernan, *Ghouls, Gimmicks, and Gold.*

24. Joseph Lewis, "A Bloody Laugh," *The Point*, February 26, 1970, 14.

25. It is interesting that *Dracula* and *The Thing* achieved prominence during times when upheaval was threatening, but that *Night of the Living Dead* achieved cultural prominence in the midst of such upheaval.

26. See Romero's discussion of the film in Gagne, *Zombies.*

27. Reynold Humphries reads this childish behavior much more deeply as indicative of a deep Oedipal complex between the brother and sister in Humphries, *American Horror Film.*

28. Wells, *Horror Genre*, 82.

29. Wood, *Hollywood*, 103.

30. R. H. W. Dillard, "*Night of the Living Dead*: 'It's Not Like Just a Wind That's Passing Through,'" in *American Horrors: Essays on the Modern American Horror Film* (Chicago: University of Illinois Press, 1987), 28.

31. Tudor, *Monsters and Mad Scientists*, 71.

32. For more on the apocalyptic overtones see Jane Caputi, "Films of the Nuclear Age," *Journal of Popular Film and Television* 16 (1988): 100–107.

33. For more on splatter films see Michael A. Arnzen, "Who's Laughing Now? The Postmodern Splatter Film," *Journal of Popular Film and Television* 21 (1994): 176–184.

Chapter 5: *The Exorcist* (1973) and *The Texas Chainsaw Massacre* (1974)

1. Quoted in Gunnar Hansen, "Foreword," in Stefan Jaworzyn, The Texas Chainsaw Massacre *Companion* (London: Titan Books, 2003), 10.

2. According to the always useful Internet Movie Database: http://www.imdb.com/title/tt0070047/trivia.

3. See, Jaworzyn, Texas Chainsaw Massacre *Companion*, 84.

4. For accounts of these hysterical reactions see, Mark Kermode, *The Exorcist* (rev. 2nd ed.) (London: BFI Modern Classics, 2003); and Paul West, *Laughing Screaming* (New York: Columbia University Press, 1995), 288–289.

5. Kermode, *The Exorcist*, 9.

6. *The Exorcist* was followed by a number of similarly themed films such as *Carrie* (1976), *The Omen* (1976), *The Amityville Horror* (1979), and *The Shining* (1980).

7. Tudor, *Monsters and Mad Scientists*, 175.

8. Carol Clover, *Men, Women and Chainsaws: Gender in the Modern Horror Film* (Princeton, NJ: Princeton University Press, 1992), 24.

9. Jones, *Horror: A Thematic History*, 43; and Christopher Sharrett, "The Idea of Apocalypse in *The Texas Chainsaw Massacre*," in *Planks of Reason: Essays*

on the Horror Film, ed. Barry Keith Grant (Metuchen, NJ: Scarecrow Press, 1984), 256.

10. Slocum-Schaffer, *America in the Seventies*, 168.

11. Ibid., 30.

12. For more on the paranoid tone of the 1970s, see David Frum, *How We Got Here* (New York: Basic Books, 2000), 37–53.

13. Slocum-Schaeffer, *America in the Seventies*, 169–70.

14. Arlene Skolnick, *Embattled Paradise: The American Family in an Age of Uncertainty* (New York: Harper Collins, 1991), 127.

15. Frum, *How We Got Here*, 160.

16. For more on the apocalyptic hysteria of the 1970s, see Frum, *How We Got Here*, 158–166.

17. For an interesting discussion of the history of apocalyptic vision in film, see Ian Christie, "Celluloid Apocalypse," in *The Apocalypse and the Shape of Things to Come*, ed. Frances Carey (Toronto: University of Toronto Press, 1999), 320–338.

18. James Berger, *After the End: Representations of the Post-Apocalypse* (Minneapolis: University of Minnesota Press, 1999), 7.

19. In terms of contemporary film, see Catherine Russell, "Decadence, Violence and the Decay of History: Notes on the Spectacular Representations of Death in Narrative Film, 1965 to 1990," in *Crisis Cinema: The Apocalyptic Idea in Postmodern Narrative Film*, ed. Christopher Sharrett (Washington, DC: Maisonneuve, 1993), 174.

20. See Russell, "Decadence, Violence and the Decay of History," 178; and Mary Wilson Carpenter, "Representing Apocalypse: Sexual Politics and the Violence of Revelation," in *Postmodern Apocalypse: Theory and Cultural Practice at the End*, ed. Richard Dellamora (Philadelphia: University of Pennsylvania Press, 1995), 109.

21. Disaster films, in particular, became popular in the 1970s, films such as *The Poseidon Adventure* (1972), *The Towering Inferno* (1974), *Earthquake* (1974), and *Airport 1975* (1974).

22. Sharrett, "Idea of Apocalypse", 261–262.

23. Thomas S. Frentz and Thomas Farrell, "Conversion of America's Consciousness: The Rhetoric of *The Exorcist*," *Quarterly Journal of Speech* 61 (1975): 40–47.

24. West, *Laughing Screaming*, 292.

25. Quoted in Jaworzyn, Texas Chainsaw Massacre *Companion*, 43.

26. Barbara Creed, *The Monstrous Feminine: Film, Feminism, Psychoanalysis* (London: Routledge, 1993), 34.

27. On this development in horror films of the seventies and eighties, see Tudor, *Monsters and Mad Scientists*, 70–71.

28. In this regard, *Texas Chainsaw* follows the lead of an earlier and equally controversial film, Wes Craven's *Last House on the Left* (1972).

29. See Kermode, *Exorcist*, 78–85.

30. The 1950s and early 1960s were filled with teen-focused creature features, such as *I Was a Teenage Werewolf* (1957) and *The Blob* (1958), and a handful of more contemporary films had engaged themes of dangerous children—such as *Bad Seed* (1956) and *Village of the Damned* (1960)—and of endangered youth, notably *Last House on the Left* (1972).

31. For more on this legacy, see West, 316–318.

32. For more on the shift from security to paranoia, see Tudor, *Monsters and Mad Scientists*.

33. Interestingly, in a recent DVD release of *Jason X* (2001), one in the long line of *Friday the Thirteenth* films, the viewer can choose to skip directly to each death scene and skip the largely superfluous plot.

Chapter 6: *Halloween* (1978)

1. Vera Dika, *Games of Terror: Halloween, Friday the 13th, and the Films of the Stalker Cycle* (Rutherford, NJ: Farleigh Dickinson University Press, 1990).

2. Interestingly, Carpenter himself adopts a similar explanation of the film. While he is dubious of the kind of "killer as repressed sexuality explanation," he does suggest that Michael is operating based on an incestuous, pseudo-Oedipal attraction to his slain sister. See Gilles Boulenger, *John Carpenter: The Prince of Darkness* (Los Angeles: Silman-Peters Press, 2001), 99.

3. The films of the 1970s, particularly the later years, dramatically display the tension between liberal hedonism and conservative paternalism. For more on the conflicted nature of 1970s American films see Peter Lev, *American Films of the 70s: Conflicting Visions* (Austin: University of Texas Press, 2000).

4. For more on the roots and growth of the disco lifestyle see Tim Lawrence, *Love Saves the Day: A History of American Dance Music Culture, 1970–1979* (Durham, NC: Duke University Press, 2003).

5. The connection between sexual liberation and feminism in the 1970s is more fully discussed in Frum, *How We Got Here*, 188–201.

6. Stephen Birmingham, *The Golden Dream* (New York: Harper Row, 1978).

7. Slocum-Shaffer makes the point, "'Narcissism' became a loaded word that expressed the sense of chaos and fragmentation that Americans felt." See Slocum-Shaffer *America in the Seventies*, 199.

8. On this point see Sheldon Waldrep, "Introducing the Seventies," in *The Seventies: The Age of Glitter in Popular Culture*, ed. Sheldon Waldrep (New York: Routledge, 2000), 3.

9. Frederick Jameson, *Postmodernism: Or, the Cultural Logic of Late Capitalism* (Durham, NC: Duke University Press, 1991), 296.

10. George Lipsitz, *The Sixties: From Memory to History* (Chapel Hill: University of North Carolina Press, 1994), 230.

11. For a good review of the rise of the religious right, see Dan Junas, "Report on the Religious Right in Washington State," Washington ACLU Web site, 1995, http://www.aclu-wa.org/issues/religious/3.html#3.0.

12. Peter N. Carroll, *It Seemed Like Nothing Happened: The Tragedy and Promise of American in the 1970s* (New York: Holt, Rinehart and Winston, 1982), 326–327.

13. For a comprehensive examination of the bogeyman and his cultural functions, see Marina Warner, *No Go the Bogeyman* (London: Vintage, 1998).

14. Warner, *No Go the Bogeyman*, 386.

15. For more on these and other horrifying figures of children's tales, see Warner, *No Go the Bogeyman*.

16. By the end of the 1970s, even the threatening figure of Dracula had been embraced as a humorous figure that fit perfectly into the disco culture in *Love at First Bite* (1979).

17. See the discussion of the Gothic tradition in Chapter 1.

18. For more on Carpenter's background see, Boulenger, *John Carpenter*.

19. See Clover, *Men, Woman, and Chainsaws*, 39–41.

20. Thus begins the infamous, "sex = death" formula that would dominate the American horror film for the next decade.

21. Hence Wes Craven's monster, Freddy, lurks in the shadows on "Elm Street."

22. Many critics have observed the importance of looking, or the gaze, in *Halloween*. On this see Clover, *Men, Woman, and Chainsaws*; and J. P. Tellotte, "Through a Pumpkin's Eye: The Reflexive Nature of Horror," in *American Horrors: Essays on the Modern American Horror Film*, ed. Gregory A. Waller (Urbana, IL: University of Illinois Press, 1987), 114–128.

23. See Boulenger, *John Carpenter*, 171.

Chapter 7: *The Silence of the Lambs* (1991)

1. Richard Tithecott, *Of Men and Monsters: Jeffrey Dahmer and the Construction of the Serial Killer* (Madison: University of Wisconsin Press, 1997), 3.

2. In my own reading, Mann's film is at least as interesting and provocative as Demme's *Silence*. However, where Demme's film is quick and highly accessible, Mann's is more contemplative and troubling. See my "Redeeming the Visual: Aesthetic Questions in Michael Mann's *Manhunter*," *Literature/Film Quarterly* 31 (2003): 10–16.

3. The story of *Silence*'s optioning is an interesting one. Dino DeLaurentis had, in optioning *Red Dragon* for the Mann film, also optioned all the subsequent novels with these characters. However, abysmal box office of Mann's film soured DeLaurentis on the sequel and he passed. Of course, after *Silence*'s unprecedented popular and critical success, DeLaurentis renewed his option for the Ridley Scott sequel *Hannibal* (2001) and the Brett Ratner prequel/remake *Red Dragon* (2002).

4. For more on Demme and his involvement on the film, see Michael Bliss and Melissa Banks, *What Goes Around Comes Around: The Films of Jonathan Demme* (Carbondale: Southern Illinois University Press, 1996).

5. Information on box office and production comes from Daniel O'Brien, *The Hannibal Files: The Unauthorised Guide to the Hannibal Lecter Trilogy* (London: Reynolds and Hearn, Ltd., 2002).

6. Amy Taubin, "Writers on the Lamb," *The Village Voice*, March 5, 1991, 56; B. Ruby Rich, "Writers on the Lamb," 55; and Judith Halberstam, "Skinflick: Posthuman Gender in Jonathan Demme's *The Silence of the Lambs*," *Camera Obscura* 27 (1991): 36–53.

7. Leonard Quart and Albert Auster, *American Film and Society* (3rd ed., exp. and rev.) (Westport, CT: Praeger Publishers, 2002), 130–131.

8. For more on Reagan's economic policies, see John A. Ferejohn, "Changes in Welfare Policy in the 1980s," in *Politics and Economics in the Eighties*, eds. Alberto Alesina and Geoffrey Carliner (Chicago: University of Chicago Press, 1991), 123–142.

9. Joseph Stiglitz, *The Roaring Nineties* (New York: W. W. Norton, 2003), 14.

10. Quart and Auster, *American Film and Society*, 130.

11. On this point, see Susan Faludi, *Backlash: The Undeclared War Against American Women* (New York: Crown Publishers, 1991), 229–256.

12. James Davidson Hunter, *Culture Wars: The Struggle to Define America* (New York: Basic Books, 1992).

13. Faludi, *Backlash*, 454.

14. Sheila Tobias, *Faces of Feminism: An Activist's Reflections on the Women's Movement* (Boulder, CO: Westview Press, 1997), 228.

15. Marsha McCreadie, *The Casting Couch and Other Front Row Seats: Women in Films of the 1970s and 1980s* (New York: Praeger Publishers, 1990), 15–30.

16. Philip Jenkins, *Using Murder: The Social Construction of Serial Homicide* (New York: de Gruyter Press, 1994).

17. Mark Selzer, *Serial Killers: Death and Life in America's Wound Culture* (New York: Routledge, 1998).

18. Philip Simpson, *Psycho Paths: Tracking the Serial Killer through Contemporary American Film and Fiction* (Carbondale: Southern Illinois University Press, 2000), 15.

19. On the abandonment of community, see Robert Putnam, *Bowling Alone: The Collapse and Revival of American Community* (New York: Simon and Schuster, 2001), 30–33, 252–258.

20. Miggs flings semen on to Starling. This "discourtesy" offends Lecter, who then "give[s] her a chance for what she wants most ... advancement of course."

21. Harris's version of Crawford includes more of his personal life (his wife's struggle with and eventual death from cancer) and hints at a more complex relationship with Starling. In Demme's version, Lecter suggests a more sexual aspect of Crawford's interest in Starling, but she dismisses this insinuation as something "Miggs would say."

22. Interestingly, the novel makes the female senator one of the antagonists, but this is downplayed dramatically in the film.

23. Roderick Hart, "Introduction: Community by Negation—An Agenda for Rhetorical Inquiry," in *Rhetoric and Community: Studies in Unity and Fragmentation*, ed. James M. Hogan (Columbia: University of South Carolina Press, 1998), xxvi.

24. Indeed, as intertextual evidence for this reading we might note that while *Silence* ends with Starling veering towards community in the form of Crawford, Harris's sequel, *Hannibal*, ends with Starling becoming Lecter's lover and taking up his crimes.

25. For more on this controversy, see my "Unmasking Buffalo Bill: Interpretive Controversy and *The Silence of the Lambs*," *Rhetoric Society Quarterly* 28 (1998): 33–47.

26. My distaste for these two post-*Silence* films is more clearly articulated in my "*Hannibal*: A Review Essay," *Scope: An On-Line Film Journal*, http://www.nottingham.ac.uk/film/journal/filmrev/films-august-02.htm; and "*Red Dragon*: A Review," *Scope: An On-Line Film Journal*, http://www.nottingham.ac.uk/film/jouranl/filmrev/films-august-03.htm.

Chapter 8: *Scream* (1996)

1. On this point, see Paul Thaler, *The Spectacle: Media and the Making of the O. J. Simpson Story* (Westport, CT: Praeger Publishers, 1997), xiv.

2. Ibid., xv.

3. This valuable box-office information comes from the Internet Movie Database, http://www.imdb.com/title/tt0117571/business.

4. Mark Jancovich, "General Introduction," in *Horror, The Film Reader*, ed. Mark Jancovich (London: Routledge, 2002), 5.

5. Paul Wells, *Horror Genre*, 97; and Humphries, *American Horror Film*, 189.

6. Jean-François Lyotard, *The Postmodern Condition* (Minneapolis: University of Minnesota Press, 1984), xxiv.

7. Brian Ott and Cameron Walter, "Intertextuality: Interpretive Practice and Textual Strategy," *Critical Studies in Media Communication* 17 (2000): 429–446.

8. Douglas Coupland, *Generation X: Tales for an Accelerated Culture* (New York: St. Martins, 1991).

9. David Gross and Sophronia Scott, "Proceeding with Caution," *Time*, July 16, 1990, 57.

10. On this point see, Stephen Earl Bennett and Stephen C. Craig (with Eric Rademacher), "Generations and Change: Some Initial Observations," in *After the Boom: The Politics of Generation X*, eds. Stephen C. Craig and Stephen Earl Bennett (Lanham, MD: Rowman & Littlefield, 1997), 1–19.

11. Neil Howe and William Strauss, "The New Generation Gap," *Atlantic Monthly*, April 1992, 79.

12. Stephen Earl Benett and Eric W. Rademacher, "The 'Age of Indifference' Revisited: Patterns of Political Interest, Media Exposure, and Knowledge among Generation X," in Craig and Bennett, *After the Boom*, 38.

13. William Strauss and Neil Howe, *Generations: The History of America's Future, 1584 to 2089* (New York: William Morrow, 1991), esp. 327–328.

14. "Stagflation" was a term coined to describe the combination of inflation and economic stagnation.

15. On this point, see Peter Sacks, *Generation X Goes to College* (Chicago: Open Court, 1996), 126–128.

16. McLuhan, for instance, makes a cameo appearance in Woody Allen's *Annie Hall* (1977).

17. See, for example, Marshall McLuhan, *Understanding the Media: The Extensions of Man* (New York: McGraw-Hill, 1964).

18. On this point, see Jean Baudrillard, *The Gulf War Did Not Take Place* (Bloomington: Indiana University Press, 1995).

19. On this point, see Frederick Wasser, *Veni, Vidi, Video: The Hollywood Empire and the VCR* (Austin: University of Texas Press, 2001).

20. Ricki Lake was host of a popular television talk show in the vein of *The Jerry Springer Show* and other exploitation talk shows.

21. For an interesting discussion of this trend in horror films, see Todd F. Tietchen, "Samplers and Copycats: The Cultural Implications of the Post-modern Slasher in Contemporary American Film," *Journal of Popular Film and Television* 26 (1998): 98–107.

22. See the discussion of the final girl in Chapter 6.

23. On Sidney's strength, see Kathleen Rowe Karlyn, "*Scream*, Popular Culture, and Feminism's Third Wave: 'I'm Not My Mother,'" *Genders* 28 (2003): http://www.genders.org/g38/g38_rowe_karlyn.html.

Chapter 9: *The Sixth Sense* (1999)

1. See, for instance, James Keller, "'Nothing that Is Not There, and the Nothing That Is:' Language and *The Blair Witch Project*," *Studies in Popular Culture* 22 (2000): 69–81; Margrit Schreier, "'Please Help Me, All I Want to Know Is: Is it Real or Not?' How Recipients View the Reality Status of *The Blair Witch Project*," *Poetics Today* 25 (2004): 205–234; and J. P. Tellotte, "*The Blair Witch Project* Project: Film and the Internet," *Film Quarterly* 54 (2001): 32–39.

2. On the pervasiveness of these apocalyptic beliefs, see the discussion in Chapter 5. In terms of the relationship between apocalyptic beliefs and the millennium, see Lisa McMinn, "Y2K, the Apocalypse, and Evangelical Christianity: The Role of Eschatological Belief in Church Responses," *Sociology of Religion* 62 (2001): 205–220; and Nancy A. Schaefer, "Y2K as an Endtime Sign: Apocalypticism in America at the *fin-de-millennium*," *Journal of Popular Culture* 38 (2004): 82–105.

3. Schaefer, "Y2K as an Endtime Sign," 98.

4. For background, see Stephen Levy, "The Bug that Didn't Bite," *Newsweek* (January 10, 2000), 41.

5. Michael Barkun, "Millennium Culture: The Year 2000 as a Religious Event," in *Millennial Visions: Essays on Twentieth-Century Millenarianism*, ed. Martha F. Lee (Westport, CT: Praeger Publishers, 2000), 17–40.

6. Martha F. Lee, "Apocalypse and Community: Rethinking the Origins of Millennialism," in *Millennial Visions*, ed. Lee, 55–68.

7. On this point see, Mark Kingwell, "(Stop) Making Sense of the Millennium: Politics and Culture at the End," in *Millennial Visions*, ed. Lee, 18.

8. Frank Kermode, for instance, notes a "sociological disposition" in relation to apocalyptic themes and figures. See his "Apocalypse and the Modern," in *Visions of Apocalypse*, eds. Saul Friedlander, Gerald Holton, Leo Marx, and Eugene Skolnikoff (New York: Holmes & Meier, 1985), 86.

9. Stephen O'Leary, *Arguing the Apocalypse: A Theory of Millennial Rhetoric* (New York: Oxford University Press, 1994), 3–19.

10. For more on these typical apocalyptic narratives see, Barry Brummett, "Using Apocalyptic Discourse to Exploit Audience Commitments through 'Transfer,'" *Southern Speech Communication Journal* 54 (1988): 58–73; and

Ronald F. Reid, "Apocalypticism and Typology: Rhetorical Dimensions of a Symbolic Reality," *Quarterly Journal of Speech* 69 (1983): 229–248.

11. Kingwell, "(Stop) Making Sense," 34.

12. Erik Doxtader, "Reconciliation: A Rhetorical Concept/ion," *Quarterly Journal of Speech* 89 (2003): 267.

13. O'Leary, *Arguing the Apocalypse*, 224.

14. I am, of course, aware that the final year of the twentieth century was 2000, but I am bowing to the overwhelming popular consensus that the century ended in 1999.

15. Charlene Bunnel, "The Gothic: A Literary Genre's Transition to Film," in *Planks of Reason: Essays on the Horror Film* (Metuchen, NJ: Scarecrow Press, 1984), 79–100.

16. Haunted house films typically engage the sense of dislocation in space and time. On this point see, Barry Brummett, "Electric Equipment for Living: Haunted House Films," *Critical Studies in Mass Communication* 2 (1985): 247–261.

17. An eloquent discussion of the phenomenon of memory can be found in Charles Scott, *The Time of Memory* (Albany: State University of New York Press, 1999).

Conclusion

1. At the time of this writing, the trade papers report that Romero has finally secured funding for a fourth *Living Dead* film and that production has begun.

Selected Bibliography

Arnzen, Michael A. "Who's Laughing Now? The Postmodern Splatter Film." *Journal of Popular Film and Television* 21 (1994): 176–184.

Ballio, Tino, ed. *The American Film Industry* (Madison: University of Wisconsin Press, 1985).

Benson, Thomas W., and Carolyn Anderson. *Reality Fictions: The Films of Frederick Wiseman* (Carbondale: Southern Illinois University Press, 1989).

Berger, James. *After the End: Representations of the Post-Apocalypse* (Minneapolis: University of Minnesota Press, 1999).

Bliss, Michael, and Christina Banks. *What Goes Around Comes Around: The Films of Jonathan Demme* (Carbondale: Southern Illinois University Press, 1996).

Bordwell, David. *Making Meaning: Inference and Rhetoric in the Interpretation of Cinema* (Cambridge, MA: Harvard University Press, 1989).

Boulenger, Gilles. *John Carpenter: The Prince of Darkness* (Los Angeles: Silman-Peters Press, 2001).

Braudy, Leo. "Hitchcock, Truffaut, and the Irresponsible Audience." *Film Quarterly* 21 (1968): 21–27.

Brummett, Barry. "Burke's Representative Anecdote as a Method in Media Criticism." *Critical Studies in Mass Communication* 1 (1984): 161–176.

Brummett, Barry. "Electric Literature as Equipment for Living: Haunted House Films." *Critical Studies in Mass Communication* 2 (1985): 247–261.

Clover, Carol. *Men, Women and Chainsaws: Gender in the Modern Horror Film* (Princeton, NJ: Princeton University Press, 1992).

Creed, Barbara. *The Monstrous Feminine: Film, Feminism, Psychoanalysis* (London: Routledge, 1993).

Dellamora, Richard. *Postmodern Apocalypse: Theory and Cultural Practice at the End* (Philadelphia: University of Pennsylvania Press, 1995).

Durgnat, Raymond. *A Long Hard Look at* Psycho (London: British Film Institute, 2002).

Flynn, John. *Cinematic Vampires: The Living Dead on Film and Television* (Jefferson, NC: McFarland and Company, 1992).

Frentz, Thomas S., and Thomas Farrell. "Conversion of America's Consciousness: The Rhetoric of *The Exorcist*." *Quarterly Journal of Speech* 61 (1975): 40–47.

Gagne, Paul R. *The Zombies That Ate Pittsburgh* (New York: Dodd, Mead and Company, 1987).

Gelder, Ken, ed. *The Horror Reader* (New York: Routledge, 2000).

Gitlin, Todd. *The Sixties: Years of Hope, Days of Rage* (New York: Bantam Books, 1987).

Grant, Barry Keith, ed. *Planks of Reason: Essays on the Horror Film* (Metuchen, NJ: Scarecrow Press, 1984).

Greenblatt, Stephen. *Learning to Curse: Essays in Early Modern Culture* (London: Routledge, 1990).

Halberstam, Judith. *Skin Shows: Gothic Horror and the Technology of Monsters* (Durham, NC: Duke University Press, 1995).

Heffernan, Kevin. *Ghouls, Gimmicks, and Gold: Horror Films and the American Movie Business, 1953–1968* (Durham, NC: Duke University Press, 2004).

Humphries, Reynold. *The American Horror Film: An Introduction* (Edinburgh: Edinburgh University Press, 2002).

Ingebretsen, Edward J. "Monster-Making: A Politics of Persuasion." *Journal of American Culture* 21 (1998): 24–34.

Jackson, Rosemary. *Fantasy: The Literature of Subversion* (London: Methuen, 1981).

Jameson, Frederick. *Postmodernism: Or, the Cultural Logic of Late Capitalism* (Durham, NC: Duke University Press, 1991).

Jancovich, Mark. *Rational Fears: American Horror in the 1950s* (Manchester: Manchester University Press, 1996).

Jaworzyn, Stefan. The Texas Chainsaw Massacre *Companion* (London: Titan Books, 2003).

Jenkins, Philip. *Using Murder: The Social Construction of Serial Homicide* (New York: de Gruyter Press, 1994).

Jones, Daryl. *Horror: A Thematic History in Fiction and Film* (London: Arnold, 2002).

Karlyn, Kathleen Rowe. "*Scream*, Popular Culture, and Feminism's Third Wave: 'I'm Not My Mother.'" *Genders* 28 (2003): http://www.genders.org/g38/g38_rowe_karlyn.html.

Keller, James. "'Nothing that Is Not There, and the Nothing That Is:' Language and *The Blair Witch Project*." *Studies in Popular Culture* 22 (2000): 69–81.

Kermode, Mark. *The Exorcist* (rev. 2nd ed.) (London: BFI Modern Classics, 2003).

King, Noel. "Hermeneutics, Reception Aesthetics, and Film Interpretation." In *Film Studies: Critical Approaches*, eds. J. Hill and P. C. Gibson (Oxford/New York: Oxford University Press, 2000), 210–221.

Kinnard, Roy. *Horror in Silent Films: A Filmography, 1896–1929* (Jefferson, NC: McFarland and Company, 1995).

Leigh, Janet (with Christopher Nickens). Psycho: *Behind the Scenes of the Classic Thriller* (New York: Harmony Books, 1995).

Lucanio, Patrick. *Them or Us: Archetypal Interpretations of Fifties Alien Invasion Films* (Bloomington: Indiana University Press, 1987).

Maddrey, Joseph. *Nightmares in Red, White and Blue: The Evolution of the American Horror Film* (Jefferson, NC: McFarland and Company, 2004).

McCreadie, Marsha. *The Casting Couch and Other Front Row Seats: Women in Films of the 1970s and 1980s* (Westport, CT: Praeger Publishers, 1990).

Modleski, Tania. *The Women Who Knew Too Much: Hitchcock and Feminist Theory* (New York: Routledge, 1988).

Naremore, James. *Filmguide to* Psycho (Bloomington: Indiana University Press, 1973).

O'Brien, Daniel. *The Hannibal Files: The Unauthorised Guide to the Hannibal Lecter Trilogy* (London: Reynolds and Hearn, Ltd., 2002).

Ott, Brian, and Cameron Walter. "Intertextuality: Interpretive Practice and Textual Strategy." *Critical Studies in Media Communication* 17 (2000): 429–446.

Phillips, Kendall R. "Redeeming the Visual: Aesthetic Questions in Michael Mann's *Manhunter*." *Literature/Film Quarterly* 31 (2003): 10–16.

Phillips, Kendall R. "Unmasking Buffalo Bill: Interpretive Controversy and *The Silence of the Lambs*." *Rhetoric Society Quarterly* 28 (1998): 33–47.

Prawer, S. S. *Caligari's Children: The Film as Tale of Terror* (Oxford University Press, 1981).

Quart, Leonard, and Albert Auster. *American Film and Society* (3rd ed., exp. and rev.) (Westport, CT: Praeger Publishers, 2002).

Rebello, Stephen. *Alfred Hitchcock and the Making of* Psycho (London: Mandarin, 1990).

Rothman, William. *Hitchcock: The Murderous Gaze* (Cambridge, MA: Harvard University Press, 1982).

Schelde, Per. *Androids, Humanoids, and other Science Fiction Monsters: Science and Soul in Science Fiction Films* (New York: NYU Press, 1993).

Schneider, Stephen Jay, and Daniel Shaw, eds. *Dark Thoughts: Philosophical Reflections on Cinematic Horror* (Lanham, MD: Scarecrow Press, 2003).

Schreier, Margrit. "'Please Help Me, All I Want to Know Is: Is It Real or Not?': How Recipients View the Reality Status of *The Blair Witch Project*." *Poetics Today* 25 (2004): 205–34.

Selzer, Mark. *Serial Killers: Death and Life in America's Wound Culture* (New York: Routledge, 1998).

Sheahan Wells, Amanda. Psycho: *Directed by Alfred Hitchcock* (London: York Press, 2001).

Silver, Alain, and James Ursini, eds. *Horror Film Reader* (New York: Limelight Editions, 2000).

Silver, Alain, and James Ursini. *The Vampire Film: From Nosferatu to Bram Stoker's Dracula* (2nd ed.) (New York: Limelight Editions, 1994).

Simpson, Philip. *Psycho Paths: Tracking the Serial Killer through Contemporary American Film and Fiction* (Carbondale: Southern Illinois University Press, 2000).

Skal, David. *Hollywood Gothic: The Tangled Web of Dracula from Novel to Stage to Screen* (New York: W. W. Norton and Company, 1990).

Skal, David. *The Monster Show: A Cultural History of Horror* (rev. ed.) (New York: Faber and Faber, 2001).

Tellotte, J. P. "*The Blair Witch Project* Project: Film and the Internet." *Film Quarterly* 54 (2001): 32–39.

Tietchen, Todd F. "Samplers and Copycats: The Cultural Implications of the Postmodern Slasher in Contemporary American Film." *Journal of Popular Film and Television* 26 (1998): 98–107.

Tithecott, Richard. *Of Men and Monsters: Jeffrey Dahmer and the Construction of the Serial Killer* (Madison: University of Wisconsin Press, 1997).

Todorov, Tzvetan. *The Fantastic: A Structural Approach to a Literary Genre* (Ithaca, NY: Cornell University Press, 1975).

Tudor, Andrew. *Monsters and Mad Scientists: A Cultural History of the American Horror Film* (Oxford: Blackwell, 1987).

Vieira, Mark. *Hollywood Horror: From Gothic to Cosmic* (New York: Abrams, 2003).

Waller, Gregory A., ed. *American Horrors: Essays on the Modern American Horror Film* (Urbana, IL: University of Illinois Press, 1987).

Warner, Marina. *No Go the Bogeyman* (London: Vintage, 1998).

Warren, Bill. *Keep Watching the Skies: Volume I* (Jefferson, NC: McFarland, 1982).

Wasser, Frederick. *Veni, Vidi, Video: The Hollywood Empire and the VCR* (Austin: University of Texas Press, 2001).

Wasson, Richard. "The Politics of *Dracula*." *English Literature in Transition (1880-1920)* 9 (1966): 24–27.

Wells, Paul. *The Horror Genre: From Beelzebub to Blair Witch* (London: Wallflower, 2000).

West, Paul. *Laughing Screaming* (New York: Columbia University Press, 1995).

Wood, Robin. "Gods and Monsters." *Film Comment* 12 (1978): 19–25.

Wood, Robin. *Hollywood from Vietnam to Reagan ... and Beyond* (New York Columbia University Press, 2003).

Index

Warner, Marina, 133, 142
Warner Brothers, 90, 102
Warren, Bill, 39, 58
Watergate, 108, 172
Wayans, Keenan Ivory, 180
Welles, Orson, 135
Wells, Amanda Sheahan, 64
Wells, H. G., 35, 36
Wells, Paul, 9, 18, 80, 97, 168
Wes Craven's New Nightmare, 165
West, Paul, 116
Westerns, 36
Whale, James, 14, 46
What Lies Beneath, 194
Wilcox, Fred, 128
Wild Bunch, The, 111
Williamson, Kevin, 165, 179
Wise, Naomi, 53
Wizard of Oz, The, 1
Women's rights, 67, 130

Wood, Robin, 3, 48, 49, 64, 98, 129
Woodstock, 81, 86, 164
Work, 17–18, 43, 45, 46, 58, 65–66, 74, 78, 87
World War I, 15–16, 20, 23, 30
World War II, 35, 36, 39, 40, 41, 44, 45, 65, 86, 169
World War III, 41

X-Files, The, 161

Y2K Bug, 185
Yablans, Irwin, 123–24
Yom Kippur War, 110
You Only Live Twice, 125
Youth, 69, 80, 81, 85, 86–88, 92, 107, 117–20, 122, 140–41, 176, 179, 207n30
Yuppies, 149–50, 151, 152, 168

About the Author

KENDALL R. PHILLIPS is Associate Professor in the Department of Communication and Rhetorical Studies at Syracuse University. His essays and reviews have appeared in such journals as *Literature/ Film Quarterly* and *Philosophy and Rhetoric*.